Grammar
Dialogues

Grammar Dialogues

An Interactive Approach

ALLAN KENT DART

American Language Institute
New York University

PRENTICE HALL REGENTS
Englewood Cliffs, New Jersey 07632

Library of Congress Cataloging-in-Publication Data

Dart, Allan Kent (date)
    Grammar dialogues : an interactive approach / Allan Kent Dart.
      p. cm.
    ISBN 0-13-634460-7
    1. English language—Textbooks for foreign speakers. 2. English
language—Grammar—1950- I. Title.
    PE1128.D346 1992
    428.2′4—dc20   90-22344
                                    CIP

Acquisitions editor: Anne Riddick
Editorial/production supervision and
  interior design: Douglas Gordon
Cover design: Suzanne Bennett
Prepress buyer: Lori Bulwin
Manufacturing buyer: Ray Keating

© 1992 by Prentice-Hall, Inc.
A Simon & Schuster Company
Englewood Cliffs, New Jersey 07632

Printed in the United States of America
10 9 8 7 6 5 4 3 2 1

ISBN 0-13-634460-7

Prentice-Hall International (UK) Limited, *London*
Prentice-Hall of Australia Pty. Limited, *Sydney*
Prentice-Hall Canada Inc., *Toronto*
Prentice-Hall Hispanoamericana, S.A., *Mexico*
Prentice-Hall of India Private Limited, *New Delhi*
Prentice-Hall of Japan, Inc., *Tokyo*
Simon & Schuster Asia Pte. Ltd., *Singapore*
Editora Prentice-Hall do Brasil, Ltda., *Rio de Janeiro*

Contents

8 *Participial Phrases* *209*

9 *Causative Verbs* *234*

10   *Complex Sentences: Noun Clauses and Indirect Speech*   *245*

Preface

Grammar Dialogues, an interactive text, is a study of grammar through contextualized dialogues. It is intended for high-intermediate to advanced students of English as a second language who are at a college, at a university, at an institute or in a continuing education program for adults. The material is also appropriate for students of English as a foreign language who are studying in a non–English-speaking country.

The Exercises

Each exercise in this book consists of a set of dialogues that focus on the points of English grammar discussed in the explanation that directly follows the exercise. The students can role-play these dialogues: one student playing the role of person A, another playing the role of person B. Sometimes there are three or four roles to play.

Here are some suggestions on how to use the materials:

1. The class can begin by breaking up into pairs or small groups.
2. To find out what the students may or may not know, the teacher can assign an exercise (or part of an exercise) as a quiz. The students can then exchange books and correct one another's work.
3. The teacher also can assign an exercise as homework. At the next class meeting, with the teacher's help, the students can correct their own work while they compare answers and practice the dialogues.
4. During the period of correction and practice, the teacher can go from group to group, helping individual students with pronunciation and demonstrating natural-sounding intonation patterns appropriate to the dialogue. The teacher also can help the students to "act out" the dialogues.
5. Following this "rehearsal," the class can perform the dialogues. More work on pronunciation and appropriate intonation patterns can take place at this time. Some students might not be quite clear on certain points of grammar, so the teacher may need to elucidate further.

The Explanations

Except for some review exercises, a grammar explanation follows each exercise. Each explanation contains concise descriptions of grammar with examples and dialogues that are meant for the students, either in small groups or in a circle, to read aloud and perform. The paragraphs in each explanation are numbered so that the students can refer to them quickly and so that the teacher or the group leader can easily assign them to be read aloud.

While going through an explanation, the teacher can work on the pronunciation of grammatical terms and the production of appropriate intonation patterns; also, he or she may wish to provide supplementary explanations, examples and written or oral exercises to illustrate a certain point further.

Depending on the level of proficiency of a class and the degree of difficulty of an exercise, either the teacher can go through an explanation with the students before they do an exercise, or the students can go through an explanation on their own (at home or in groups in class) as part of the assignment.

Planning a Lesson

Depending on the nature of a particular class, the teacher may find that it is not necessary to follow the order of the exercises as presented in this book. However, because the book is semiprogrammed and the students will constantly review the old material within the context of the new, the teacher should try to adhere to the order as closely as possible.

To give the teacher an idea of how he or she might plan a lesson, let me describe the program I usually follow for my classes. I use the material for a multiskills course in which the students meet for 3 hours, 4 days a week, in a 14-week semester. Every morning, the students bring in copies of *The New York Times*, which we skim. This activity leads to reading or writing assignments or to a period of conversation practice focusing on an article in that day's paper.

The students continuously work on assignments, compositions and essays. On many mornings, they tape their written work on the chalkboard, compare their work and consult with me about any problems.

The second half of each meeting is usually devoted to the grammar dialogues. The students role-play the dialogues that they have done for homework. In the last 15 minutes or so of class, I frequently assign conversation topics, or the students find topics of interest to themselves.

Acknowledgments

I must thank the administration of the American Language Institute, New York University, for supporting my efforts and allowing me to test the material in my classes.

To Anne Riddick and Tina Carver at Prentice Hall Regents, I wish to express my appreciation. I am also grateful to the numerous anonymous reviewers of the manuscript for *Grammar Dialogues*. Their constructive criticism and thoughtful suggestions were most helpful.

For their fine editing, special thanks go to Doug Gordon and Ronald Boudreau.

For their assistance and encouragement, I wish to express my indebtedness to Linda Markstein, Patty Duffy, Clarice Kaltinick and Phyllis Skalski.

I feel an especially strong sense of gratitude toward the students in my classes at the American Language Institute, who participated in various stages of development of the manuscript over a period of years. I would like to thank them all.

Allan Kent Dart
Brooklyn, New York

Working in a Group

The explanations and exercises in *Grammar Dialogues* are designed to be used in pairs or in small groups. While studying English grammar, you are interacting with others and developing your communication skills. So that a group will work together smoothly, a leader can be chosen (either by the group or by the teacher) to take care of giving turns and to make sure that everyone participates.

When your group is having a discussion or a debate, the group leader can act as a moderator, imparting order to the meeting and making certain that everyone contributes.

Correcting an Exercise

To facilitate correcting an exercise, it is a good idea for you to use a pen or pencil that differs in color from the one that you used to write your answers. In the following example, note how each mistake is crossed out rather than erased. Also note how each punctuation mark is circled for reading ease and how each addition is inserted above the place it belongs and is indicated by a caret (∧).

Example

even though / we / have / no / money / bank / we / still / plan / to go / trip
we / want / to stay / home

A: What are your and your wife's summer plans?

B: *Even though we don't have no money in the bank. we have still planned to go on a the trip. We don't want to stay at the home.*

Formal and Informal Style

The terms **formal** and **informal** are frequently used in this text. Formal usage is found most commonly in formal writing—for example, in a research paper for a course at a university or in an essay or article for a magazine that takes itself seriously. Informal style is found in a personal letter, a gossip column in a newspaper or a work of fiction. Compare the following:

FORMAL   Sir, the conditions under which we are working are intolerable.
INFORMAL   Boss, the conditions we're working under are hard to take.
FORMAL   Let us look at the question put forward and discuss it.
INFORMAL   Let's look at the problem and talk about it.

When you speak, you most often use an informal style. When you write, you must adopt a style that is appropriate to the subject matter and the audience for which your writing is intended. For instance, it would be inappropriate to use a formal writing style in a college newspaper article about a basketball game; likewise, it would be inappropriate to use an informal writing style for a *Los Angeles Times* or *Chicago Tribune* editorial discussing a serious social or political issue.

Nouns and Pronouns

❑ **1.1** **Agreement of Nouns, Pronouns,
Verbs and Expressions of Quantity**

Circle each correct verb form. In a few cases, both answer choices are acceptable.

Example
A: Don't you think some of the coffee breaks (*have* / *has*) been too long recently?
B: I certainly do, Professor. I couldn't agree with you more.
C: Yeah, there ('*s* / *are*) a lot of lazy guys around here.

1. A: Half of the workers in this plant (*is* / *are*) union members.
   B: And they make more money than we nonmembers do.
   A: Right, and that isn't fair. Why, none of those union people (*work* / *works*) as hard as we do.

2. A: Ten dollars for a movie (*is* / *are*) much more than I can afford. How about you?
   B: Listen, that's too high. Even five dollars (*is* / *are*) too much for me.
   C: Not one of the movies playing in town (*is* / *are*) worth a dime. They couldn't pay me a thousand dollars to go to any of them.

3. A: Hey, what's wrong? What on earth is going on?
   B: I don't know, but the police (*is* / *are*) knocking at the front door.
   C: Well, none of us (*has* / *have*) done anything wrong.

4. A: The statistics in this report somehow (*strike* / *strikes*) me as wrong. What do you think?
   B: Oh, yes, I'm sure. In fact, I'm positive.
   A: Oh? Just why are you so certain?
   B: Statistics (*was* / *were*) my major at the university.

5. A: None of the president's suggestions (*was* / *were*) acceptable to the prime minister.
   B: Yes, I know, Ambassador. What do you think of the suggestions?
   A: Frankly, not one of them (*make* / *makes*) any sense, I feel.

6. A: I'm worried about my girlfriend. I haven't heard from her for weeks.
   B: Well, no news (*is* / *are*) good news, as they say.
   A: Well, I'm afraid, in my case, that no news (*is* / *are*) bad news. I've never had any luck in love.

7. **A:** Two-thirds of a cup of cream (*go / goes*) into the chicken gravy.
   B: Hey, listen, there (*'s / are*) a lot of calories in that much cream.
   A: Oh, come on, you don't have to worry about calories. Why, you're as skinny as a string bean.

8. **A:** You've had your head buried in that book for days. Why do you like it so much?
   B: Each of the stories (*is / are*) about love and romance.
   A: Oh, really! Can't you think about anything else?

9. **A:** In the days of the horse and carriage, thirty miles a day (*was / were*) good time.
   B: Gee, Grandpa, that wasn't very fast, was it?

10. **A:** The number of refugees in the detention camps (*is / are*) shocking, isn't it? What can be done?
    B: Well, the United Nations (*is / are*) looking into it.
    A: I've heard a number of refugees (*has / have*) already died.

11. **A:** Every man, woman and child in the country (*carry / carries*) an ID card. The government is very strict and hard.
    B: Yes, everyone (*has / have*) to follow a lot of regulations and rules. We're almost slaves of the state.
    A: All of us (*live / lives*) in a constant state of fear.

12. **A:** The poor (*is / are*) victims of an unjust and greedy society.
    B: Yes, the rich (*want / wants*) everything for themselves.
    C: Oh, come on. People in the United States (*is / are*) living well, in general.
    A: Yes, but not everyone (*is / are*), that's for sure.

13. **A:** Ummm, yum, this is delicious. What's in this soup?
    B: There (*'s / are*) vegetables and lots of spices.
    A: Boy, the French really (*know / knows*) how to cook, don't they? Everyone in France (*eat / eats*) well.

❏ 1.2 Agreement of Nouns and Verbs

1. One noun subject takes a singular verb; two (or more) noun subjects connected by *and* take a plural verb:

> An apple *is* good for you.
> A lemon and an orange *are* acidic.

A plural noun subject also takes a plural verb:

> *Do* bananas grow up or down?

2. When a prepositional phrase follows a noun subject, the verb that follows must agree with the noun subject (not with the noun in the prepositional phrase). Compare the following:

> *The plot* in that movie *keeps* you on the edge of your seat.
> *The actors* in that movie *keep* your attention throughout.
>
> *The child* in the garden *is* my granddaughter.
> *The children* in the garden *are* playing hide-and-go-seek.

❏ 1.3 Agreement with Expressions of Quantity

1. We often put **expressions of quantity** such as *some of* and *half of* before a noun or pronoun subject; the verb that follows must agree with the subject:

Some of *the dialogue* in that movie *is* a little boring.
(Some of *it is* boring.)

Some of *the actors* in that movie *are* rather amateurish.
(Some of *them are* amateurish.)

Half of *the apple* on this plate *is* yours.
(Half of *it is* yours.)

Half of *the apples* in that basket *are* rotten.
(Half of *them are* rotten.)

These are some other expressions of quantity:

a lot of	fifty percent of	one-third of
a majority of	most of	two-thirds of

2. *A number of* is an expression of quantity that is always followed by a plural noun or pronoun plus a plural verb:

A number of *good movies* (*them*) *have* been made recently.
A number of *good actors* (*them*) *are* up for Oscars this year.

3. *The number of* is always followed by a plural noun plus a singular verb:

The number of *accidents* on the nation's highway *is* shocking.
The number of *cars* on our streets *increases* ten percent a year.

4. A verb agrees with the noun or pronoun subject in expressions of quantity with *all of:*

All of *my time* (*it*) *is* spent on my school studies.
All of *the students* (*them*) *are* trying their best.

When we use a noun subject, we may omit the preposition *of:*

All (of) *my money* goes to food and rent.
All (of) *the people* want honesty in government.

But with a pronoun subject, we cannot omit *of:*

All of *it* goes quickly.   [Never *All it.*]
All of *them* want an end to corruption.   [Never *All them.*]

5. *Every* or *each* plus a singular noun determines a singular verb:

Every *book* in my teacher's bookcase *is* in reference to grammar.
Each *student* in the school *carries* an ID card.

6. *Each of* plus a plural noun or pronoun always takes a singular verb:

Each of *our four children has* a unique personality.
Each of *the students' teachers gives* a lot of homework.
Each of *us spends* a lot of time at the library.

7. *One of* or *not one of* plus a plural noun is always followed by a singular verb:

One of *the proposals* in this memo *is* absolutely insane.
Not one of *his friends has* offered help during this crisis.

We frequently use *only* with *one of:*

Only one of our ideas has made us any money.
Only one of my Christmas presents was something I wanted.

8. A singular verb always follows *everyone, everybody* and *nobody:*

> *Everyone* on this planet *wants* to have peace and prosperity.
> *Everybody,* at least almost everybody, *desires* an end to war.
> *Nobody* in the world *is* going to be here forever.

9. Because *none* has the meaning of "not one," formal usage requires that a singular verb follow *none of* plus a plural noun:

> None of [Not one of] *the men and women* here *is* married.
> None of [Not one of] *his ideas is* very imaginative.

However, *none of* followed by a plural verb has become so common in modern informal usage that a singular verb following *none of* may sound incorrect to a native speaker's ears. For example, many English-speaking people might think the following sentences sound strange and unnatural:

> None of *her children is* spoiled.
> None of *my friends takes* advantage of me.

Many native speakers would perhaps feel more comfortable hearing a plural verb following *none of:*

> None of *the grapefruits* in this basket *are* any good.
> None of *the players* on the team *are* following the rules.
> None of *us are* happy with the government's decision.

However, in formal usage, both spoken and written, a singular verb following *none of* is usually more accurate and precise:

> *None of* the conclusions reached in this paper *is* supported by facts or examples.
>
> *None of* the experiments conducted during this project *has* brought forth any new approach to the treatment of mental illness.

❑ 1.4 Agreement with Expletive *There*

When the word *there* is an **expletive,** a singular verb follows when the following noun is singular. Informally, we often use *there's,* the contraction of *there is:*

> *There's* a large soup bowl on the counter near the sink, and *there's* a small platter on the table in the pantry.

Formal usage requires that a plural verb precede a plural compound subject or a plural noun:

> *There are* a large bowl and a small platter in the cupboard.
> *There are* some forks, spoons and knives in the drawer.

In informal usage, however, we frequently hear and see a singular verb:

> *There's* a water kettle and a frying pan on the stove.
> *There's* some children at the door yelling trick-or-treat.

❑ 1.5 Agreement Irregularities with Some Nouns

There are a number of irregularities in the determining of singular or plural nouns:

1. The word *news* is singular; the word *people* is plural:

> The *news is* startling; the *people are* shocked.

The word *police* is plural:

> The *police are* always running after someone.

2. Singular verbs usually follow expressions of time, distance and money:

> *Two hours* of hard exercise *is* enough for anyone.
> *Three minutes is* a long time to hold one's breath.
> *Seven hundred miles is* easy to drive in a day.
> *Twenty dollars is* too much to pay for any movie.

3. *The United States* and *the United Nations* always take a singular verb:

> *The United States has* many magnificent coastlines.
>
> Many people feel that *the United Nations is* a great force for making peace in the world.

4. A singular verb follows a noun ending in *-ics* when the noun refers to an academic area of study:

> *Linguistics deals* with the intricacies of language.
> *Physics is* the study of the interactions between matter and energy.
> *Mathematics has* never been an easy subject for me.
> *Ethics is* the study of morals and values.

5. A plural verb may follow certain nouns ending in *-ics* when they refer to a situation other than an academic area of study. Compare the following:

> *Economics is* the study of material wealth.
>
> VERSUS
>
> The *economics* of running a business *give* me a headache.
>
> *Statistics is* the study of numerical data.
>
> VERSUS
>
> The *statistics* coming in from the government *are* forecasting good times for everyone in the nation.

6. Nouns of nationality that end in *-ese, -ch* or *-sh* can mean the name of a language; they are followed by a singular verb:

> *Chinese is* spoken by more than a billion people.
> *French is* no longer the most important language of diplomacy.
> *Polish is* a Slavic language.

7. When such nouns of nationality are preceded by the definite article *the,* the words refer to the people who speak the language, so a plural verb follows:

> *The Vietnamese are* no longer living in a divided nation.
> *The French are* famous for their life-style.
> *The English are* known for their wry sense of humor.

8. Certain adjectives preceded by *the* can be used as nouns that refer to groups of people; a plural verb follows:

> *The rich are* getting richer, and *the poor have* been forgotten.
> *The blind have* a kind of sixth sense; they see in other ways.

❏ 1.6 *He or She*

Circle the words that you think are most appropriate. Be prepared to explain your choices as shown in the example.

Example

sexist   *informal*

A: Everyone in this country must pay (*his* /(*his or her*)/ *their*) fair share of taxes.

B: Well, I must say I couldn't agree with you more. ((*The*)/ *A*) number of people who don't pay their taxes ((*is*)/ *are*) shocking.

C: Yes, the government ((*has*)/ *have*) got to do something soon.

1. A: My cat's name is Tom. Without a doubt, (*he* / *it*) is the cleverest cat in (*his* / *its*) neighborhood. People (*love* / *loves*) to play with (*him* / *it*) because (*he* / *it*) is so friendly and never scratches.

    B: My cat's name is Alice. (*She* / *It*) is the most curious cat I've ever seen. Why, (*she* / *it*) can do anything.

    C: You know, everyone in my circle of friends (*has* / *have*) a cat, and I can't stand cats.

2. A: Prime Minister, Her Majesty's government (*has* / *have*) requested that a special fund be set aside for the protection of wildlife in our forests. And most of the people of the nation (*support* / *supports*) the request.

    B: But where on earth will we get money for it? It doesn't grow on trees, you know.

    A: Yes, ma'am, I know, but the people (*do* / *does*) want it.

    B: Yes, but the people (*don't* / *doesn't*) want to pay more taxes.

3. A: The Vanderbilder family (*is* / *are*) famous for (*its* / *their*) wealth and power, but (*it's* / *they're*) also well known for (*its* / *their*) philanthropy.

    B: Yes, everyone in this city (*know* / *knows*) that (*his* / *her* / *his or her* / *their*) welfare depends on the good welfare of the Vanderbilder family. (*It's* / *They're*) running this town.

4. A: Everyone in my close circle of friends (*have* / *has*) some kind of problem in (*his* / *her* / *his or her* / *their*) love life. (*All* / *All of*) them (*is* / *are*) running after rainbows in the sky.

    B: Yes, not one of them (*have* / *has*) been using (*his* / *her* / *his or her* / *their*) head.

5. A: Nobody (*is* / *are*) allowed to enter the university library without (*his* / *her* / *his or her* / *their*) ID card.

    B: Also, when a student (*leave* / *leaves*) the library, (*he* / *she* / *he or she* / *they*) (*is* / *are*) subject to a bag check by a security guard. Not everyone (*is* / *are*) honest these days.

6. A: What happened at the end of the performance?

    B: The audience (*was* / *were*) standing up. (*It* / *They*) (*was* / *were*) applauding wildly and stomping (*its* / *their*) feet.

7. A: How terrible! Someone (*have* / *has*) put (*his* / *her* / *his or her* / *their*) dirty hands on that freshly painted wall.

    B: Don't blame me, Mom. I've been outside all day.

8. A: In the United States, the public (*has* / *have*) demanded that taxes be lowered. (*It* / *They*) (*need* / *needs*) some relief from the heavy tax burden.

    B: Yes, (*all* / *all of*) the citizens (*want* / *wants*) a change, and (*it* / *they*) (*want* / *wants*) it now.

    C: Right. None of them (*is* / *are*) willing to pay more than (*he* / *she* / *he or she* / *they*) (*is* / *are*) already paying.

❑ 1.7 Avoiding Awkwardness

Recast each awkward-sounding sentence. Do the exercise orally or write your answers on a separate sheet of paper.

Example

When a student wishes to ask a question, he or she should raise his or her hand in order to get his or her teacher's attention.

When students wish to ask questions, they should raise their hands in order to get their teacher's attention.

1. When an employee of the International Trends Corporation submits his or her letter of resignation, he or she must submit it in triplicate to his or her supervisor.

2. Everyone in this city has a right to affordable housing for his or her family. Why must someone in our rich country not have a place to call his or her home?

3. When a parent answers a child's question, he or she should give his or her child an honest and straightforward reply. He or she shouldn't waste his or her time, nor should he or she waste his or her child's time.

❑ 1.8 Indefinite Nouns and Pronouns

1. We use a singular pronoun to refer to a singular noun:

> A *man* is calling; *he* has a message for you.
> A *woman* is waiting for me; *she*'s to be my future wife.

We use a plural pronoun to refer to a plural noun:

> The *citizens* are rioting; *they* want more food and jobs.
> The *people* want action; *they* demand an audience with the leader.

2. A singular noun frequently does not indicate whether a person is male or female; we call such a noun an **indefinite noun:**

> A *worker* has rights.
> A *freelance worker* works hard.

Traditionally, in the English language we have used a singular masculine pronoun or a possessive adjective to refer to an indefinite noun:

> When a *worker* is sick, *he* has a right to be paid during *his* illness.
> A *freelance worker* works for *himself;* nobody pays *him* while *he* is sick.

However, in recent years this usage has come into disfavor both because it is obviously sexist and because it is often not an accurate description. For example, in a company in which half of the work force is women, the use of *he* or *his* in reference to an indefinite noun looks and sounds arrogant and offensive.

To avoid any suggestion of sexism, we can use *he or she* or the rather clinical-looking *s/he*. We may also use *him or her* (*him/her*) or *himself or herself* (*him- or herself*):

> When a *worker* is sick, *he or she* has a right to be paid during *his or her* illness.
>
> A *freelance worker works for him- or herself;* nobody pays *him or her* while *he or she* is sick.

The overuse of these devices, however, can be awkward. We can avoid this clumsiness by recasting the sentence. One way is to change the indefinite noun to a plural noun:

> When *workers* are sick, *they* have a right to be paid during *their* illness.
> *Freelance workers* work for *themselves;* nobody pays *them* when *they* are sick.

3.   These are the **indefinite pronouns,** which are always singular:

one	everybody	somebody	anybody	nothing
no one	everything	something	anything	
everyone	someone	anyone	nobody	

4.   Traditionally, as with indefinite nouns, we have used masculine pronouns and possessive adjectives to refer to indefinite pronouns:

> *Nobody* in the office has submitted *his* resignation yet.
> *Everyone* in this class has a right to *his* personal views.
> *One* has to be careful with *his* valuables these days.

To be more in tune with modern times, today we would more likely say or write:

> *Nobody* in the world wants to lose *his or her* home.
> Doesn't *everyone* have a right to *his or her* political beliefs?
> *One* has to be careful with *his or her* (or *one's*) credit cards.

5.   Very often it is best for us to recast a sentence containing an indefinite pronoun in order to avoid awkward construction. As with indefinite nouns, we can change an indefinite pronoun to a plural noun. Compare the following:

> At Christmas, *everyone* in the company receives a bonus in *his* pay envelope, something extra *he* can spend on *himself* and *his* family.
>
> VERSUS
>
> At Christmas, all of the *employees* in the company receive a bonus in *their* pay envelopes, something extra *they* can spend on *themselves* and *their* families.

6.   In informal usage, not considered acceptable by strict grammarians, we often hear (and sometimes read) plural pronouns and possessive adjectives used in reference to an indefinite pronoun:

> *Everyone* is upstairs in *their* rooms by *themselves* studying.
> *Somebody* put *their* dirty shoes on my beautiful new sofa.

Such informality is inappropriate in formal writing.

7.   Often the singular subject pronoun *you* has the same meaning as *one*, the indefinite pronoun. Compare the following:

> *One* has to be careful when *one* is traveling by *oneself.*
>
> VERSUS
>
> *You* [meaning "one"] have to be careful when *you* are traveling by *yourself.*

English-speaking North Americans rarely use *one* in this manner. To our ears, it can sound false and pretentious. It is quite common in British usage, however.

8.   When we do not know the sex of an animal, we use the pronoun *it* or the possessive adjective *its:*

> What a beautiful cat! Is *it* a Persian? What's *its* name?

When we know the sex of a creature, we very often personify the animal by using masculine or feminine pronouns and possessive adjectives:

> A: What a beautiful dog! Is it a *he* or a *she?*
> B: It's a *he; his* name is Rover.
> A: What kind of dog is *he?*
> B: Oh, *he's* just a mongrel. *His* sister, who's at the vet's now, looks just like *him.* I don't know what's wrong with *her; she* just won't eat *her* food.

9. We sometimes personify ships and automobiles, in addition to animals. They are considered feminine:

> **A:** Look at *her* plow through the waves.
> **B:** Yes, *she*'s a magnificent ship.
>
> **A:** What a beautiful car!
> **B:** And *she*'s a great racer.

10. We also sometimes personify certain countries (in a somewhat literary style):

> **A:** Ah, beautiful France, *she* will always remain in my memories.
> **B:** India will always remain in mine. How ancient *her* culture is!

☐ 1.9 Collective Nouns

1. A **collective noun** describes a group of people, animals or things that are considered to be a single unit. In American English, such nouns are usually followed by a singular verb; however, we most often refer to the word with a plural pronoun or possessive adjective:

> The Smith *family is* large. *They*'re celebrating *their* Fourth of July at a big family picnic in the park.
>
> That *couple is* living in *their* trailer up in the mountains.
>
> The *faculty is* on strike; *they* want more pay.
>
> The *committee has* finally made a decision; *they*'ve made up *their* minds at last.
>
> The *team* is practicing hard; *they*'re going to win the next game.
>
> The *audience is* booing; *they*'re angry with the bullfighter.

2. However, we sometimes use *it* or *its* when we are referring to the collective noun as a single unit rather than as a group of individuals:

> The Smith *family* is large. *It* has *its* fingers in every important financial pie in the country.
>
> The *committee* has made *its* decision.
>
> Our *team* is the best. *It* will never lose a game.

3. More formally, particularly in British usage, we may use a plural verb after a collective noun and refer to the collective noun as a group of individuals; we refer to the word with plural pronouns and possessive adjectives:

> My *family are* spread out all over the country; *they*'re all following *their* own particular life-styles.
>
> That *couple are* living in separate houses now; *they*'ve broken up for good.
>
> The *group are* coming along now; *they*'re making progress.

4. The British often use a plural verb with the collective nouns *public* and *government:*

> Her Majesty's *government have* been in support of new legislation to help the poor in the inner-cities.
>
> The *public have* called for a greater lowering of taxes.

But on the American side of the Atlantic, people always think of these two words as singular:

> The *government is* hiding something; the *public has* a constitutional right to know what it is.

❑ 1.10 We Ourselves

Supply in each blank the appropriate reflexive pronoun. Frequently, a preposition preceding a pronoun will be required. Use the prepositions in the following list:

about   by   in   with
at   for   of

Example

A: She has no sense of humor; she takes ___*herself*___ so seriously.

B: Yes, it's impossible for her to laugh ___*at herself*___.

1. A: Why is the dog always scratching _____?

    B: He's got fleas, I think.

2. A: Look! You've cut _____.

    B: Yes, while I was shaving _____.

3. A: Have all your children graduated?

    B: Oh, yes, and we're very, very proud _____. We gave up a lot

    of nice things _____ in order to send our kids to college.

4. A: Who originally introduced me to you?

    B: You _____ did. Don't you remember? You just walked up to

    me and introduced _____.

5. A: Why is she always feeling so sorry _____?

    B: She's very self-centered. She just wants to be the center of attention. I'm not very

    fond of her _____.

6. A: What! Why are you, a junior officer, in command of this ship during a storm? The

    captain _____ should be on the bridge.

    B: Well, frankly, ma'am, he's in his cabin all _____, and he's

    blind drunk, so I've had to take command _____.

    A: Why, that's terrible. I'm absolutely shocked. The captain should be

    ashamed _____.

7. A: I'm so angry _____.

    B: Why?

    A: I went to an important meeting yesterday, and I talked _____

    too much.

8. A: Just who elected the dictator to his position?

B: He elected _____.

A: _____?

B: Yes, he was able to push _____ into his powerful position

all _____, without help from anyone.

A: How are the people of this nation going to get rid of this snake?

B: We will, but we want to do it _____.

We _____ want to determine our destiny in our own way.

9. **A:** How did that guy in apartment 35G kill _____?

B: He just opened a window and threw _____ out.

A: My, my, my.

10. **A:** How do I stop this machine?

B: Don't worry, it'll turn _____ off automatically. It'll

turn _____ on again automatically, too.

A: Wow! What a fantastic machine! Does it also plug _____ in?

B: No, it doesn't have to. It runs on batteries. I have to put those

in _____.

11. **A:** But, Mommy, some neighborhood kids broke the kitchen window.

B: Now listen, boys, you _____ are responsible for this broken

window, and you know it. Don't lie to me.

A: But, Mom, we didn't break the window _____. Our baseball

did it.

B: Well, your baseball didn't hit _____, did it?

A: O.K., Mom, we give up.* What's the punishment?

B: Wait until your dad gets home. He's going to give it to you _____.

A: Oh, come on, Mother, give us a break.† It's just a broken window. We didn't

mean to do it.

❑ 1.11 Reflexive Pronouns

1. A **reflexive pronoun** refers back to the subject of a sentence:

> *People* in our town enjoy *themselves* on New Year's Eve.
> No *computer* computes by *itself.*

*Surrender.

†Give us another chance.

These are the reflexive pronouns:

oneself	ourselves
myself	yourselves
yourself	themselves
herself, himself, itself	

2.   We often use a reflexive pronoun to emphasize a subject. In what can be a rather formal (and somewhat stiff) style, the pronoun may follow the subject directly:

I myself, and nobody else, am going to accomplish this feat.
The president himself was present at the astronauts' landing.

Or the pronoun may appear at the end of a clause or a sentence:

The prime minister addressed the striking workers *herself.*
He does all the cleaning *himself,* even though he has a housekeeper.

3.   We frequently use reflexive pronouns as objects of certain verbs:

In his depression, Hamlet *killed himself.*
All of us have *enjoyed ourselves* immensely.
Don't *cut yourself* with that sharp knife, little boy.

4.   We also frequently use reflexive pronouns as objects of prepositions:

I'm just furious *at myself.*
They're always worrying *about themselves* and their possessions.
Just look *at yourself* in the mirror. What do you see?

5.   Idiomatically, the preposition *by* plus a reflexive pronoun means "alone":

It isn't much fun for one to travel *by oneself* [alone].
We were *by ourselves* [alone] when we made the decision.

6.   Try not to confuse the idiom *by oneself* with the emphatic use of reflexive pronouns. Compare the following:

The king wishes to make the statement to the news media *himself.*   [emphasis]

VERSUS

He's in the other room *by himself* writing it.   [meaning "alone"]

7.   As with other pronouns, masculine and feminine reflexive pronouns may be combined; however, such combinations can look awkward:

Everyone in my class lives by *himself or herself.*
BETTER   All my classmates live by *themselves.*

An actor must have a great deal of confidence in *him- or herself.*
BETTER   Actors must have a great deal of confidence in *themselves.*

2
Verbs, Adverbs and Types of Questions

❏ 2.1 Contrasting Verb Tenses

Supply in each blank the appropriate form of the verb given in parentheses. Use only the verb forms described in section 2.2.

Example

A: What's that couple dancing?

B: (*do*) They *'re doing* _____ the tango.

A: What an exciting dance!

B: And sexy!

1. A: Listen, Mr. Know-it-all, I'm beginning to get angry. What you're saying is

   embarrassing me. (*make*) You _____ a fool of me.

   B: Oh, I'm truly sorry. (*put*) I didn't realize I _____ my

   foot in my mouth.*

2. A: (*have*) The people of the United States _____ a

   constitution for more than a couple of hundred years.

   B: (*have*) Well, Switzerland _____ one for about 700

   years.

3. A: Katherine Gibson is certainly a woman who likes variety in her life. She never

   looks the same.

*Said the wrong thing.

13

B: Isn't that true? (*do*) Every time I see her, she _____ her hair in a different style.

4. **A:** It's a fascinating world, isn't it?

   B: It certainly is. Just think. (*make*) Right now, somewhere on earth, an important discovery _____.

5. **A:** How was your day yesterday?

   B: (*shop*) I _____ downtown from early in the morning to late in the afternoon, (*find*) and I _____ a beautiful winter coat for myself.

6. **A:** Good morning, ladies and gentlemen. Welcome to the first day of your exercise class. (*make*) I promise you that by the time this course comes to an end, you _____ a great deal of progress.

   B: We all hope so, Jane.

7. **A:** (*have*) Since the revolution in that country, the people _____ _____ a democratic form of government.

   B: (*enjoy*) Yes, they _____ peace and prosperity for quite a few years now.

8. **A:** What are your plans for after work?

   B: (*stop*) On my way home, I _____ at the bakery to pick up a birthday cake. (*come over*) A friend of mine _____ _____ to my place tonight. (*be*) It _____ his birthday, (*give*) so I _____ him a surprise birthday party.

9. **A:** Listen, our office has just got to get some kind of decision from your office by the end of the week.

   B: Don't worry. (*make*) I'm certain a decision _____ by the end of the week. At least we hope so.

10. **A:** Why weren't you in class that day a couple of weeks ago?

    B: (*hurt*) My arm _____ me that morning (*fall down*) because I _____ the night before.

11. **A:** What's the weather forecast for today and tomorrow?

    B: (*rain*) It _____ for the rest of the day, (*pass over*) but in the early evening the storm _____ our area and move out to sea. (*shine*) The sun _____

tomorrow morning, (*become*) but it _____ cloudy

in the afternoon.

12.   A: (*make*) Since the end of their revolution in the early 1980s, many improvements

_____ in their society, so the revolutionary

leaders say.

   B: I wonder what the people have to say.

13.   A: Tell me, Grandpa, what's on your mind?

   B: (*think / celebrate*) Oh, I _____ how hard it is to

believe that when your grandmother and I _____

our golden anniversary next September, (*live*) we _____

_____ together for fifty years (*know*) and _____

each other for sixty. It seems like only yesterday that we got married, (*be*) and yet

it _____ almost fifty years ago. (*go by*) How

fast time _____!

   A: (*think / cry*) Oh, Grandpa, I _____ that I

_____.

❑ 2.2   The Uses of the Six Verb Tenses

1.   There are six verb tenses in the English language; each tense has a continuous form. A verb phrase can be in the active or the passive voice. These are the six tenses:

the present (continuous) tense	the present perfect (continuous) tense
the past (continuous) tense	the past perfect (continuous) tense
the future (continuous) tense	the future perfect (continuous) tense

2.   We use the **simple present tense** for the following:

   a.   A factual statement:

A giraffe *has* a long and elegant neck.
The best wine in the world *is produced* in France.

   b.   A habitual activity or occurrence:

Our church *gives* free meals to the homeless once a week.
Hundreds of criminals *are arrested* every day.

   c.   A scheduled event in the future:

The class *begins* at nine o'clock sharp tomorrow morning.
The ship *sets* sail for Pago Pago at midnight tomorrow.

3.   We use the **present continuous tense** to express the following:

   a.   An event that is taking place now or temporarily:

We'*re beginning* a new exercise now.
Rented computers *are being used* for the time being.

b.   An event that is taking place in the future:

The movie *is coming* to an end in a few minutes.
The spy *is being shot* at dawn.

4.   We use the **simple past tense** for the following:

a.   An event that took place at a definite time in the past:

Marie Antoinette *lost* her head at the guillotine on October 16, 1793.
Independence *was declared* on July 4, 1776.

b.   An event that took place over a period of time in the past:

World War II *lasted* from 1939 to 1945.
The people of the nation *were led* by a dictator for forty years.

c.   A habitual activity that occurred in the past:

When he was a child, he *went* to Hebrew school every Saturday.
Mail *was delivered* twice a day in the old days.

5.   We use the **past continuous tense** for *emphasizing* the following:

a.   The occurrence of an event in the past; in this use, the simple past tense and its continuous form are interchangeable:

Women *were wearing* (or *wore*) ballgowns at the White House reception last night.
During the party, the guests *were being served* (or *were served*) the finest of food and drink.

b.   The duration of an event at a specific point in the past:

A: Where were you at nine o'clock last night?
B: I *was eating* dinner then.
A: And the children?
B: They *were sleeping* in their beds.

In this use, the past continuous tense is usually required.

6.   We also use the past continuous tense for expressing the following:

a.   Two actions happening at the same time in the past:

The audience *was applauding* wildly while the performers *were giving* their bows.
The patient *was crying* while she *was being examined* by the doctor.

b.   An action in progress interrupted by a single action in the past:

As I *was getting out of* the taxi [action in progress], I suddenly *felt* a pain in my back [interruption].

When I *walked* into the kitchen [interruption], the host and hostess *were having* a fierce argument [action in progress].

In this use, the simple past tense and its continuous form are often interchangeable, but there is usually a difference in meaning. Compare the following:

When I walked into the room, everyone *was laughing.*
(They started laughing *before* I entered the room.)

When I walked into the room, *everyone laughed.*
(They started laughing *when* I entered the room.)

Note: Of all the six continuous tenses, only the present and the past continuous tenses occur in the passive voice.

7. We use the **simple future tense** for an event that will occur in the future:

> "In the end, good *will triumph* over evil," the priest said in his Sunday sermon.
> Our lives *will be made* richer when we marry, I promise.

8. We employ the **future continuous tense** when we wish to *emphasize* the following:

   a. The continuous nature of an event in future time:

   > We'*ll be studying* hard for a long time.
   > All of us *will be praying* for peace and prosperity.

   b. An action in progress interrupted by another action in the future:

   > I'*ll be sleeping* soundly when you *get* home tonight.
   > The flowers *will be blooming* when you *return* in the spring.

9. *Be going to* plus a verb is also commonly used for future events. The verb phrase may be active or passive:

> Nothing special *is going to happen* tomorrow.
> Some things *are going to be delivered* tomorrow.

10. The future (continuous) tense and *be going to* are essentially interchangeable:

> You *will (are going to) make* a great success of your life.
> I'*ll (am going to)* be seeing you soon.

However, *will* gives much greater force to a statement. Besides simple futurity, *will* expresses the following:

> PROMISE   I *will love* you forever.
> DETERMINATION   We *will defend* our country with our lives.
> PREDICTION   The world *will come* to an end tomorrow.

11. When an action is deliberately planned, a native speaker most often uses *be going to*. In other words, the action is the result of a previous plan:

> I have an invitation to stay with a friend of mine in Connecticut. I'*m going to go* there this weekend. The taxi is waiting for me downstairs, and I have my luggage on the elevator. I'*m going* to the airport to catch my plane.

When an action is not deliberately planned, we usually use *will*:

> A: The taxi left without me, and I don't have time to take a bus to the airport.
> B: Here, I'*ll take* you in my car.
> A: Also, I don't have enough money to pay for my ticket.
> B: Your roommate *will lend* you some.
> A: And I lost my friend's number in Connecticut.
> B: Don't worry. Information *will have* it.

12. We use the **present perfect tense** to express the following:

   a. An event before an event in the general present:

   > When I *get* home, my wife *has gone* to work.   [before I get home]

   b. The duration of an event beginning in the past and continuing to the present and probably into the future:

   > I *have been* in this class since the first day of school.
   > [I am still here, and I'll most probably be here for the rest of the semester.]

Brunei *has been* independent for only a few years.
[It still is, and it will most surely remain so in the future.]

c.   Events that occur at an indefinite time in the past; the time of the action is not given:

"The Eagle *has landed.*"   [Among the first words spoken by Neil Armstrong when he landed on the moon.]

"I *have seen* the promised land."   [Spoken in a speech by Martin Luther King, Jr.]

Although we use the present perfect tense to express events at an indefinite time in the past, these events are directly related to events in the present. There is a relation of cause and effect:

Cause	Effect
The Eagle *has landed.*	We *are* now on the moon.
I *have seen* the promised land.	I now *know* the truth.

d.   Repeated events in the past that might be repeated again in the future:

I *have traveled* around the world twice, and I hope to go again.

Important discoveries *have been made* in recent years, and many more will be made in the future.

13.   For expressing the duration of an event from the past to the present, the present perfect tense and the **present perfect continuous tense** are essentially interchangeable; we use the continuous form for *emphasis:*

He *has been smoking* (or *has smoked*) since he was sixteen.
We *have been living* (or *have lived*) in the same house for 75 years.

However, when the two forms are interchangeable, we tend to favor the continuous form.

14.   For expressing the temporary nature of an event, the present continuous tense and the present perfect continuous tense are interchangeable:

They'*ve been working* (or *are working*) at night temporarily.
He'*s been renting* (or *is renting*) his furniture for the time being.

15.   We use the **past perfect tense** to express the following:

a.   An event that occurred before another in the past:

When she *fell* in love, she *had been* in love before.
When I *spoke* to him last, he *had been fired* from his job.

b.   The duration of an event before another in the past:

He *had worked* for the phone company for twenty years when he finally *retired.*

c.   Repeated events before a single event in the past:

When I finally *got* to Montreal, I'*d taken* three different planes.

16.   We use the past perfect tense most often in connection with a verb in the simple past tense:

He *had won* a million dollars when he *won* a million more.

Because the day *had been* long and difficult, my wife and I *were* very tired that evening.

However, the past perfect tense may appear by itself in a narrative to show an event that took place before a specific point in the past:

All of us were terribly excited when we got the news. We were cheering and waving, and in our excitement we were kissing strangers on the street. The church bells were ringing for victory; our soldiers were coming home. The war *had finally come* to an end.

17.   We use the **past perfect continuous tense** for emphasizing the duration of an event before an event in the past; it is basically interchangeable with the past perfect tense:

> When the train finally *came,* I *had been waiting* (*had waited*) for a couple of hours.
>
> It *had been raining* (*had rained*) for forty days when it suddenly *stopped.*

However, when the two forms are interchangeable, we most often favor the continuous form.

18.   When expressing duration with the past perfect continuous tense, we nearly always use a stated duration of time:

> When we got to San Francisco, we'*d been driving* **for six days.**
>
> When the patient regained consciousness, he'*d been lying* in a coma **for more than two years.**

19.   We do not use the **future perfect tense** as frequently as we use the other tenses. We use it to express the following:

   a.   An event before an event in the future:

> When I get home, I *will have eaten.*   [before I get home]
>
> When you get to the office, the mail *will have been delivered.*   [before you get to the office]

   b.   The duration of an event before an event in the future:

> When people *celebrate* the Fourth of July in 2076, the United States *will have been* an independent nation for 300 years.

   c.   Repeated events before an event in the future:

> By the time the twenty-first century comes to an end, many unimaginable changes *will have taken* place in the world.

20.   For expressing duration and emphasis, the **future perfect continuous tense** is basically interchangeable with the future perfect tense; the continuous form only gives much greater emphasis:

> When we finally get home, we *will have been traveling* (*will have traveled*) for more than three years.
>
> When my wife and I celebrate our next anniversary, we *will have been living* (*will have lived*) together for 25 years of perfect bliss.

However, when the two forms are interchangeable, we usually use the continuous form.

❑ 2.3   Negative Verb Phrases, Questions and Adverbs

Supply in each blank an appropriate form of the verb given in parentheses. Use only the verb forms described in section 2.6. Also use an adverb and a noun and pronoun subject when they are provided.

Examples

   a.   **A:**   (*you / do*) How ___*do you do*___? My name is Mr.
   Wisdom.

B: (*you / kid*) *Are you kidding* _____ me? (*you / get*) Where on earth _____ *did you get* _____ a name like that?

b. A: I'm a very cautious person.

B: (*ever / make*) So am I. I _____ *don't ever make* _____ a deal with a person (*have*) who _____ *doesn't have* _____ an honest face.

1. A: (*my boss / just / call*) _____ a few minutes ago?

B: Yes, he did, and he's coming into the office soon, so you'd better look busy.

2. A: (*someone / walk*) How many times _____ on the moon?

B: (*you / expect*) Just how _____ me to know that? I can't remember that kind of trivia. (*you / look*) Why _____ it up in your encyclopedia?

A: But, Mom, it's so out of date. It's older than you are.

B: (*you / have*) Young man, how come _____ more respect for me?

3. A: I have to be very quiet in the afternoon. I just can't make any noise at all.

B: Why's that?

A: (*usually / take*) My roommate _____ a nap then. (*always / take*) Ever since he became my roommate, he _____ a nap in the afternoon.

B: That must be inconvenient for you.

A: It is, but I have one thing to be grateful for.

B: What's that?

A: (*snore*) He _____.

B: Ha, ha, ha.

4. A: May I ask you a rather personal question?

B: Of course, as long as it's not about my age. What is it?

A: (*your late husband* / ever / go out with*) _____ _____ another woman?

B: Never! (*be / always*) He _____ very faithful, at least to my knowledge.

*Dead husband.

5. **A:** (*have*) Jack and Jill _____ a very big family, it

    seems. They already have three, don't they? And isn't she pregnant again?

    B: Yes, she is. (*push*) You know, whenever I see them, they _____

    _____ a baby carriage.

6. **A:** (*now / write*) So, Professor Kronenberg, I hear you _____

    _____ a book about the American Revolution. (*it / be*) How long

    _____?

    B: Oh, just guessing, I'd say about a thousand pages.

    A: My! (*take*) That _____ a long time to write.

    B: At least five years or so, I imagine.

    A: (*finally / finish*) I'm sure that when you _____

    your project, (*do*) you _____ a great deal of

    research.

    B: (*spend*) Yes, I _____ a lot of time at the library.

7. **A:** (*your father / serve*) _____ in the army during

    World War II?

    B: (*start*) When the war _____ in 1939, (*even /*

    bear / yet) he _____ .

❏ 2.4 Contrasting Verb Tenses

Follow the directions for section 2.3.

> ***Example***
>
> **A:** What a wonderful soprano!
>
> **B:** Incredible! (*ever / hear*) She must have the most beautiful voice that
>
> I _*have ever heard*_____ .

1. **A:** Good morning, darling.

    B: (*you / feel*) Well, good morning, dear, how _____

    _____?

    A: (*wake up / yet*) I _____ , but I will after a

    few cups of coffee.

2. **A:** (*you / sit down*) Juan, why _____? Take

    it easy and relax for a while.

B: I can't, Maria, I have to clean up the kitchen.

A: You don't have to worry about that. (*do*) The dishes _____ _____ by the children while you took your shower, (*sweep*) and I _____ the floor.

3. **A:** (*go*) I _____ to Europe on my vacation this coming summer.

   B: Oh, really? (*tell*) You _____ me that when I spoke to you last. (*you / tell*) Why _____ me?

   A: (*yet / make*) Well, I _____ any plans when I saw you last.

   B: Oh, how exciting! I wish I could go with you.

4. **A:** (*make*) Last night, my neighbors upstairs were having a party, and let me tell you that so much noise _____, I had to call the police.

   B: You shouldn't have done that.

   A: Why not? I couldn't sleep, and I had to get up early.

5. **A:** (*do*) At this time, some very important research _____ _____ at this university.

   B: (*have*) That's because it _____ such strong financial support from the federal government since the early 1980s.

6. **A:** (*do*) You know, Mr. Cartel, when we sign this contract before us, your company and mine _____ business together for more than thirty years.

   B: (*be*) Yes, Mr. Monopoly, and it _____ quite a profitable association.

7. **A:** (*you / get*) Hey, Bill, how _____ lost last night? (*be / you*) _____ drunk?

   B: (*you / joke*) _____? (*never / drink*) I _____ when I drive.

   A: (*just / kid*) Yes, I know, I _____. (*you / lose*) Well, anyway, how _____ your way?

   B: (*get*) Well, when I _____ to the traffic

interchange just before the bridge, (*make*) I _____

_____ the right turn, and quite suddenly I was in unknown territory.

8. **A:** (*he / ever / have*) When your grandfather had his operation last spring,

_____ one before?

B: Not ever! (*never / examine*) Why, when he went into the hospital last May,

he _____ by a doctor before.

9. **A:** Could I ask you a personal question?

B: It depends on how personal it is.

A: (*you / be*) How many times _____ in love?

B: That's too personal. (*you / want*) Anyway, why _____

_____ to know?

A: Oh, just curious.

❏ 2.5 Contrasting Verb Tenses

Follow the directions for section 2.3.

Example

A: Janet, why isn't there any ice cream in the fridge?

B: (*already / eat*) It *'s already been eaten* _____ by the

children, Dave.

A: Darn it!

B: (*you / have*) Why *don't you have* _____ an apple?

A: Thanks a lot.

1. **A:** (*travel*) I'm afraid I _____ much in

my life.

B: (*you / ever / be*) _____ in Europe?

A: (*never / be*) No, I _____ there, (*die*)

and I _____ to go.*

2. **A:** (*that student / fail*) Professor, why _____

_____ your course this semester?

B: (*rarely / do*) Since the very first day of class, he _____

*Eager to go.

_____ any homework. (*even / write*) In fact, he _____

_____ one composition.

3. A: (*go on*) Just what _____ in your

     office these days?

  B: (*know*) Who _____? (*yet / tell*)

     Nobody _____ me what's up,

     (*expect*) and I _____

     anyone to; (*be / just*) I _____

     an ordinary secretary.

4. A: What! (*your husband / still / pay*) _____

     _____ his federal income taxes?

  B: That's right. (*be*) They _____ due

     almost six months ago, (*still / pay*) and he _____

     _____ them.

5. A: (*tell*) Son, for the past few hours I _____

     _____ you what I think you should do. (*you / think*)

     What _____?

  B: Just why do I have to listen to your advice, Dad?

  A: (*I / be*) _____ your father?

6. A: (*go*) I _____ for a swim in the lake

     this afternoon. Would you like to go?

  B: (*sound*) Why, that _____ nice. I'd

     love to.

  A: (*you / swim*) _____ very well?

  B: (*take*) No, I _____ swimming lessons

     all last summer, (*still / learn*) but I _____

     _____ how to swim.

  A: (*you / learn*) _____ anything at all?

  B: (*even / learn*) I _____ how to float.

7. A: What an absolutely marvelous day!

  B: (*it / be*) _____? (*ever / like*) When the

     weather's nice like this, I _____ to

     stay inside. Let's go somewhere.

8. **A:** Bella Donna Rolanda is so fashionable! So elegant! So perfect! So impeccable!

   B: The height of fashion, my dear. (*just usually / come out of*) Whenever I see her on Madison Avenue, she _____ some very expensive beauty salon.

9. **A:** How's your new apartment?

   B: So-so. (*have*) I _____ enough room. (*fix*) Also, the plumbing, which _____ since the building (*build*) _____ almost fifty years ago, (*always / leak*) _____ .

   A: (*you / do*) What _____ about it? (*you / call*) Why _____ your landlord?

   B: (*you / try*) _____ to pull my leg?* You know what a cheap man my landlord is.

10. **A:** (*be / you*) _____ very busy at work yesterday?

    B: Not at all. (*get*) When I _____ to my office, (*just / paint*) it _____ , (*be / still*) and the walls _____ all wet; (*do*) I _____ anything at all for the whole morning. (*still / have*) Today I _____ _____ a place to work. (*lay*) Since ten o'clock this morning, they _____ _____ new carpet on the floor.

11. **A:** (*we / get out of*) Why _____ the house and go for a walk?

    B: (*still / make*) I can't, I've got lots of things to do in the kitchen, and the beds _____ , and it's almost eleven o'clock in the morning.

    A: (*you / forget*) Oh, come on, why _____ _____ the beds and the kitchen and go out with me?

    B: (*you / help*) Why _____ me? (*go out*) And then we _____ .

*Kid me.

A: (*kill*) Oh, but my back _____ me this

morning.

B: (*always / have*) You know, you _____

a way of getting out of work.

12. A: (*we / have*) Darling, _____ breakfast

together tomorrow morning?

B: (*get up*) By the time you _____,

sweetheart, (*already / leave*) I _____

the house. (*see*) I _____ you until

tomorrow night when I (*get*) _____

home at about ten.

A: (*be*) Well, we _____ able to see each

other then, either. (*already / go*) By ten o'clock I _____

_____ to bed. (*probably / sleep*) I _____.

☐ 2.6 Negative Verb Phrases and Questions

1. In the simple present and past tenses, except for the verb *be,* for negative verb phrases in the active voice we use the **auxiliary verbs** *do, does* and *did,* which we combine with the adverb *not;* we often use them in a contracted form:

> Two and three *do not* (*don't*) make six.
> That word *does not* (*doesn't*) mean a thing.
> They *did not* (*didn't*) build Rome in a day.

Note: Auxiliary verbs are often called **helping verbs** because they assist the main verb in performing different functions.

2. We combine *not* with auxiliaries in negative verb phrases in all the other tenses; we also frequently use them in a contracted form:

> It *is not* (*isn't*) raining much these days.
> We *will not* (*won't*) be seeing you soon.
> I *have not* (*haven't*) been taking it easy lately.
> The number of robberies *has not* (*hasn't*) declined.
> We *had not* (*hadn't*) done anything by that time.

3. We use *do, does* and *did* in questions in the simple present and past tenses; they precede the subject:

> *Do you* do much exercise?
> How often *does your roommate* help to clean the house?
> What on earth *did you* do to your hair?

4. In all the other tenses, the subject follows an auxiliary as well:

> *Will you* be here before the sun sets?
> How long *have you* been living in your place?
> How much money *had you* spent by that time?

Exception: When an interrogative pronoun (information word) is the subject of a sentence, the verb follows the subject directly:

> ***Who*** *gave* you that beautiful black eye?
> ***How many people*** *live* on earth?
> ***What*** *has happened* to your orchid plant?

❏ 2.7 Frequency Adverbs

1.　We use adverbs to modify verbs. **Frequency adverbs,** which describe the frequency of an event, very often occur (particularly with the simple present tense). These are the frequency adverbs:

Affirmative		Negative	
always	sometimes	rarely	almost never
almost always	usually	hardly ever	(not) ever
frequently	occasionally	seldom	
often	generally	never	
most often			

2.　In the simple present and past tenses, frequency adverbs usually follow the verb *be*:

> When the kids get up, they*'re always* full of fun and energy.
> It*'s almost never* cold in Los Angeles.
> When she was a child, she *was almost never* sick.

All other verbs are preceded by a frequency adverb:

> When he says hello, my boss *seldom has* a smile on his face.
> We *rarely went* swimming when we were in Alaska.

3.　In the other tenses, a frequency adverb follows an auxiliary:

> From the beginning of our relationship, she *has always* been faithful and loyal.
> We *will never* betray our trust in each other.

4.　In questions, frequency adverbs come after the subject:

> When you wake up from a nap, how do *you usually* feel?
> While he was working for you, was *he always* diligent?
> When you were at school, what time did *you usually* get up?

In negative verb phrases, frequency adverbs usually follow the adverb *not*:

> I'm afraid that I'm *not always* being told the truth.
> Our city has*n't always* been so full of crime.
> They do*n't often* go to church anymore.

5.　When *ever* occurs, the verb phrase is negative:

> I*'m not ever* here when you are.
> When she sleeps, she *doesn't ever dream.*

However, this is not true when the subject of a sentence is a negative word (or words):

> ***Nothing*** *has ever happened* in this town.
> When I dial that number, ***no one*** *ever answers.*

And this is not true in sentences with adjective clauses containing verb phrases in the present or past perfect tenses that follow nouns that are modified by adjectives in the superlative degree:

That must be one of the funniest jokes that I *have ever heard.*
It must have been the finest wine that I *had ever drunk.*

Ever may occur in both affirmative and negative questions:

Have you ever ridden (Haven't you ever ridden) on an elephant?
Do you ever do (Don't you ever do) the crossword puzzle?

6.   Usually, we use the frequency adverb *always* in the simple present or past tenses to express the frequency of a habitual activity:

The class *always begins* at nine o'clock.
When I was a child, dinner *was always served* at six.

However, to **emphasize** the frequency of a habitual activity, we use *always* in the present or past continuous tenses:

Bankers *are always worrying* about interest rates.
While we were in Seattle, it *was always raining.*

❏ 2.8 *Yet,* *Still* **and** *Even*

1.   We use the adverb *yet* most often in the final position of simple sentences or in the final position of clauses. The verb is negative:

She *hasn't quit* her job *yet.*
I *haven't called* the office *yet,* but I'll do it as soon as I can.

However, on occasion the adverb may directly follow a negative auxiliary:

I can't give you a sensible answer because I *haven't yet* been asked a sensible question.
When I called the hospital, the patient *hadn't yet* woken up.

2.   We almost always place *yet* at the end of questions:

Have you tipped the waiter *yet?*
Has a reservation been made *yet?*

But on occasion in the perfect tenses, we place *yet* after the subject:

Has *the contract yet* been signed?
By that time, had *you yet* made a decision?

3.   In the simple present and past tenses, the adverb *still* precedes the verb:

Though she's afraid of heights, she *still goes* mountain climbing.
They *still loved* each other when they got a divorce.

With other tenses, it almost always follows an auxiliary:

I've begged my company not to do it, but they *have still* transferred me to another city.
He'll pay a million in taxes, but he*'ll still* have two.

But for emphasis, we might put the adverb before the verb phrase:

She's disciplined her son, but she *still has had* problems with him.

4.   *Still* most often follows the verb *be:*

I *am still* a student.
All of my friends *are still* single.

In negative verb phrases, *still* usually precedes the verb *be:*

> They *still aren't* married.
> The food *still isn't* here.

For greater emphasis, however, we sometimes put the adverb after the verb:

> They *are still* not married.
> The food *is still* not here.

5. *Still* follows the subject in questions:

> Does *your child still* have braces on her teeth?
> Although that bill is wrong, have *you still* paid it?

6. *Still* precedes negative verb phrases:

> Though he might appear happy, he *still hasn't found* happiness.
> We *still haven't made* our first billion.

Still also precedes verb phrases containing frequency adverbs:

> She's lived in New York State for ten years, but she *still has never gone* to New York City.

> He's always been very good to her, but she *still has always been* very mean to him.

7. We use the adverb *even* for emphasis; it usually occurs in negative verb phrases:

> That fellow isn't telling you the truth. He doesn't have a million dollars. Why, he *doesn't even have* a dime. In fact, he *doesn't even have* a place to live in.

But we sometimes use it in affirmative verb phrases:

> They've decided to sell their car, their furniture and their apartment in town. They *have even decided* to sell their house in the country.

☐ 2.9 Adverbs of Indefinite Time

1. We often use **adverbs of indefinite time** with the perfect tenses. They usually follow an auxiliary:

> The children *have already* gone to bed.
> She*'s just* been promoted to a new job.
> When he died, he *had recently* won the lottery.
> This terrible movie *has finally* come to an end.

2. We can put these adverbs, except for *just,* in initial or final position:

> *Recently,* we've changed our phone number.
> We've put in a new swimming pool *recently*.

> *Already,* the new year has begun.
> My calendar has become full of appointments *already*.

> *Finally,* spring has come at last.
> The birds and the flowers have returned *finally*.

Note the commas when the adverbs are in initial position.

3. In questions, adverbs of indefinite time can follow the subject:

> Has *Daddy just* gotten home?
> Have *you finally* finished your project?

Or we can put these adverbs in final position:

> Have you washed the dishes *already?*
> Has your boss gotten angry *recently?*

4.   We also use adverbs of indefinite time with verb phrases in the simple past tense. When the adverb is *just, finally* or *already,* we may use an expression of definite time:

> I *just found* a new job *yesterday.*
> They *finally bought* a new car *last week.*
> I *already took* my vacation *two months ago.*

5.   When we use expressions of definite time, we must use the simple past tense. In formal usage, if we do not use such expressions and if an event is fairly recent, we most often use the present perfect tense. This usage does not exactly represent better grammar; it only suggests a greater degree of formality. Compare the following:

> **Formal**
>
> A: *Have you already typed* the letter, Ms. Quick?
> B: Yes, I have, sir, and it's ready to be signed.
>
> A: *Has the mail just come?*
> B: No, I don't believe so, Mrs. Post.
>
> **Less Formal**
>
> A: *Did you already type* the letter?
> B: Yeah, I did.
>
> A: *Did the mail just come?*
> B: No.

6.   We may also observe such a distinction with the adverb *yet:*

> **Formal**
>
> A: *Have you had* dinner *yet?*
> B: No, I haven't.
>
> **Less Formal**
>
> A: *Did you have* dinner *yet?*
> B: Not yet.

❏ 2.10 Negative Questions

1.   In **negative questions** in quite formal usage, *not* follows the subject. *Why* is the usual information word. Most often, we put the stress on *not:*

> Do *you* **not** listen to your conscience?
> Why did *the government* **not** do something about the situation?

Adverbs follow *not:*

> Do you *not ever* use suntan lotion to protect your skin?
> Have you *not always* been a student at this school?

But *still* precedes *not:*

> Children, have you *still not* made your beds?

2.   In informal usage, a subject follows a negative auxiliary:

> *Don't you* want to go to the game?
> Now listen, everyone, *haven't you* made enough money for a day?

3.   Adverbs follow the subject:

> Hasn't *she recently* inherited a lot of money?
> Didn't *you already* do your homework a few hours ago?

But *still* always precedes *not* in the perfect tenses:

> Oh, no, have you *still not* stopped smoking?
> What! Had he *still not* gotten up by lunchtime?

4. Also informally, we substitute *aren't I* for the very formal *am I not:*

> FORMAL   *Am I not* the ruler of this land?
> INFORMAL   *Aren't I* a foolish person sometimes?

5. When we ask a negative yes/no question—in other words, a question asking for a yes/no answer—it is often just for the sake of conversation (we expect people to agree with us):

> A: *Isn't that* a lovely sunset?
> B: It certainly is. It's breathtaking.

Or we may use the form to express surprise:

> A: *Isn't this* my toothbrush I'm using?
> B: No, it's mine.

6. With negative information questions, we may simply ask for information:

> A: Why *haven't you* paid the gas bill?
> B: I haven't had any money.

Or we can express annoyance:

> A: Wah! Wah! I want another ice cream cone.
> B: Bobby, why *don't you* grow up? You're acting like a little baby.

Or we can express a great deal of anger:

> A: How dare you insult me? Why *don't you* get out of this room? Now!
> B: O.K., O.K., take it easy; I'm leaving.

7. In the simple present tense, negative information questions with *why* can take the form of a polite request or suggestion:

> A: Why *don't you* get up, dear?
> B: Oh, Dad, I'd like to sleep a little bit more.

> A: Why *don't we* take a little break?
> B: Didn't we just have one?

8. We often use *how come* (meaning "why") in negative questions; note that the subject precedes the negative auxiliary:

> A: How come *you don't* like pizza?
> B: It doesn't like me.

> A: How come *the police haven't* come?
> B: Nobody has called them.

❑ 2.11 Emphasizing Ourselves

Supply in each blank an appropriate verb phrase. Use a verb chosen from the following list. Use an adverb when it is given in parentheses. Frequently, a pronoun subject (*you, he, I* and so on) of your own selection will be required. Some verbs will appear more than once.

ask	do	give	like	say
be	eat	go	live	see
buy	find	have	make	take
cost	get	kid	pay	

Example

A: Why ___*do you say*___ your former roommate is a lazy guy?

B: (*ever*) Listen, not once ___*did he ever do*___ anything while he ___*was living*___ with me.

1. A: How _____ the movies, Grandpa?

   B: Not since 1968 _____ a film. (*just*) They _____
   _____ as good as they _____
   when I _____ a young man. How about you?
   How _____ the movies?

   A: Actually, only sometimes _____; they
   _____ a lot these days, you know, (*just*) and
   I _____ a student without much money.

   B: _____ me for a loan, by any chance?

2. A: Ma'am, this little ivory statue is only a hundred dollars.

   B: _____ me? Only a hundred dollars! Why, it's not
   worth that. Just because I'm a tourist, you think you can take advantage of me.
   Not a penny more than ten dollars _____ for it.

   A: It's a deal, ma'am. (*just*) You _____ yourself a
   genuine ivory statue.

3. A: Why _____ that your boyfriend is cheap?

   B: Oh, he's not really cheap, he's just rather tight with his money. For example, only
   once in a great while _____ at a restaurant, (*ever*)
   and not once since I first met him _____ me to a
   movie, (*ever*) and never _____ me a birthday
   present.

   A: Listen, why _____ a new boyfriend? You're too
   good for him.

4. A: (*often*) _____ at a restaurant?

   B: Oh, rarely; almost never, in fact. Only once in a blue moon* _____
   _____ to one; they're just too expensive, you know. (*ever*) Only on
   very special occasions, I must say, _____ a meal
   at a restaurant. How about you?

*Once in a great while.

A: *(almost always)* I _____ a meal at one; rarely

_____ at home. As a matter of fact, I can't cook.

B: Why _____ dinner at my house some evening?

I _____ you a good home-cooked meal. *(even)*

I _____ a cake if you'd like.

A: I'd love to, any time. Not often _____ the

opportunity of having a good home-cooked meal. Oh, by the way,* I _____

_____ chocolate cake the best.

5. A: *(often)* _____ sushi, sashimi and things like those?

B: Not very often, only sometimes _____ a yen† for

raw fish.

A: *(ever)* _____ snake or dog?

B: *(ever)* Never, never _____ snake, *(ever)* and

never _____ dog. Why, a dog is man's best friend.

And snake! Why, I hate snakes. Just the idea of it disgusts me. Ugh!

❑ 2.12 Negative Openings

1. When we use a negative frequency adverb at the beginning of a sentence or a clause, the word order that follows is that of a question; we call the pattern a **negative opening:**

> *Never do I worry* when I walk on the streets at night.
> When I say hello to my neighbor, *seldom does she respond.*
> *Rarely did he complain* during his serious illness.

2. We frequently employ a negative opening with the adverb *not* combined with *once, often* or *ever:*

> Not **once** *have I ever made* a truly serious mistake.
> Not **often** *does one get* something for nothing.
> Not **ever** *have you looked* as beautiful as you do now.

3. We also use *not* combined with certain prepositional phrases:

> Not **for a long time** *have I had* such a meaningful experience.
> Not **for a day** *has my roommate felt* well.
> Not **since last week** *have we seen* our boss.

4. We frequently combine the adverb *only* with *sometimes* and certain adverbial expressions:

> *Only sometimes do I have* an appetite for something sweet.
> *Only once in a while does my neighbor mow* his front lawn.
> *Only once a day (week, month, year) do I drink* champagne.

*Incidentally.

†A yearning; longing; a strong desire.

5. We may also combine *only* with prepositional phrases:

> *Only* **at home** *do I truly relax.*
> *Only* **in New York** *do you find* so many fascinating people.

6. We use negative openings only when we wish to emphasize how we feel—in other words, how happy, surprised, angry or disappointed we are.

❏ 2.13 Emphasizing Ourselves

Supply in each of the blanks an appropriate verb phrase. Use a verb or an adverb when it is given in parentheses. Use a pronoun subject—such as *he, she,* or *we*—when it is required. Try not to overuse the emphatic form; use it where you think it is most effective.

> *Example*
>
> A: (*resemble*) Whom _____*do you resemble*_____ more, your mother or your father?
>
> B: (*look like*) Well, I _____*do look like*_____ my mother a bit, (*resemble*) but I _____*resemble*_____ my father much more.

1. A: My children like to help me out in the house. I don't know what I'd do without them. (*your twins / ever / do*) _____ any chores around the house?

    B: Frankly, they're quite spoiled and lazy. (*seldom / do*) They _____ _____ much of anything, (*do*) but they _____ _____ the dishes from time to time; (*do*) however, when they _____ them, (*do*) they _____ _____ them very well.

2. A: (*be*) How _____ your trip to Alaska last summer?

    B: (*have*) We _____ a fabulous time, (*have*) but we _____ a few problems.

    A: Like what?

    B: (*have*) Well, we _____ three flat tires on our way up to Anchorage, (*run out of*) and we _____ gas a couple of times.

    A: (*sound*) Oh, that _____ so bad.

    B: (*forget*) Oh, and I _____; (*break down*) our car _____ when we (*finally / get*) _____

_____ to Anchorage. (*be*) But there _____

_____ one thing that we (*be*) _____

very grateful for.

A: What was that?

B: (*never / get*) We _____ lost, not even once. (*use*)

We _____ a great map.

3. A: (*be*) How _____ your trip to London last

summer? (*have*) _____ a good time?

B: (*have*) Well, I'd say that we _____ an

interesting time rather than a good time. (*be*) Because we _____

_____ so busy with things connected to business, (*get*) we _____

_____ much of a chance to see anything. (*even / see*) Why,

we _____ the changing of the guards at

Buckingham Palace, (*pay*) and not once _____ a

visit to one of those famous London pubs.

4. A: How does Beverly Bell like her new job?

B: (*like*) Unfortunately, she _____ her boss much;

(*make*) however, she _____ very good money.

(*get*) It's a union plant, and she _____ good

union wages. (*offer*) Also, the company _____

excellent benefits to its workers. (*be*) It _____ a

cheap outfit.

A: (*do*) What _____?

B: (*work*) She _____ on an assembly line.

A: (*that / get*) _____ boring and tedious? (*hate*)

_____ all that noise?

B: (*make*) Sure she does, but she _____ darned

good money, and, believe me, (*need*) she _____

it.

5. A: (*everything / go*) How _____ on your last

vacation?

B: (*have*) Not smoothly, but we _____ a pretty

good time despite everything.

A: (*go*) What _____ wrong?

B: (*have*) Well, first off,* not once _____ a sunny

day. (*make*) When we _____ plans for our trip,

(*know*) we _____ that August is the rainy

season in the Magic Islands. And the mosquitoes! (*bite*) I _____

_____ all the time.

A: (*think*) Well, what _____? (*ever / go back*)

_____ to the Magic Islands?

B: (*ever / go back*) Perhaps, maybe in another season, but never, never,

never _____ to that terrible hotel.

☐ 2.14   The Emphatic Form with the Simple Present and Past Tenses

1. For emphasis when we speak, we put a **stress** on the auxiliary verb:

> He's never been in Asia, but he **has** been in Europe.
> They won't do the job for fifty, but they **will** do it for a hundred.

For emphasis when we write, we underline the word:

> She isn't painting much these days, but she is writing.

For emphasis in print, we *italicize* the auxiliary verb:

> We hadn't planned to go to Alexandria, but we *had* planned to go to Cairo.

2. Since auxiliary verbs do not occur in affirmative verb phrases in the active voice with the simple present and past tenses, we use the auxiliary *do, does* or *did* to make the **emphatic form.** We put a stress on the auxiliary:

> I don't do housework, but I **do** *do* the gardening.
> She never wears lipstick, but she **does** *wear* a little bit of eye shadow.
> He didn't win first prize in the contest, but he **did** *try*.

3. We most often use the emphatic form in clauses introduced by *but* or *however:*

> We hated the play, *but* we did like the actors.
> He's very much a hermit; *however,* he does appear in public from time to time.

Or we use the form in one of a pair of clauses coordinated by *but* or *however:*

> She *does want* to be a success; *however,* she doesn't want to work for it.
> Oh, yes, I *did like* that spicy food, *but,* unfortunately, it didn't like me.

4. We use the emphatic form less frequently in other types of clauses:

> If she *does marry* that man, I'll be very surprised.
> Everything was expensive in Tokyo, so we *did spend* a lot.

5. We sometimes use frequency adverbs with the emphatic form:

> I *never did go* to the Vatican when I was in Rome.
> When we go out with them, we *always do have* a great time.

*To begin with; first.

6. We often use the emphatic form by itself when it contrasts with something already said or written:

> A: You didn't wash your hands, young man.
> B: I *did wash* them, Daddy, I did.
>
> A: You know, dear, I think you're beginning to lose interest in me.
> B: Listen, darling, I *do love* you, truly.

7. We frequently use emphatic adverbs such as *definitely*, *certainly* and *really* with the emphatic form:

> A: My, your son looks so much like you.
> B: Yes, indeed, he *certainly does resemble* me.
>
> A: My son isn't doing enough homework, Ms. Brooks?
> B: That's right, Mrs. Ramirez, he *definitely does need* to do more work outside of class. He *really does require* it.

8. In their enthusiasm, speakers and writers have a tendency to overuse the emphatic form. Compare the following:

Overused

I *did lose* a lot of money at cards; however, I *did win* quite a bit at roulette, but I *did lose* all of it at the horse races the next day.

Better

I lost a lot of money at cards; however, I *did win* quite a bit at roulette, but I lost all of it at the horse races the next day.

❑ 2.15 Seeking Confirmation

Supply in each blank an appropriate verb phrase or tag ending. Use each verb and adverb that is given in parentheses. Frequently, a pronoun subject of your own selection will be required. Practice the appropriate intonation patterns.

> *Example*
>
> A: (*see*) Yes, I must say that I _____ *have seen* _____ many, many things all over the world in my very long life.
>
> B: (*travel*) You _____ *have traveled* _____ a great deal, *haven't* _____ *you* _____, Mr. Quest?

1. A: O.K., class, let's have a little history quiz. (*be*) First off, who _____ _____ Charles Lindbergh? Now raise your hands. Yes, you, Tom.

    B: I'm not quite sure. (*fly*) He _____ across the Atlantic Ocean, _____?

    A: That's right, Tom. (*do*) Now, when _____ it?

    B: (*be*) Ummm, let me think, now, let's see, it _____ in 1935, _____?

C: That's not right, Mr. Fujioka. (*be*) It _____ in

1927, _____ it?

A: (*raise*) That's right, David, but you _____ your

hand, _____?

2. A: The mechanic down at the garage wants a thousand dollars for repairing my right

fender. (*charge*) He _____ too much, _____

_____?

B: I'm afraid so. (*that guy / look*) You know, frankly, never _____

_____ honest to me.

A: (*look*) Yes, he _____ a little crooked,* _____

_____?

3. A: (*need*) Even though I _____ it for work all the time,

(*always / borrow*) my girlfriend _____ my car.

(*always / expect*) Also, she _____ me to take her to

the best and most expensive restaurants in town.

B: (*just / take*) She _____ advantage of the fact that

you love her so much, _____?

A: (*really / think*) _____ so?

B: Listen, I know that woman well. (*go out with*) _____

her for a couple of years before you came along?

4. A: Listen, Mom and Dad, why should I have to listen to your orders all the time?

(*get*) I _____ sick of it. (*leave*) Why _____

_____ me alone?

B: (*be*) I _____ your father, _____?

C: (*be*) And _____ your mother? (*be*) _____

_____ the woman who brought you into this world?

B: (*deserve*) _____ some respect and loyalty from you,

our oldest son?

A: (*ever / show*) But you _____ me any respect,

_____?

5. A: (*seldom / have*) Your neighbors _____ guests,

_____?

*Dishonest.

B: (*be*) Well, you know, they _____ rather strange

people, _____?

A: (*ever / see*) Yes, you _____ them around,

_____?

B: (*ever / see*) Never, why, not once _____ them

on the street, (*ever / see*) and only two or three times _____

_____ them in their yard. They're very spooky.

A: (*just / like*) They _____ to be by themselves,

_____?

❏ 2.16 Tag Questions

1. We use **tag questions** in much the same way that we use negative questions:

> **A:** Look at that blue sky, the lovely and light floating clouds, and the cherry blossoms. My!
> **B:** *It's a beautiful day, isn't it?*   [Isn't it a beautiful day?]

2. The final part of a tag question is called a **tag ending.** When a statement is positive, we usually use a negative tag ending:

> **A:** Are you sure I don't have to set this dial?
> **B:** It's automatic, *isn't it?*

When a statement is negative or contains a negative adverb, we use a positive tag ending:

> **A:** I think you're exaggerating the issue. Just why do you think we need population control?
> **B:** Are you serious? The world's population *isn't getting* any smaller, *is it?*
> **A:** She *seldom does* much around the house, *does she?*
> **B:** Right, but she does do a great deal in the garden.

3. As with negative questions, with negative tag endings we may observe either a formal or an informal style. Compare the following:

Formal

> **A:** Just why do we have to listen to you?
> **B:** What? I'm the group leader, *am I not?*
> **A:** How do I know how much money my husband makes?
> **B:** You prepare his taxes, *do you not?*

Informal

> **A:** Must you have everything for yourself?
> **B:** You're right. I am being selfish, *aren't I?*
> **A:** After I gave the waiter the tip, he ran out the door and disappeared.
> **B:** You tipped the wrong guy, *didn't you?*

4. We often follow the emphatic form of the simple present and past tenses with tag endings:

> **A:** We might get married, but I'm not so sure.
> **B:** Pay attention now, and listen to me. You *do love* her, *do you not?*

A: Oh, no, Mom, I didn't do that. Really, Mother, I didn't, believe me.

B: You did, you *did lie* to me, *didn't you?* I can tell it in your eyes. You can't hide a thing.

5.   When we ask a tag question and if we are certain of the answer, which we most often are, our intonation of the tag ending is down:

A: It's a perfectly lovely day, *isn't it?*

B: Absolutely splendid! Everything is just right.

When we are not certain of the answer, our intonation is up:

A: The economy isn't going to get worse, *is it?*

B: Frankly, I'm not sure, it's hard to say.

❏ 2.17   Telling People What to Do

Supply in each blank an appropriate verb phrase. Use the verbs in the following list, some of which will occur more than once; also use each adverb that is given in parentheses. Use a pronoun subject of your own choice when it is required. Use the polite word *please* when it is appropriate or necessary.

be	drink	go	know	meet	take
call	drive	have	leave	pay	tease
come	enjoy	join	look	quiet down	wait
do	give	kid	make	show	wash

Example

A: _____*Show*_____ me your driver's license, _*please*_.

B: I'm sorry, officer; I _____*left*_____ it at home by mistake.

A: Well, then ____*please show*____ me some other kind of

identification.

1.   **A:** Children, all that unnecessary noise _____ me

crazy. _____, kids. (*just*) And the two of

you _____ so filthy and dirty.

_____ at your boots. (*ever*) Where on earth

_____? _____ to

the bathroom right now, Bobby and Betty, _____,

and _____ your hands and face.

B: Ah, Mom, _____ us a break. (*always*) You

_____ us orders.

2.   **A:** Hi, my name is Peter Bouchard; my friends _____

me Pete.

B: Hi, my name is Patricia Blair; (*just*) _____ me

Patty, _____.

A: You _____ a new student on the campus,

_____? You _____

_____ here last semester, _____?

B: No, I _____ here last semester; I'm a brand-new

student.

A: _____ many friends on campus?

B: No, I _____ a soul;* I'm rather lonely.

A: Why _____ my social club?

You _____ a lot of nice kids, I promise.

_____ with me now. (*just*) I _____

_____ on my way there.

B: Well, I'm a rather shy person, and I _____ new

people too easily.

A: Oh, come on, you _____ too shy to speak to

me, _____?

3. A: Unfortunately, we have to go now; our kids _____

for us at home. It _____ nice seeing you all.

It _____ a lot of fun: great party, great food,

fabulous people and marvelous music.

B: _____ all our love to everyone at home, dear.

A: O.K., Mom.

C: Yes, and _____ safely, son.

A: _____ me, Dad? My wife _____

_____ us home. I _____ too much

alcohol.

C: Yes, son, you _____ a little too much

tonight, _____?

A: Oh, come on, Dad, _____ me a break. (*just*)

I _____ myself. I _____

_____ a fool out of myself, _____?

*A person.

4. **A:** Class! _____ and _____

    attention. This classroom sounds like Grand Central Terminal.

    B: Yes, sir.

    C: O.K., Mr. Wisdom.

    A: (*ever*) Now, listen, young man, _____ me that again.

    All right, let's begin. Teddy! _____ that gum out

    your mouth before I _____ it for you. Darn it,

    José, _____ silent for just a minute if you can. And

    Abdul, _____ Emma. That _____

    nice, _____? Now let's go on.

❏ 2.18 The Imperative Mood

1. We use the **imperative mood** for making requests or commands in the present. The verb always remains a base form (simple form of a verb):

> *Wash* your hands before leaving the bathroom.
> *Keep* your hands on your lap.

2. It is very often best that we use the polite word *please* in such commands and requests. It may appear at the beginning of the sentence or, if the sentence is short, at the end:

> *Please clean* the whole house with a strong disinfectant.
> *Shut* the door, *please.* It's drafty in here.

Note: We use a comma when *please* is in final position.

3. We also use the imperative mood for giving instructions:

> *Roast* the turkey at about 350 degrees—not any hotter.
> *Carve* the bird with a finely sharpened carving knife.

4. In the imperative mood, we do not usually include the subject of a sentence (always second person singular or plural), but it is understood:

> [*You*] Please take those dirty boots off the sofa.
> [*You*] Stop smoking so much of that poison, I beg you.

Do not (don't) makes a negative phrase:

> *Don't touch* that fragile lamp, please.
> Please *do not* ask so many outlandish questions.

5. Frequency adverbs precede the verb in commands and requests:

> Please *always lock* the windows before leaving the house.
> *Always take* care of your old friends, *never be* disloyal and don't *ever talk* about them behind their backs.

6. We frequently employ the emphatic form of the simple present tense with the imperative mood:

> Please *do do* something around the house once in a while.
> *Do sit down* and rest yourself, please.

Note: In the imperative mood, we use the verb *be* with the auxiliary verb *do:*

> Please *don't be* so picky with your food.
> Children, *do be* on time when you have an appointment, please.

7. A person's name or title is a polite addition to a command or a request, so we often use it:

> *Ma'am,* please do allow me to introduce myself.
> Don't make a fool out of yourself, *Andy,* please.

☐ 2.19 Making Suggestions and Requests

Supply in each blank either an appropriate form of a verb from the following list or an appropriate response. Use each adverb that is given in parentheses. Use a pronoun subject of your own choice when it is required. Use the polite word *please* when it fits; however, do not overuse the word.

answer	clean	go	play	take
be	close	have	ring	turn on
build	dance	leave	run	use
buy	do	listen	spend	
cancel	get	make	stay	

Example

A: ___*Shall I turn on*___ the lights? ___*Isn't*___
it a little dark in here?

B: ___*Please do*___, dear, thank you.

1. A: Well, what do you think, Moto? _____ to the
movies tonight, or _____ home? It's up to you.

   B: _____ to the movies, Yoko. It's nice and cozy
here, and it's so cold out tonight. _____ a nice
evening at home, for a change. I'm tired of going out.

   A: Moto, that sounds nice. _____ a big fire in the
fireplace?

   B: What a wonderful idea! _____.

   A: What _____ for dinner, Moto?

   B: I don't care, Yoko, it's up to you.

2. A: Ummm, Peggy, (*just*) _____ to that great
music.

   B: Yeah, great! _____, _____?

   A: Oh, _____ yet. _____
_____ some drinks at the bar first, _____?

B: O.K., but _____ too much time over drinks. I

feel like dancing tonight, don't you?

A: I always do when I'm with you, Peggy.

B: Oh, Jason, you're such a flatterer.

3. A: Well, kids, I'm afraid I've got bad news this morning. I've got to go to the office

today; I've got lots of things to catch up on.

B: But, Mom, it's Saturday! You should stay home and rest.

C: Yeah, you should take it easy. You work hard at the office.

A: I know, boys, but I've just got to go to the office,

so _____ the Saturday chores

and _____ the usual errands?

B: But, Mom, I _____ baseball in the park with

the gang. I _____ the pitcher today.

C: Yeah, and I _____ to the movies with a bunch

of kids from school.

A: Well, I'm sorry to have to disappoint you, boys,

but _____ your plans

and _____ something for me, for a change?

B: O.K., Mother, if we have to. Somebody else _____

_____ to be the pitcher today.

C: Yeah, O.K.

A: Good, now that that's settled, let me tell you what I want you to do today.

First, _____ all of the beds, and

then _____ the breakfast dishes?

Then _____ all the dirty clothes down to the

basement and _____ all the laundry.

And _____ a mess in the basement? There's an

extra amount of laundry this week, for some reason. It's probably because you

two insist on using so many towels every day.

B: What kind of soap _____?

A: It's down in the basement by the washing machine. _____

_____ more than you need. After the laundry, _____

_____ to the store. _____

anything that isn't on this shopping list. _____

any junk food. Is that understood?

B: But, Mom!

A: Well, let's see, is there anything else? Oh, yes, this is *very*

important. _____ the cat's litter box?

B: But, Mother, ugh! I hate to do that.

C: _____, Mom, the phone _____

_____. _____ it?

A: No, dear, _____ _____, I will.

[On the phone]

D: Hi, Barbara, great news! You don't have to come into the office today. The boss

can't make it, and we can't do anything without her.

A: O.K., Lan Ling. Thanks. Yes, I'll be right there.

C: Who was that on the phone, Mom?

A: Oh, just someone from the office, dear. They want me to get there as fast as I can.

☐ 2.20   *Let's*; Polite Requests with *Shall, Will* and *Would*

1.   In suggestions, *let's* (*let* plus *us*) may precede a verb in the imperative mood. In negatives, *not* precedes the verb. *Let's* or *let's not* is a frequent response to such suggestions:

    A: It's unbelievably cold. *Let's get* home fast.
    B: Yeah, *let's*. Come on, *let's run*.
    C: *Let's not*, I'm out of breath. *Let's* slow down.
    D: Oh, please, *let's not argue*. It's too cold.

2.   *Shall I* or *Shall we* means "do you want me (us) to" when it precedes a verb in the imperative mood:

    Shall I (*Do you want me to*) *reveal* my secret?
    Shall we (*Do you want us to*) *go* for a walk in the moonlight?

In a way, we are asking for permission. *Please do* or *please don't* is the most polite response to *shall I:*

    A: *Shall I open* the window?
    B: *Please do,* Dad. We need some fresh air.

    A: *Shall I tell* you a little bit of gossip?
    B: *Please don't.* I hate idle gossip.

Let's or *let's not* is the most polite response to *shall we:*

    A: *Shall we become* husband and wife?
    B: Oh, *let's*. That sounds like fun.
    A: *Shall we have* a large wedding in a church?
    B: *Let's not. Let's elope.*

3. We use *shall we* with *let's* in tag questions:

    A: *Let's listen* to a little bit of soft music, *shall we?* And *let's stay* home by the fire this evening, *shall we?*

    B: Sounds absolutely lovely. *Let's.*

4. We use *will you* (*please*) before a verb in the imperative mood:

    A: Darn it, Pluto. *Will you get out of* the kitchen?

    B: *Bark, bark, bark.*

    A: Children, *will you please get up* right now?

    B: Ah, Grandma, it's too cold to get out of bed.

5. *Would you* (*please*) may also precede a verb in the imperative mood:

    A: I'd like to tell you more about the problems I'm having with my wife.

    B: *Would you please change* the subject? The problems you're having with your wife are none of my business.

6. *Would you* (*please*) *not* makes for a very strong request:

    A: *Would you please **not** step* on my feet when you're dancing with me?

    B: And *would you please **not** try* to lead me? I'm the man, aren't I?

3

Articles and Prepositions

❏ 3.1 *A* and *An* Versus No Article

Fill in each blank with *a, an* or a horizontal line (meaning no article is required).

Example

A: Just what are you looking for in __*a*__ companion?

B: __—__ intelligence, __*a*__ good set of values and __*an*__ honorable reputation.

1. A: What's the most distinctive feature of _____ giraffe?

   B: _____ elongated neck.

   A: How about _____ elephant?

   B: Besides its size, _____ long trunk.

2. A: Why are you going to _____ auction tomorrow?

   B: I'm very interested in _____ antique furniture.

   A: Are you interested in _____ antiques as _____ investment?

   B: It's really just _____ hobby, but I've made quite _____ lot of money

   collecting _____ old furniture, I must admit.

3. A: What must _____ person who wants to be _____ lawyer or _____ banker

   have?

   B: Well, one thing is for sure—_____ honest face.

4. A: What do we usually find in _____ democratically governed country?

   B: _____ open society and _____ free life-style.

5. A: What kind of book is *Gone with the Wind?*

47

B: It's _____ historical novel, _____ account of life in the South before, during and after the Civil War.

6. A: What's one of the most important things going on at _____ university?

   B: _____ scientific research, most certainly.

7. A: What do the models in fashion magazines such as *Vogue* and *Bazaar* always have?

   B: _____ beautiful hair, _____ long legs, _____ captivating smile, _____ sparkling eyes and _____ good set of teeth.

8. A: According to the Bible, what did God create on the sixth day of Creation?

   B: _____ human being.

9. A: What are some of the things that France is famous for?

   B: _____ wonderful food, _____ beautiful fashions and _____ lovely perfume. And, of course, _____ charming women.

10. A: What does everyone have? It's that thing that makes us completely different from one another.

    B: Ummm, let's see, _____ unique personality? _____ soul?

11. A: If you like to cook and eat, what's _____ very nice thing to have?

    B: _____ herb garden by the kitchen door and _____ dishwasher.

12. A: Oh, really? How often do you see _____ psychiatrist?

    B: Once _____ week I have _____ one-hour session.

    A: How much is _____ session?

    B: I pay _____ two-hundred dollars for _____ visit.

    A: Goodness gracious! That's _____ awful lot of money. What's your psychiatrist like? _____ man or _____ woman?

    B: _____ man; he's _____ European, from Vienna.

    A: Well, I hope you're getting your money's worth.

13. A: When the Civil War came to _____ end in 1865, what did the United States finally become?

    B: _____ united nation and _____ free one.

❏ 3.2 *A* and *An*

1. *A* is called the **indefinite article,** and we use it before a singular noun or an adjective that begins with a consonant sound:

   a kitchen table   *a good* idea

2.   We use *an*, the alternate form of *a*, before a singular noun or an adjective that begins with a vowel sound:

> *an early* class   *an ostrich* feather

A has the meaning of "one," and it may occur with countable nouns in phrases such as *a thousand people* and *a hundred dollars*.

3.   A word beginning with a consonant letter (all the letters of the alphabet except the vowels *a, e, i, o* and *u*) usually begins with a consonant sound; however, certain nouns and adjectives begin with a consonant letter but have a vowel sound. For example, most nouns and adjectives beginning with the consonant *h* have a consonant sound:

> *a happy* home   *a house* plant   *a half* hour

However, the following words beginning with *h* have a vowel sound:

> *an hour* meeting   *an honest* lawyer   *an heir*
> *an honor*   *an homage*   *an heiress*

Herb may begin with either a vowel or a consonant sound; *an herb,* however, is more common:

> Sage is *an (a) herb,* and so is rosemary.

An hotel and *an historical* occur in British usage; in the United States, we most often use *a hotel* and *a historical.*

4.   Most words that begin with the vowel *u* have a vowel sound:

> *an ugly* duckling   *an utter* fool   *an unnecessary* question

However, a few nouns and adjectives beginning with the vowel *u* have a consonant sound (pronounced *you*):

> *a university*   *a universal* concept   *a useful* machine
> *a united* stand   *a unique* idea   *a Ukrainian*

5.   *European* and *one* begin with the vowels *e* and *o*, respectively, but have a consonant sound:

> *a European* vacation   [pronounced *your*]
> *a one*-day affair   [pronounced *won*]

6.   We never use *a* or *an* before a plural countable noun or an uncountable noun:

> little *mice*   love *stories*   beautiful *bread*

❑ 3.3 Place, Time and Direction

Supply a preposition in each blank. Use only those in the following list.

> above   around   below   from   of   over   under
> among   at   between in   on   to   with

Example

A: Daddy, does the sun always rise _____*in*_____ the east?

B: Yes, son, it does, and it always sets _____*in*_____ the west.

A: Is the sun far _____*from*_____ us?

B: Yes, about 93,000,000 miles, I think it is.

A: Why don't people build a rocket and go _____*to*_____ the sun?

B: If they did that, the rocket would melt; the sun is very hot.

A: Couldn't they go _____*at*_____ night?

1. A: Where's the atlas?

    B: _____ the top shelf _____ the bookcase.

    A: Is it the blue book lying _____ its side?

    B: No, it's the large red one _____ the Bible and the dictionary; there's a yellow cookbook directly _____ it.

2. A: Where shall I put the TV set?

    B: Hmm, let's see. Don't you think _____ the corner _____ the living room would be a good place for it?

    A: Next _____ the stereo?

    B: Right. Isn't that the best place?

3. A: Well, I'm ready to do it. Where shall I sign my name _____ this contract?

    B: _____ the last page _____ the bottom line _____ my signature, please.

4. A: _____ that painting _____ a man standing _____ the trees and animals, why does he have a ring _____ his head?

    B: That's not a ring; it's a halo. That's a portrait of Saint Francis. Saints are always portrayed _____ a halo.

5. A: What a beautiful necklace Madame France is wearing _____ her neck!

    B: Indeed, and look at the bracelets _____ her wrists.

    A: And the lovely baby orchids _____ her hair.

6. A: Where did you hear that? What terrible news!

    B: _____ the car radio _____ my way home _____ work.

    A: Isn't it _____ this evening's newspaper?

    B: I didn't see it, but it'll be _____ TV for sure.

7. A: I want to get _____ a subway station. Are we close _____ one?

    B: Yes, there's one _____ the corner _____ Lexington Avenue and 68th Street. You can easily walk there; it's not _____ all far _____ here.

8. **A:** Have you found that letter from the Tax Department yet?

   B: Yes, _____ some old papers and letters _____ the top

     drawer _____ my desk _____ the bedroom.

9. **A:** _____ the receiving line _____ the reception _____

     the embassy this evening, where should the ambassador stand?

   B: _____ the end.

   A: And his wife?

   B: _____ his right side, according to protocol.

❑ 3.4 More Prepositions

Supply a preposition in each blank. Use only those in the following list.

about	between	from	out	to
across	by	in	over	up
at	during	of	since	with
along	for	on	through	

Example

A: Will the poor ever have a better way ___*of*___ life?

B: As long as the rich continue to be so selfish and greedy, the gap *between*

    them and the poor will remain a wide one.

1. **A:** What's the weather forecast _____ tomorrow?

   B: It'll probably be raining _____ the rest _____ the day,

     but _____ the early evening the storm will pass _____ our area

     and move _____ _____ sea. The sun's going to be shining

     tomorrow morning, but it'll become cloudy _____ the afternoon. Unless

     the forecast changes, I'm not going to make any plans _____ tomorrow

     evening. I certainly don't want to go _____ _____ the rain.

2. **A:** Mommy, where do potatoes grow?

   B: _____ the ground, dear.

   A: Where do cows and sheep live?

   B: _____ a farm. Can't you stop asking so many questions, honey?

3. **A:** Did your father serve _____ the army _____ World War II?

   B: No, when the war started _____ 1939, he hadn't even yet been born.

     He's not *that* old.

A: Did he see any action _____ Vietnam?

B: Oh, yes, _____ that time he'd already been _____ the

army _____ a couple _____ years, so he saw a

lot _____ action _____ the early stages _____ the

war.

4. A: When I was _____ Malaysia last January, I went _____* a

monsoon. Have you ever been _____ one?

B: Yes, a terrible one. I went _____ a very long one when I visited

Nepal _____ 1978. I arrived _____ Katmandu _____

June 6th, and the monsoon got there three days later. When it finally ended, it

had been raining _____ more than four months, and several villages had

been destroyed completely _____ landslides and floods, and quite a few

people had been killed.

5. A: Daddy, I get confused _____ prepositions.

B: Everybody does, Bobby, it just takes practice.

A: _____ example, where's my nose?

B: _____ the middle _____ your face.

A: How _____ my brain?

B: _____ your head.

A: Well, how _____ my head?

B: _____ your shoulders.

A: And where are they?

B: _____ the top _____ your body.

A: How _____ my feet?

B: They're _____ the floor, where they ought to be. Now stop asking me so

many questions, please. You're making me dizzy.

6. A: What does your book _____ famous aviators have to say _____

Charles Lindbergh?

B: Well, first it says that _____ 1927 Lindbergh was the first person to

fly _____ the Atlantic Ocean _____ a solo flight _____

New York _____ Paris.

A: Oh, I thought it was _____ 1937.

Went through means "experienced."

7.   A: If this question isn't too personal, may I ask why you and your wife got a

divorce?

B: No, I don't mind talking _____ it. It's been some time _____

our divorce, and discussing it doesn't bother me so much now.

A: Yes, I know, _____ my own experiences _____ life, that time is

a great healer. So just what went wrong _____ your marriage?

B: _____ spite _____ the fact that we were deeply _____

love _____ each other, we just didn't get _____.* We were

arguing _____ the time we got _____ _____ the

morning _____ the time we went _____ bed _____

night. Despite our inability to agree _____ anything, we did manage to

have lots _____ good times. Although my former wife treated me

terribly _____ our marriage, I was always good _____ her, and

I was always good _____ her father, even though he was probably the

main cause _____ the divorce. Oh, _____ the way, this little

talk we're having is confidential, isn't it? Just _____ you and me?

A: Oh, _____ course, I won't mention a thing _____ anyone.

❑ 3.5 Types of Prepositions

1.   We use a **preposition** to connect one part of speech with another:

We're getting close *to* the end *of* our trial.

2.   We form a **prepositional phrase** by combining a preposition with a noun or a pronoun:

A great many things are happening *in the world.*
This is a secret *between you and me.*

3.   A **place preposition** shows where a person, place or thing is:

The president is *at the White House today.*
Their office is *at 1 Washington Square North in the Village.*

4.   We often use place prepositions in **expressions of place,** which usually contain a preposition plus *the* plus *of:*

The North Pole is *at the top of the world.*
He interrupted us *in the middle of our conversation.*

5.   A **time preposition** can refer to one point in time:

We went to the theater together *on Saturday.*
Our plane arrived on time *at noon.*
They met *in September* and were married *in May.*

*Get along means "have a harmonious relationship."

Or we can use it to refer to extended time, expressing duration:

I've been working on this project *since Christmas last year.*
They're never able to see each other *during the work day.*

6. **Prepositions of direction** refer to movement:

I always *walk to work from my apartment building.*
I live in a sixth-floor walk-up; I'*m going up and down* the stairs all day and all night long.

❑ 3.6 Prepositions and *A* and *An* Versus No Article

Supply in each blank *a, an,* a horizontal line (meaning no word is required) or a preposition chosen from the following list.

about	between	for	of	to
around	by	from	on	until
at	down	in	out of	with

Example

A: Does your roommate have _____*an*_____ excellent educational background?

B: Not really, but she does have _____*a*_____ high school diploma, so she doesn't find it difficult to find _____—_____ service jobs. She's working _____*at*_____ _____*a*_____ fast-food place now.

1. A: Must I stop drinking and smoking, Dr. Moy?

   B: I think you should, Mr. Crawford. _____ alcohol isn't good _____ you, and _____ cigarettes are even worse.

2. A: Do _____ lot _____ people _____ your country speak English?

   B: No. It's spoken _____ places _____ tourists, but it isn't spoken much _____ _____ rural areas.

3. A: Shakespeare presents the world _____ us _____ _____ marvelous way, doesn't he? His plays are _____ reflection _____ real life.

   B: Yes, but they're not always so easy _____ me to understand.

4. A: Where do you work?

   B: I'm _____ guard _____ the Museum _____ Modern Art. It's _____ 53rd Street _____ Fifth and Sixth Avenues.

5. A: How long are you going to be studying _____ this university?

B: I'll be here until I have _____ excellent understanding of the English

language. As long as I have _____ problems _____ grammar

and writing, I'm going to remain _____ the university's program

_____ students _____ English as _____ second

language. I won't drop _____ _____ school unless I

run _____ _____ money. I'll stay here as long as I

get _____ allowance _____ my parents.

6. **A:** How was your summer _____ France?

 B: I didn't have many opportunities _____ sightseeing. I usually spent

most _____ my time studying. As soon as I arrived _____

Paris, I enrolled _____ _____ course _____

_____ private language institute. Even though I spoke _____

little bit _____ French, I was still put _____ _____

beginners' class. After _____ couple _____ weeks, however, I

was transferred _____ _____ more advanced group, and

_____ the end _____ the summer, I was speaking the language

well enough to get _____* _____ _____ fair

amount _____ success _____ everyday French society.

7. **A:** You've never studied art history or appreciation _____ _____

formal situation, have you?

 B: What do you mean _____ formal?

 A: Well, _____ _____ university or _____ institute.

 B: Oh, _____ that way, no, but although I don't know much _____

art _____ _____ formal way, I do very much like to look

_____ _____ pictures. _____ spite _____ my

busy schedule _____ the office, I still manage to spend _____

least _____ couple _____ hours _____

week _____ different museums _____ New York

City. _____ art is _____ important part _____ my life,

even though I have little intellectual understanding _____ it.

8. [On the phone]

 A: Hi, Mom, I'm calling _____ Bangkok, _____ Thailand.

Get by means "succeed."

B: Oh, hi, dear, are you O.K.? Is everything going well?

A: Just great. I arrived _____ Bangkok three days ago, and I'm

staying _____ _____ former classmate _____

mine _____ the University of Toronto. He's _____ wonderful

guide; he's even teaching me how to speak _____ little bit _____

the Thai language. _____ Bangkok I'm going to take the

train _____ _____ Singapore. _____ my way I'm

going to make _____ stops _____ Penang and Kuala Lumpur.

B: How was your stay _____ Taiwan?

A: Unfortunately, I was sick _____ bed _____ _____

cold _____ more than _____ week, so I didn't get

much _____ _____ chance to see things. But, listen, Mom, I

have to go; I'm _____ my way _____ the train station so that I

can get tickets _____ Kuala Lumpur. I'll call you _____ there.

I love you. Bye.

B: Oh, dear, I love you, too. Bye.

❏ 3.7 *The* Versus No Article

Fill in each blank with *the* or a horizontal line.

Example

A: Where does one usually get a tooth pulled?

B: ___*The*___ dentist's, certainly not at ___———___ home.

1. **A:** We love to go to _____ Caribbean Islands on our holidays.

   B: Which islands do you like best?

   A: Well, I do like _____ Aruba and _____ Martinique very much.

2. **A:** Jean, what two countries are located on _____ Iberian Peninsula?

   B: Oh, that's easy, Mrs. Blake, _____ Spain and _____ Portugal.

3. **A:** Where can we find some of _____ largest rain forests in _____ world?

   B: In _____ South America.

4. **A:** Gee, where are you going? It's early.

   B: It's late; I'm going to _____ bed. I'm exhausted.

5. **A:** When it gets hot in the afternoon, the flies settle on _____ ceiling.

   B: I just don't understand how they get through _____ screens.

   C: Yeah, how do they do that?

   A: Listen, kids, it's because you're always leaving _____ door open.

6. **A:** Where do you usually do your homework?

   B: At _____ home, but sometimes I do it at _____ library.

   A: Don't you ever do it at _____ school?

   B: No, there are always too many distractions.

7. **A:** Where's _____ Mt. Everest?

   B: Isn't it in both _____ Tibet and _____ Nepal?

   A: Yes, and where are they?

   B: In _____ Himalayas, aren't they?

8. **A:** Where's _____ Khartoum?

   B: It's the capital of _____ Sudan.

   A: Excuse my ignorance, but where's that?

   B: It's in _____ Africa, below _____ Egypt. It's in _____ Khartoum where _____ Blue Nile and _____ White Nile meet and become _____ Nile River.

9. **A:** What's _____ deepest lake in the world?

   B: _____ Lake Baikal.

   A: Where on earth is that? Is it in _____ Soviet Union?

10. **A:** _____ Amsterdam is the capital of _____ Netherlands.

    B: Really? I think _____ Hague is.

    A: Oh? I'd better look it up in the encyclopedia.

11. **A:** Where's _____ Hudson Bay?

    B: It's in _____ Canada, way up in _____ north.

12. **A:** Do you know how many countries there are on _____ equator?

    B: No, but I bet that you do.

13. **A:** Where are _____ Hawaiian Islands?

    B: In the middle of _____ Pacific Ocean.

    A: Are they in _____ Western Hemisphere?

    B: I'm not sure about that.

14. **A:** Where's _____ Bay of Bengal?

B: It's an arm of _____ Indian Ocean off the coasts of _____ India

and _____ Burma.

☐ 3.8 *The* Versus No Article; *The* with Geographic Locations

1. We use the definite article *the* with names for objects with which we are familiar in our surroundings:

    the door   *the* radio   *the* lights   *the* kitchen

We also use *the* for objects in our natural environment:

    the birds   *the* trees   *the* flowers   *the* mountains

Pronunciation note: When *the* precedes a word that begins with a vowel sound, we often pronounce it so that it rhymes with *he* or *she:*

    The heiress is embarrassed.   *The end* of the film is exciting.

2. We do not use *the* with certain names of places in our surroundings:

    at *home, work, church, college* or *school*   in *jail, prison* or *bed*

3. The names for people of certain occupations as well as their places of business or services require *the:*

    the dentist (*the* dentist's)   *the* baker (*the* bakery)

4. We use *the* with adjectives in the superlative degree:

    the biggest   *the* most handsome   *the* best

5. Ordinal numbers require *the:*

    the first time   *the* second chance   *the* third man

6. We do not use an article with the names of countries:

    China   Greece   Egypt

Exceptions: The Netherlands [Holland], Sudan (or *the* Sudan) and *the* Philippines.

7. We use *the* with names of countries when the name refers to a political union:

    the United States of America   *the* Dominican Republic
    the Republic of Mexico   *the* Union of South Africa

8. The names of cities do not require *the:*

    Istanbul   Ottawa   Lima

Exception: The Hague, capital of South Holland.

9. A foreign article appears with the names of a few cities:

    Los Angeles   *Las* Vegas   *Le* Havre

10. We use *the* with the names of rivers, canals, oceans and seas:

    the Nile River   *the* Suez Canal   *the* Black Sea   *the* Pacific Ocean

11. No article accompanies the names of lakes:

    Lake Louise   Lake Chapala   Mirror Lake

Exceptions: The Lake of Lucerne, *the* Lake of Constance and *the* Great Salt Lake.

However, we use *the* with the name of a group of lakes:

>   *the* Great Lakes   *the* Finger Lakes

12. *The* does not accompany the names of bays and sounds:

>   Hudson Bay   Tokyo Bay   Puget Sound

We do use *the*, however, with the names of some bays in *of* phrases:

>   *the* Bay of Bengal   *the* Bay of Naples   *the* Bay of Pigs

13. The names of gulfs are given in *of* phrases with *the:*

>   *the* Gulf of Mexico   *the* Gulf of Thailand

Exception: The Persian Gulf.

14. *The* does not usually appear with the name of an island:

>   Catalina Island   Bermuda   Long Island

Exceptions: The island of Manhattan and *the* island of Majorca.
    However, we use *the* with the name of a group of islands:

>   *the* Caribbean Islands   *the* Thousand Islands

15. We use *the* with the name of an archipelago, a desert, a forest, a canyon or a peninsula:

>   *the* Malay Archipelago   *the* Gobi Desert   *the* Black Forest
>   *the* Grand Canyon   *the* Iberian Peninsula

16. We use *the* with the name of a range of mountains (we do not often use the word *mountains*):

>   *the* Alps   *the* Himalayas   *the* Andes

The name of a single mountain is usually preceded by *Mt.*, an abbreviation of mountain; we do not use *the:*

>   Mt. Everest   Mt. Fuji   Mt. Rushmore

Exception: The Matterhorn.

17. We use *the* with points on the globe:

>   *the* North Pole   *the* equator   *the* meridian

18. *The* occurs with the name of a geographic area:

>   *the* South   *the* Middle West   *the* Far East

But no article occurs with the name of a continent:

>   Asia   Africa   Europe   North America

❑ 3.9 *A, An* or *The* Versus No Article

Supply in each blank *a, an, the* or a horizontal line.

>   ***Example***
>
>   A: Sandra and Conrad Mellon have two children—___*a*___ daughter and ___*a*___
>   son. Both children are college students.
>
>   B: Oh, where are they going————— good schools?

A: Yes, _the_ son is studying at _the_ University of Michigan,

and _the_ daughter just entered ———— Columbia University

last fall.

1. A: What do you think is _____ single most important event of _____

twentieth century?

B: Oh, I'd say _____ World War II, wouldn't you?

A: Well, how about _____ Russian Revolution?

C: Looking at _____ whole century, how about _____ First World War?

2. A: What do you usually do in _____ evenings?

B: _____ homework.

A: Is it difficult?

B: Not really, but, I must say, _____ homework assigned this morning isn't so

easy.

3. A: What do you usually do on Sunday mornings?

B: I go to _____ church.

A: Oh, I didn't know you're interested in _____ religion.

B: Yes, very, I believe in _____ God.

4. A: Where were you yesterday?

B: I had to attend _____ day-long meeting.

A: Was _____ meeting about the new reorganization of the company?

B: Yes, and it was _____ complete waste of my time.

5. A: What's _____ formula for _____ water?

B: Let's see, it's H_2O, isn't it?

A: _____ carbon monoxide?

B: Oh, I can't remember; it's on the tip of my tongue.

6. A: How was your day yesterday?

B: I met _____ wonderful woman. I must tell you all about her.

A: Is she _____ woman I saw you with yesterday at the mall?

B: _____ very same woman. Isn't she lovely?

7. A: What would appeal to you right now? What do you have _____ appetite for?

Have _____ yen for something special?

B: Well, _____ orange would be good, and so would _____ apple.

A: _____ apples and _____ oranges in the refrigerator are fresh from the store today.

8. A: What is _____ important international organization in _____ New York City?

   B: _____ United Nations and _____ few dozen more.

   A: How about in _____ Switzerland?

   B: Isn't _____ Red Cross's headquarters there?

9. A: Have you read _____ article in _____ *New York Times* about your native country recently?

   B: Yes, just _____ other day, in fact.

   A: What was _____ article about?

   B: It was about _____ political situation in _____ capital.

10. A: Of all _____ musical instruments, which is your favorite?

    B: That's hard to say. Perhaps _____ piano.

    A: Do you have _____ piano?

    B: No, and I certainly wish I did.

Now read aloud each of the following dialogues and stress one *the,* whichever one you think is most appropriate.

11. A: Housing is the most important thing that we must discuss at the meeting tomorrow.
    B: I'm sorry, Mr. Mayor, but I disagree. The need for jobs in the community is the thing that we must talk about.

12. A: The violinist we heard last week wasn't very inspired, was he?
    B: I agree, but the violinist we're going to hear at the recital tonight is the violinist of the century, according to many of the music critics.

13. A: You're really very much in love with your girlfriend, aren't you?
    B: Oh, yes. The more I get to know her, the more I fall in love with her. It's difficult to put into words, but she truly is the woman of my dreams and the answer to all my prayers—the only reason for my existence.

❑ 3.10 *The* Versus No Article; More Place Names

1. We use *the* with a university or college when the name of the school follows in an *of* phrase:

   the University of California   *the* College of Arts and Crafts

No article occurs with the names of other colleges and universities:

   Harvard University   Smith College

2. We use *the* with libraries, museums and galleries:

> *the* Library of Congress   *the* Metropolitan Museum of Art
> *the* Tate Gallery

3. *The* appears with buildings, bridges, tunnels, towers, statues and monuments:

> *the* Chrysler Building   *the* Statue of Liberty
> *the* Golden Gate Bridge   *the* Eiffel Tower
> *the* Lincoln Tunnel   *the* Washington Monument

4. We do not use *the* with stations, terminals and airports:

> Victoria Station   Grand Central Terminal   Dulles Airport

Nor do we usually use *the* with the names of centers and plazas:

> Rockefeller Center   Grand Army Plaza

Exception: The World Trade Center.
     And we do not use *the* with streets, avenues, boulevards and parks:

> Baker Street   Park Avenue
> Yellowstone National Park   Sunset Boulevard

❑ 3.11   Other Uses of *The*

1. We use *the* in the following instances:

   a.   The names of parts of the body:

> *the* head   *the* legs   *the* stomach   *the* feet

   b.   Official titles:

> *the* captain   *the* king   *the* president   *the* general

   c.   Names of organizations:

> *the* Boy Scouts   *the* Red Cross   *the* United Nations

   d.   Names of government agencies:

> *the* Internal Revenue Service   *the* State Department

   e.   Names of law enforcement agencies:

> *the* Chicago Police Department   *the* FBI

> *Exception:* Scotland Yard.

   f.   Names of historical periods, events or epochs:

> *the* Russian Revolution   *the* Middle Ages   *the* Renaissance
> *the* Second World War   (but *World War II*)

   g.   Names of political parties:

> *the* Socialist Party   *the* Royalist Party

> But we often use the plural form of the political party and omit the word *party:*

> *the* Communists   *the* Tories   *the* Democrats

   h.   Names of musical instruments:

> *the* flute   *the* violin   *the* piano

   i.   Names of newspapers:

> **The Los Angeles Times**   **The Washington Post**   **The Observer**

  j. With plural names of a family when we are referring to two or more members of the family:

  the Vanderbilts   *the* Kennedys   *the* Smiths

  k. Names of planets:

  the planet Earth   *the* planet Saturn   *the* planet Pluto

  But we do not use an article when we drop the word *planet:*

  Mars   Uranus   Jupiter   Mercury

  We use *the* with *earth* when we refer to the land or the soil:

  All of us are living on *the* earth [land].

2. We also use *the* in time expressions:

the beginning	in *the* morning	in (*the*) spring	*the* past
the middle	in *the* afternoon	in (*the*) fall	*the* present
the end	in *the* evening	in (*the*) summer	

❑ 3.12 *The* Versus *A* or *An*; Particular Versus General; Stressed *The*

1. We do not use an article before a plural countable noun or an uncountable noun when the noun describes some thing in general:

  Oranges provide a great deal of vitamin C.
  Perfume can be very seductive.

We do use *the*, however, with such a noun when the noun describes something in particular, as in nouns modified by adjective clauses and prepositional phrases:

  The oranges that I bought turned out to be sour.
  The perfume in this bottle has lost its fragrance.

2. *The* can precede a countable noun that represents a class or group (for example, a kind of snake, a kind of insect or a kind of flower):

  The rattler can be a very dangerous snake.
  The butterfly has inspired many artists and poets.
  The orchid is the most beautiful of all flowers.

However, we more commonly use *a* or *an* in this manner:

  A cypress (sometimes *The*) is a lovely tree.
  A Rolex (sometimes *The*) is a finely made watch.
  An antelope (sometimes *The*) is an extremely fast animal.

The emphasizes the class or group, whereas *a* or *an* emphasizes the individual member of a group. *A* or *an* has the meaning of "any" in this case:

  A (*Any*) Cadillac is a great temptation to car thieves.
  An (*Any*) elephant will eat its owner out of house and home.

3. We use *the* when we are referring to a person or thing mentioned previously; in other words, we use it for **the second time something is mentioned:**

  A boat came into the harbor, and *a ferry* collided with *the boat;* then *the ferry* ran into *a barge,* and *the barge* sank.

A woman walked into the room; *a man* walked up to *the woman* and shook her hand. *The man* was the woman's husband.

4. To emphasize the uniqueness of a person, place or thing, we use stressed *the,* which sounds like *the* when it precedes a noun beginning with a vowel sound; it rhymes with *bee* or *fee:*

Mr. Sherlock Holmes says the name of the man who bought the poison is ***the*** key to the mystery.

Dr. Watson says Holmes has ***the*** mind of the century.

❑ 3.13 Reviewing Verb Tenses and Articles and Prepositions

Compose a sentence using each set of given words as a cue. Supply an appropriate form of a verb; then, when required, place in the sentence *a, an, the* or an appropriate preposition chosen from the following list. Transcribe any punctuation that is used. Do not add any words other than auxiliary verbs, articles and prepositions; do not change the order in which the cues are given.

about	down	in	on	to
around	for	of	since	up

Examples

a.   life / be / short, / so / I / want to enjoy every minute / it.

A: _Life is short, so I want to enjoy every minute of it._

I / feel / same way.

B: _I feel the same way._

b.   who / build / pyramids?

A: _Who built the pyramids?_

slaves / build / them, / they?

B: _Slaves built them, didn't they?_

1.   my husband / be / extremely neat person.

A: _____

so / be / mine.   almost never / he / ever / forget to make / his bed after he / get / mornings.

B: _____

_____

my husband / be / just / opposite; he / hardly ever / make / his.

C: _____

_____

2.   what / everyone / country / want?

A: _____

people / nation / desire / end / poverty, / yet / government / do / little / problem.

B: _____

_____

3.   Martha and Homer White / have / reputation / being cheap.   whenever / they / give / party, / they / ever / serve / expensive food / their guests.

A: _____

_____

_____

be / that / true?   Smiths / be / same way; / they / spend / dime / food.

B: _____

_____

4.   Sandra, / who / be / first people to reach / summit / Mt. Everest?   and / when / they / do it?

A: _____

_____

oh, that / be / hard question, / it?

B: _____

5.   before / Russian Revolution, / many / rich / understand / problems / poor.

A: _____

_____

that situation / still / exist / everywhere / world today, / it?   not much / change / then, / it?

B: _____

_____

4

Modal Auxiliaries and Related Idioms

❑ 4.1 Advisability, Obligation, Recommendation and Expectation

Supply in each blank an appropriate verb phrase with *should* or *ought to*. Use the base form given in parentheses. Use an adverb when it is given. Use a subject pronoun of your own choice when it is required. Practice both *should* and *ought to,* but focus on *should.*

Example

A: Hey, Helen, wait a minute. I want to pick up a pack of smokes.

B: (*smoke*) Oh, please, you ___*shouldn't smoke*___, ___*should*___ ___*you*___? (*quit*) You ___*ought to quit*___ right now, today.

A: Give me a break, Helen, I'm going to, I'm going to.

1. A: You certainly did make a stupid mistake when you did that, I must say. You just weren't using your head, were you?

   B: (*do*) What _____ instead?

   A: (*consult with*) _____ your lawyer before you did any business with those guys? They're the biggest crooks in town. Some people say they're even part of the Mafia.

   B: (*tell*) You _____ me about all of this.

   A: (*ask*) Well, you _____ me.

2. A: When I got to the boss's meeting yesterday afternoon, it was almost over.

B: (*get*) I know, you _____ there on time; she was furious. Why on earth were you so late?

A: I'd overslept; my alarm clock didn't go off for some reason.

[Two days later]

A: The boss seems a little angry at me today, doesn't she?

B: (*be*) Don't you think she _____? Really! (*stand*) You _____ at the coffee machine when she came into the office this morning. (*sit*) You _____ at your desk.

A: But I'd already finished everything that I had to do.

B: (*still / stand*) You _____ there, talking to all the women in the office; it wasn't the right time for taking a coffee break.

A: I just can't stand this office. (*be*) The boss _____ so strict.

B: (*be*) Perhaps, but you _____ so lazy. Let me tell you a little secret. (*fire*) The boss tells me that you _____.

3. **A:** There's a lot of traffic in town today, isn't there?

   B: (*drive*) Yes, so please slow down; you _____ so fast.

   A: (*go*) Oh, I'm sorry, how fast _____?

   B: (*go*) Not more than the limit of 35 miles an hour, and we _____ _____ one bit faster. Listen, I want to get where we're going as much as you do, but I want to get there alive and kicking.*

4. **A:** (*wear*) You know, Jennifer, you _____ a white dress to Maria's wedding last Saturday afternoon; it was completely inappropriate.

   B: Why not? (*wear*) What color _____ instead?

   A: Any color but white. (*always / reserve*) That _____ _____ for the bride, _____?

   B: Oh, Auntie, you're so old-fashioned.

   A: Well, perhaps, but I do know what's right and what's wrong.

   B: (*criticize*) Oh, really, Auntie, you _____ me so.

*Alive and kicking means "alive and well."

Why, look at the bride, *she* wore a white dress, and she'd already been married three times.

A: I know, dear, and wasn't that shocking? (*do*) She _____

_____ that, _____?

B: Oh, Auntie! Were you born in the nineteenth century?

5. A: Well, this is my plan. I'm going to take my savings—almost thirty thousand—and invest them in a new computer company.

B: (*do*) Hey, wait a minute, you _____

that, _____? After all, what happens if the company goes out of business? Then you won't have any savings for a rainy day.*

(*put*) You _____ all your eggs in one

basket,† _____?

❑ 4.2 An Overview of Modal Auxiliaries

1. **Modal auxiliaries** add a special meaning to the base form that they always precede:

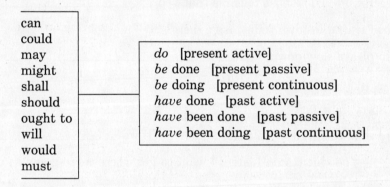

```
can
could
may        do   [present active]
might      be done   [present passive]
shall      be doing   [present continuous]
should     have done   [past active]
ought to   have been done   [past passive]
will       have been doing   [past continuous]
would
must
```

2. In negatives the adverb *not* follows modal auxiliaries, often in a contracted form:

A: What did you say?
B: I *can't* (*cannot*) be with you tomorrow.
A: I can lift these weights above my head.
B: Oh, you *couldn't* do that; you're just a weakling.
A: Well, General, are we going to surrender?
B: We *won't* surrender until our last man or woman falls.
A: Yes, that's exactly what I'm going to do.
B: Don't do it, you *mustn't* disobey your parents.

Note: Mayn't, mightn't, shan't and *oughtn't to* rarely occur in North American English.

---

*A day on which you might have no money.
†Invest everything in one thing.

3. We often use adverbs after modal auxiliaries:

>   A: You *should always* be loyal to your friends.
>   B: Of course, never will I betray any of them.
>
>   A: I'm going to steal some money from my roommate.
>   B: I *could never* do something like that.

Or we use adverbs after *not* in negatives:

>   A: Well, are you going to apologize?
>   B: Yes, I *mustn't ever* tell a lie again.
>
>   A: Why don't you go out with me tonight?
>   B: I'm sorry, I *can't usually* go out in the evenings.

We also use adverbs after subjects in questions:

>   A: Kids, why are you so hyperactive? Can *you never* sit down?
>   B: We're just normal kids, Uncle Luis.
>
>   A: Yes, that's what I want to do, and I don't want to do anything else.
>   B: Must *you always* have your own way?

4. The adverb *still* can precede or follow a modal auxiliary:

>   A: You're doing very well these days, aren't you?
>   B: Yes, but I *still must* work extremely hard.
>
>   A: There's nothing seriously wrong with her, is there?
>   B: No, but she *should still* see a doctor.

It always precedes negative modals:

>   A: Though we're making good time, we *still might not* get there on time.
>   B: But we *still mustn't* slow down. We've got to try to make it.

5. We place subjects directly after modals in questions:

>   A: Oh, I suddenly feel disoriented.
>   B: Here, *may I* help you?
>   A: Yes, thank you. I do feel a little dizzy.
>   B: *Should you* not sit down and rest a bit?
>
>   A: *Can you* still go out tonight even though you're exhausted?
>   B: Are you joking? I'm going to be the star of the clubs tonight.

In negative questions when a modal and *not* are contracted, we place the subject directly after the contraction:

>   A: I'm sorry, I can't make it to your birthday party.
>   B: Why *can't you* make it? You shouldn't break your promise, should you?
>
>   A: Are you really going to wear a red dress when you marry?
>   B: Why *shouldn't I* wear one? Red is my best color.

When an information word (or words) is the subject of a sentence, we place the modal directly after the information word:

>   A: *Who can* lift this piano?
>   B: Only Mr. Atlas could do that.
>
>   A: *How many people should* be invited to the wedding?
>   B: None. Let's elope, shall we?

❏ 4.3 *Should* and *Ought To*

1. *Should* and *ought to* have the same meaning. They may refer to present, future or past time:

> A: What are you thinking about, Great-grandmother?
> B: Just that children *should* (*ought to*) respect their elders.   [present]
>
> A: We're having dinner at the White House tomorrow evening.
> B: That *should* (*ought to*) be very exciting.   [future]
>
> A: Look at all those broken street lamps.
> B: They *should* (*ought to*) have been repaired a long time ago.   [past]

In North American English, we use *should* much more frequently than *ought to;* in fact, we almost never hear questions with *ought to:*

> A: *Ought I* to have called the office about this matter?
> B: You're from Britain, aren't you? I can tell by the way you're using the language.

Negatives with *ought to* are just as rare:

> A: We *ought not* to waste our time, ought we?
> B: Yes, we should get to work right away.

However, in general present time, we commonly use affirmative verb phrases with *ought to:*

> A: Yes, I did do that, Mommy, and I'm sorry.
> B: You *ought to* be ashamed of yourself, young man.

2. We use *should* or *ought to* to express a weak kind of the following:

   a. Advisability:

   > A: You *should take* better care of your health.
   > B: I know, but I'm still not going to stop smoking.

   b. Obligation:

   > A: We *should help* those who can't help themselves.
   > B: Yeah, but I've got to take care of myself first.

   c. Recommendation:

   > A: You *ought to* see that hockey game.
   > B: Sorry, but that game is too violent for my taste.

   d. Expectation:

   > A: We're going to Paris in the spring.
   > B: If it doesn't rain, that *should be* nice.

3. In past forms with *should* or *ought to*, we may express advisability, expectation or obligation, but it is understood that the advice was not followed, the expectation was not met or the obligation was not fulfilled:

> A: Napoleon *ought not to have gone* to Waterloo. His generals had advised him not to.
> B: That's easy for you to say. You have historical hindsight.
>
> A: World War I *should have been* the war to end all wars.
> B: Isn't that what they used to say: "The war to end all wars"?
>
> A: Mrs. Grave's feelings are hurt because you haven't written her.
> B: Yes, I *should have sent* her a letter of sympathy, but I was just so busy that I forgot to.

❑ 4.4 Necessity Versus No Necessity and Prohibition

Using *must* or *have to*, fill in each blank with an appropriate verb phrase. Use the base forms and adverbs that are given. Use a pronoun subject of your own choice when it is required.

> **Example**
>
> A: (*walk*) I ___*don't have to walk*___ to school; I have a bicycle.
>
> B: (*walk*) Well, I ___*must walk*___ to work; it's doctor's orders. She says I need to get as much exercise as I can, and walking is one of the best ways.

1. A: Yes, I'm going to be traveling in the tropics for a few months.

   B: (*be*) Well, when one travels in the tropics, one _____ _____ very careful of the water. (*never / eat*) Also, you _____ _____ uncooked vegetables, (*ever / eat*) and you _____ _____ salads. Also, unless you're in a deluxe hotel, (*ever / have*) you _____ ice in your drinks.

2. A: I have a very small apartment. It's more like a small closet, actually, but it's quite cozy and nice.

   B: (*do*) Good, then you _____ much cleaning, _____?

   A: (*buy*) Yes, that's right, but I _____ one more piece of furniture; the place is already starting to look like a junk shop.

3. A: What on earth are you trying to do?

   B: Wind this watch.

   A: (*do*) You _____ that, _____? Isn't it automatic?

   B: No, this is my late father's watch. It's almost fifty years old, from the days before automatic watches.

   A: Oh, really? How nice! Does it run very well?

   B: Not very well, unfortunately. (*take*) It _____ in to the watchmaker's once in a while, I'm afraid. I just wear it for sentimental reasons.

4. **A:** Yes, ma'am, this scarf is made of the finest French silk.

   B: (*dry-clean*) _____?

   A: Yes, of course, ma'am, it's a very fine silk.

   B: (*dry-clean*) Then I don't want it; I don't like things that _____

   _____. I like things that I can wash.

   A: (*ever / wear*) Then, ma'am, you _____ silk.

   B: (*all kinds of silk / dry-clean*) Oh, _____?

   A: (*never / wash*) Oh, no, indeed not, but very fine scarves such as these, which are

   on sale today by the way, _____ in water.

   B: You know, I think you've sold me on this scarf, and I'm going to take it. (*never /

   come*) I _____ into this store again. Whenever I

   do, I always spend too much money.

   A: Ha, ha, ha.

5. **A:** (*always / lag behind*) Jamie, _____ when

   we are walking on the street together? (*try*) You _____

   _____ to keep up with me. (*fall behind*) You _____

   _____. (*try*) If you do, you _____ to catch

   up with me.

   B: O.K., Daddy, I'll try, (*always / walk*) but _____ so

   fast? My legs aren't as long as yours. After all, I'm just a little boy, and you're a

   big man.

   A: You're a smart kid, Jamie. Did you know that? Yeah, O.K., I'll slow down a bit.

   (*walk*) I _____ as fast as I usually do when I'm

   walking by myself.

6. **A:** Jackson, this information is top secret—for our eyes only. (*never / reveal*)

   It _____ to anyone.

   B: (*keep*) _____ it a secret from my wife, too?

   A: Your wife doesn't like to gossip, does she?

   B: Williams, I find that question insulting to my wife, and I'd like you to take it

   back.

   A: (*know*) O.K., O.K., I'm sorry, but just to be on the safe side, your wife

   _____ the secret, _____?

   B: Oh, I suppose not, but she'll eventually find out from your husband, so it won't make any difference in the long run, will it? You know, my wife finds out

everything from your husband.

❑ 4.5 *Must* Versus *Have To*

1. We use the modal auxiliary *must* to express the following:

   a. Necessity:

   > A: Yes, I actually do think that I'm going to kill myself.
   > B: You *must* seek professional help—perhaps a psychiatrist?

   b. Prohibition:

   > A: Oh, just look at how I'm losing all of my hair.
   > B: You *must not* worry about such foolish things.

   c. Deduction:

   > A: I'm living in Paris now, spending a great deal of money, and loving my life. Oh, and the romance!
   > B: That *must* be very nice, Nicole.

   d. Recommendation:

   > A: This book is all about the present situation in your native country. You absolutely *must* read it. Here's my copy.
   > B: Thanks, that's nice of you, but I've already read it.

2. For necessity, we use *must* for only present and future time:

   > A: Look at all the cockroaches in the sink. Ech!
   > B: Yuck! Yes, we *must* get rid of them right away.

   > A: I don't have time to discuss it now, but I *must* tell you about my new love affair when I see you again.
   > B: Oh, sounds interesting. I'm just dying to hear every word.

3. For expressing necessity in the past, we must use the past form of the idiom *have to* plus a base form:

   > A: We had a lot of termites in our house.
   > B: No kidding? Did you *have to* call an exterminator to get rid of them?

   > A: The dentist *had to* pull out six of my teeth.
   > B: Didn't you *have to* go to the hospital for that?

4. Essentially, for expressing necessity in the present, the modal auxiliary *must* and the idiom *have to* have the same meaning; however, *must* conveys a much greater degree of necessity:

   > A: All of us *must* (*have to*) think about the future, yet we *must* (*have to*) live in the present.
   > B: How true! But it's so difficult to do, isn't it?

5. The negative form of *have to* has a completely different meaning from the negative form of *must*. *Do not have to* or *does not have to* means *"**no necessity.**" Must not* means *"**prohibition.**"* Compare the following:

   > A: Well, what do you think we should do?
   > B: We *mustn't* surrender. Our enemy will kill us all.
   > C: You're joking! We *don't have to* surrender. Aren't we winning?

❑ 4.6 Deduction Versus Expectation

Using *must, should* or *ought to,* put an appropriate verb phrase in each blank. Use the base forms given in parentheses, and use adverbs when they are given. Use pronoun subjects of your own choice when required.

Example

A: My boyfriend says he's going to give me a car for my birthday.

B: (*be*) You ___*shouldn't be*___ so gullible. Why, he doesn't even have a dime to his name. (*pull*) He ___*must have been pulling*___ your leg when he told you that.

1. A: Oh! Wow! My stomach is beginning to growl; it almost hurts. I am so hungry!

    B: (*be*) Well, you _____ hungry; you haven't eaten anything since yesterday morning at breakfast. (*growl*) Your stomach

    _____. Why are you on this crazy diet? I love you the way you are. (*be*) You _____ a little crazy.

    A: Oh, what do you know about diets? Are you a doctor?

2. A: What's wrong?

    B: I can't find your number in my address book. (*forget*) I _____

    _____ to write it down.

    A: (*think*) Gee, you _____ much of me if you even forgot to write my number down.

    B: Oh, come on, man, a person can be forgetful at times, can't he or she?

    A: (*be*) You _____ a feminist.

    B: Why all of a sudden do you say that?

    A: Don't all feminists say things like "he or she"?

    B: (*be*) Why _____ so macho? It makes me sick.

    (*spoil*) Your mother, sisters and aunts _____ you when you were a boy.

    A: Oh, come on, I was just joking. (*take*) You _____ any offense. Really, I'm a nice guy, believe me. I'm not macho.

    B: (*do*) O.K., I _____ it, but I'll forgive you this time.

3. A: While I was dancing with Jackie, she was always stepping on my toes.

B: (*do*) She _____ it on purpose.*

A: Why do you say that?

B: Didn't you know that she doesn't care for you very much?

A: (*be*) Well, I _____ surprised; she's never been very nice to me. It makes me sad.

B: (*be*) Hey, listen, you _____ sad, _____

_____? There are a lot of other women on campus who are just

dying to go out with you. You're a BMOC.†

A: Yeah, ha, ha, ha, but I'm not interested.

4. **A:** My! The children are certainly being very quiet upstairs, aren't they?

   B: (*do*) Too quiet. I know those kids; they _____

something wrong.

   A: Hey, kids, what are you doing up there?

   C: We're just playing marbles, Dad.

   D: Yeah, and I'm winning.

   B: (*keep*) Well, that _____ them quiet for a while.

5. **A:** Hey, Boss, a guy who says he's Napoleon Bonaparte wishes to speak to you.

   B: (*pull*) You _____ my leg.

   A: No, seriously, that's who he says he is.

   B: (*be*) Well, he _____ either drunk or crazy, or both.

Oh, go ahead, show him in. Why not?

   A: Ha, ha, ha, April Fool's Day.

   B: Oh, I completely forgot about it. (*be*) I _____ the

biggest fool of all.

6. **A:** I tried to make some bread yesterday, but the dough never rose.

   B: (*use*) You _____ enough yeast.

   A: (*use*) How much _____?

   B: Don't ask me. I know next to nothing about making bread.

*Intentionally.

†Big man on campus.

☐ 4.7 *Must* Versus *Should* or *Ought To*

1.   For expressing a recommendation, *must* conveys much greater force than *should* or *ought to*. Compare the following:

> A: You *must* read this letter at once; it may determine whether or not you're going to be fired.
> B: What are you talking about? Let me see that, please.
>
> A: You *should* see that movie, it may interest you.
> B: *Must* I?
> A: No, but it's rather amusing.
>
> A: You *ought to* practice on the piano more, Timmy.
> B: Ah, but gee whiz, Mom, give me a break, will you?
> A: O.K., Tim, you can forget about the piano, but you *must* do your homework before we sit down to dinner.

2.   Remember that with *should* or *ought to*, we may express an expectation in present, future and past, but this expectation is often not met:

> A: We're having dinner this evening at the Good Appetite. We've heard it's rather good.
> B: Oh, it *ought to* be good, if the cook isn't drunk, which he sometimes is. [future]
>
> A: She's married to the richest and best-looking man in town.
> B: She *should* be happy, shouldn't she?   [present]
> A: Yes, but she isn't. He's so very cruel to her.
>
> A: We went to Hawaii on our vacation, but we had an absolutely rotten time.
> B: You *should* have had a great time. Hawaii is fabulous.   [past]

3.   There is no expectation when we make a deduction with *must;* such a deduction is made in response to some kind of good evidence that is known to the speaker or writer:

Good Evidence	Deduction
Her temperature is 105.	She *must* be seriously sick.
He's a commentator on the BBC.	He *must* speak well.

4.   For negative deductions, we most often use *must not*. We more commonly use the contraction *mustn't* to express prohibition:

Good Evidence	Deduction
The map says there's a station here, but there isn't one.	Oh, you *must not* be using one of the new maps. That station was torn down just a year ago.
Her poor husband is bedridden.	She *must not* have much time for herself, taking care of him all the time.

5.   We cannot project deductions with *must* for the future; we can only express expectation with *should:*

> A: Her temperature is 105, but she's been given some very effective medication.
> B: Good, her temperature *should* be going down soon.
>
> A: We're going to a party way up in the Hollywood Hills tonight.
> B: Hey, man, that *should* be cool. You *should* have a great time.

6.   However, we frequently make a deduction about an event or a condition in the past; the evidence can refer to present or past time:

Good Evidence	Deduction
He's looking unbelievably young these days, isn't he?	He *must have had* a face lift. No one that old could look that young without one.
When I said what I did, she absolutely glared at me.	You *must have said* something really terrible; she never gets angry with anyone. She's a living angel.
I told her that she was ugly.	You *must not have been using* your head, you stupid guy.

Note: In North American English, when we make deductions with *must*, there is no question form.

❑ 4.8 Conjecture Versus Deduction

Using *may, might* or *must*, fill in each blank with an appropriate verb phrase. In only one sentence will you require a subject pronoun.

Examples

a. A: These snapshots of last week's picnic aren't very good, are they?

   B: Not very, you're right. Let's see. Hmm, it's hard to say. (*use / shake*) Well,

   you <u>*may not have been using*</u> the right kind of film, or

   you <u>*might have been shaking*</u> the camera. You know, I don't really

   know what's wrong here.

b. A: How do you do? My name, I'll have you know, is Alexander the Great.

   B: (*be*) Sir, you _____ *must be* _____ out of your mind.

1. A: Ummm, yum, yum, does that look good! I love a good salad. Now you're doing

   fine, Dave, just be very careful with that paring knife.

   B: Oh, I'm always, always very careful, Uncle Claude.

   [Two minutes later]

   B: Look, my finger is bleeding.

   A: (*cut*) You _____ it while you were slicing those

   tomatoes. I told you to be careful.

2. A: He just doesn't understand the value of money. He has a lot of it, but he just

   throws it away.

   B: (*bear*) He _____ with a silver spoon in his

   mouth.*

*Born rich. Often used in reference to those who abuse their good fortune.

3. **A:** Jane didn't want to go out last night for some reason.

    B: Why not?

    A: Oh, who knows? (*rain*) It _____ a little too hard

    for her. It's very hard to tell what that woman is thinking about, isn't it?

    B: Yes, and she's so darned selfish at times, isn't she?

    A: Terribly, almost unbelievably, in fact. (*spoil*) She _____

    _____ a great deal when she was a little girl.

    B: Oh, I'm sure she was. (*give*) She _____

    everything that her little heart desired.

    C: You know what?

    A and B: What?

    C: (*be*) You two guys _____ the biggest gossips I

    have ever met, talking about Jane the way you do.

4. **A:** My girlfriend and I were going to meet at the ticket counter at Union Station last

    night, but she never showed up.

    B: (*wait for*) _____ her at the wrong ticket

    counter?

    A: No, there's only one.

    B: Have you heard from her since then?

    A: No, and I've been calling and calling. (*happen*) Something serious _____

    _____ to her.

    B: Now, now, don't get so dramatic. (*say*) Listen, Bud, do you think Janet

    _____ to you, indirectly, that she doesn't want

    to go out with you anymore?

    A: (*be*) You _____ nuts; Janet is crazy about me.

    B: (*be*) Oh, well, I _____ nuts, (*be*) but you

    _____ very smart if you don't know that Janet

    has been going out with other guys—one of whom, in fact, is your best friend.

    A: But you're my best friend.

    B: Right.

5. **A:** (*believe*) He says he has a million in the bank, Cindy, and I _____

    _____ him. He has such an honest face.

    B: Perhaps, but he just loves to kid around, and, frankly, he's not always so truthful.

(*pull*) He _____ your leg when he told you that
he had a million, believe me.

❑ 4.9 *May* or *Might*

1.   We frequently use the modal auxiliary *may* and its other form, *might*, to express conjecture, or make a guess. We make conjectures with *may* or *might* in response to some very weak evidence. Essentially *may* and *might* have the same meaning. Conjectures with these two modals can refer to the present:

Weak Evidence	Conjecture
Why is everyone getting out of the water?	There *might* be a shark.
Why don't they ever say hello?	They *may not* like you.

Or the conjectures can refer to the past. The evidence can refer to the present or past:

Weak Evidence	Conjecture
Why is that guy laughing?	Who knows? He *may have just heard* a joke.
Why did she leave you?	Oh, she *might have found* someone else; I'm not sure.

2.   For coming events, we use *may* or *might* to express future possibility as well as conjecture:

A: I *may* be getting promoted in a few months.
B: Yes, I hear they're moving you into a corner office.

A: We're not sure yet, but we *might* have twins.
B: Great! The more, the merrier.

May has no question form when we express conjecture.

3.   However, in rather formal usage, we do use *might* in questions, but direct questions with *might* can sound somewhat stiff and unnatural. Such questions do not often occur in North American English:

A: But these statistics are wrong, aren't they? I thought we made more than 300 million last year.
B: Sir, if I can be frank, *might you have made* a mistake?
A: What? *Might I be* wrong?

4.   For expressing conjecture and future possibility, we frequently use *may* or *might* in indirect questions in which the modals are placed in noun clauses that follow independent clauses:

A: I wonder why there are all those new cracks in the wall.
B: *Do you think* that there *may* have been an earthquake?

A: Yes, I'm going to marry that man, no matter how cruel and awful he is to me.
B: *Don't you think* that you *might* be making a mistake?

❑ 4.10 Asking Politely for Permission

Fill in the blanks with appropriate verb phrases using *may* or *might* and *can* or *could*. Use the polite word *please* when it seems most appropriate. Use the verbs given in parentheses. Each verb phrase will require a subject pronoun.

Example

A: (*ask*) _____*May I ask*_____ you a plain and straightforward question?

B: (*make*) Why, yes, of course, but _____*could you please make*_____ it a question that isn't too personal?

1. A: Waiter, waiter, oh, please, waiter! Where *is* that guy?

   B: Yes, ma'am. (*bring*) _____ you something?

   A: You served us the soup, but you didn't give us any spoons.

   (*bring*) _____ us two, before the soup gets cold?

   B: Yes, ma'am, right away.

   C: Oh, and waiter.

   B: Yes, sir.

   C: (*stop*) _____ chewing gum when you are around our table? It ruins my appetite.

   B: It's not gum, sir, it's chewing tobacco.

2. A: Good morning, do you see something you like? (*help*) _____ _____ you?

   B: Yes, thank you. (*show*) _____ the diamond necklace that's on display in your Fifth Avenue window?

   A: Why, yes, of course, but for right now here's one in this case that's somewhat similar to the one in the window. (*show*) _____ it to you?

   B: Yes, please do.

   A: Ah! Here it is! Isn't it the loveliest thing you've ever seen?

   B: Oh, lovely! (*try*) _____ it on?

   A: Of course, here, let me help you put it on.

   B: Thank you. I love it. How much is it?

   A: It's $135,000. Of course, it's an exclusive with us—one of our newest designs.

   B: I'll take it. You know, I just love shopping at Tiffany's. You have such lovely things, and they're at such fair prices.

   A: Yes, ma'am.

3. A: Here, porter, this bag is too heavy for me. (*put*) _____ _____ it on your cart with the others?

B: It'll cost you another five dollars, Miss.

A: (*ask*) Listen, _____ you a polite question?

B: Why, of course, Miss. What is it?

A: Isn't five dollars a bag highway robbery?

B: Well, Miss, _____ you a polite question? Don't I need to make a living, too?

4. **A:** Mr. and Mrs. Smith, Bob Blake, a friend of mine from my college fraternity, and his girlfriend and I are going up to Canada for the weekend, where we're going to stay in my friend's parents' mountain cabin. (*your daughter / go*) _____ with us?

B: Are your friend's parents going to be there?

A: Well, uhm, no, they're down in Florida for the winter.

B: Are you kidding? Our daughter's just a baby.

C: You must be nuts. She's eighteen.

5. **A:** (*stop*) O.K., kids, now _____ moving around so much? I'd like to take this picture of you. (*hold*) Carmelita, _____ _____ still* for just a second? (*take*) Juanito, _____ _____ that sour look off your face? You look as if you're going to a funeral.

B: (*take*) Come on, Dad, _____ the picture?

A: (*say*) Here we go—_____ cheese?

❑ 4.11 Polite Requests for Permission with *May* or *Might* and *Can* or *Could*

1. In more formal (and more polite) usage, we use the modal auxiliary *may* to ask for permission. We use only the first and the third person (singular or plural) in such requests. The second person (singular or plural) never occurs. We sometimes add the polite word *please*.

First Person

A: *May I* tell you about some of my recent adventures?
B: Please do. Your stories are always so interesting and funny.

A: *May we* please adjourn now? We've said everything there is to say at this meeting, haven't we?
B: Let's call it a night, shall we?

Third Person

A: *May your daughter* marry me?

*Not move.

B: Why, of course, son, we'd be proud to have you in the family.

A: My children so enjoy playing with yours. *May they* come over this afternoon and play?

B: That would be nice, and please do come yourself so that we can have some tea and a little chat. It's been ages.

2. *Might* also sometimes appears in a polite request for permission, but its use is very formal in tone, so we rarely use it in our everyday conversation:

A: *Might I* please ask you a few questions?

B: Yes, but please do keep them to the point.

A: *Might we* delay the start of the meeting?

B: But isn't it better that we start now and get it over with?

A: Mr. and Mrs. Franklin, *might your daughter* marry our son?

B: To tell you the truth, my husband and I don't think it would be a good idea. Your son takes after you, a very conservative and formal man. Our daughter thrives on informality and an easy-going life-style. Neither of us thinks the two of them would ever get along.

3. In less formal (and a bit less polite) usage, the modal auxiliary *can* appears in requests for permission:

A: *Can I* give you a tip?

B: Sure, but the last tip you gave me wasn't any good. I lost my pants as well as my shirt on that horse.

A: *Can we* play on your team tomorrow, please?

B: Hey, man, sure, as long as you bring your own bats, mitts and balls.

4. We may also use the modal auxiliary *could* in such requests; when we do, we make a very strong request:

A: Mom, *could I* have another cookie, please? Pretty please with sugar on it.

B: Why, honey, if you insist, of course you may.

A: *Could we* please come and see you tonight, at midnight?

B: But is it so urgent?

A: *Could Timmy* come over to your house today and play?

B: I don't know; frankly, he misbehaved terribly the other day.

A: *Could your kids* please leave our kids alone?

B: Why, what do you mean? Your kids are always picking on ours.

5. Like the modal auxiliaries *will* or *would*, we may use *can* or *could* to precede a verb in the imperative mood. In this case, there is a second person. It is often best to use *please*. Such requests are much more insistent than requests made with *will* or *would*:

A: Listen, *can you* please move over a bit?

B: You're kidding, I can't, I'm up against the wall already.

A: *Could you* please quiet down, boys and girls? You're acting like a bunch of monkeys.

B: Oh, relax, Mr. Rogers, it's the last day of school.

❏ 4.12 Ability

Fill in the blanks with appropriate forms of *can, could* or *be able to*. The subject pronouns *you* and *one* frequently occur.

Examples

a. **A:** Yes, Mohammed, just why was Magellan disappointed?

   B: (*finish*) He _____*couldn't finish*_____ his voyage around the world.

b. **A:** Listen, you're not strong enough to walk, are you?

   B: (*hardly / get up*) Oh, my, I_'*m hardly able to get up*___, I'm afraid. (*even / lift*) I ___*can't even lift*___ my arm, I'm so weak.

1. **A:** (*an average person / stay under*) How long _____ _____ water?

   B: I wonder. (*stay under*) _____ water as long as five minutes?

   C: (*stay under*) Oh, no, people _____ water that long, _____?

2. **A:** Hey, Teddy, I've just learned a neat new game. Let's play it.

   B: O.K., how do you play it?

   A: (*hold*) First, how long _____ your breath?

   B: I don't want to play; I know that game. It always makes me dizzy.

3. **A:** Why aren't you going in to teach today?

   B: (*hardly / speak*) I _____ a word; I've got bronchitis. But I'm getting better; (*speak*) I _____ _____ at all yesterday.

4. **A:** That's right. When I arrived in the United States, (*speak*) I _____ _____ any English at all.

   B: (*even / speak*) _____ a single word?

   A: (*say*) Oh, I _____ hello, goodbye and a few words like that, but that was it.

5. **A:** (*a hen / usually / lay*) James Williams, how many eggs a day _____ _____?

   B: (*lay*) I'm not sure, Mrs. Kim, but a hen _____ just one a day, _____?

   A: To tell you the truth, I'm not so sure myself.

6. **A:** (*go*) _____ with me to a jazz concert at

Carnegie Hall tomorrow night and dinner later in the Oak Room at the Plaza

Hotel?

B: (*say*) Oh, I'd love to, but I _____ yes right

now. We've been very busy at the office lately, (*go*) and I _____

_____ with you, but I'm not really sure yet. (*call*) I

_____ you later in the afternoon and let

you know.

7. **A:** Yes, it certainly is true.

B: What is, Grandpa?

A: (*fool*) "You _____ people some of the time,

(*fool*) but you _____ them all of the time."

That's what Will Rogers said way back in the thirties.

B: What's another old saying, Grandpa? I love to hear you tell them.

A: Well, let's see. Oh, yes, this is one of my old favorites: (*lead*) "You _____

_____ a horse to water, (*make*) but you _____

_____ him or her drink."

B: What does that mean?

A: (*force*) That you _____ someone to do

something that he or she doesn't want to do.

8. **A:** (*understand*) _____ everything in

Professor Black's ethics class last semester?

B: Everything? Are you kidding? (*hardly / understand*) I _____

_____ a word. What on earth was he talking about?

A: Oh, come on, I don't believe you; you're a smart guy. (*even / understand*)

_____ a word?

B: (*ever / understand*) Really, not one of his theories _____

_____. They were just too abstract for me.

9. **A:** (*never / make*) Ever since I moved to this part of town ten years ago,

I _____ any friends. It's a very unfriendly

place.

B: Really? (*even / make*) _____ friends with

one person?

A: (*even / find*) No, why, I _____ a friendly

dog or cat in this dreadful neighborhood.

10. A: Didn't you have enough money to go on a trip last summer?

B: (*afford*)* Oh, yes, I _____ to go on a trip,

(*afford*) but I _____ to spend any time

away from my garden. Gardening is much more interesting to me than traveling,

now that I have gotten older.

☐ 4.13 Expressing Ability with *Can* or *Could*

1. We very often use the modal auxiliary *can* to express the ability to do something; *cannot* (*can't*) expresses the lack of ability:

A: Would you please help me lift this?
B: I'm sorry, but I *can't lift* that; I've got a bad back.
A: Mr. Atlas *can lift* a piano by himself.
B: And Mrs. Atlas *can play* the piano quite well.

For past time, we use *could* and *could not* (*couldn't*):

A: Did you attend your son's graduation?
B: Unfortunately, we *couldn't be* there.
A: Why, I must say, you're speaking English very well now.
B: Thank you. Just a couple of years ago, I *couldn't speak* the language at all.

2. *Could not* (*couldn't*) means that we did not have the ability to do something:

A: I *couldn't* understand a word of that play.
B: My wife and I *couldn't* make any sense out of it, either.

Could very often means that we had the ability to do something, but we did not or could not take advantage of this ability:

A: When I was living in Florida, I *could* go swimming every day, but I was too busy working.
B: That's just the way it was when I was living in London. I *could* see all kinds of plays and go to all kinds of concerts, but I just didn't have enough money to do all those things.

If we actually did do something in the past that we had the ability to do, we usually use the simple past tense:

A: When I was in California, I *went* surfboarding every day.
B: And when I was in Paris, I *saw* all kinds of paintings and *bought* all kinds of beautiful clothes and perfume.

3. With *can*, we may express a physical or a learned ability:

A: How much weight can you bear on your back?
B: On level ground I *can carry* about eighty pounds.

*We most often use *afford* with *can* or *could*.

A:　Yes, I *can* type and *can* take shorthand, but I *can't* do math, except when I'm using a calculator, of course.

B:　I'm sorry, but we're looking for a person who *can* do math well.

We also use *can* to express that we have the power as well as the ability to do something; we use only this meaning of *can* when we are expressing events in the future:

A:　Our factory *can* turn out a million units next year.

B:　And we *can* buy all of them.

A:　We *can* do everything in the world that we want to do.

B:　Yes, we're truly free spirits, aren't we? We *can* do everything that our little hearts desire.

❑ 4.14　*Be Able To*

1.　For expressing ability, the idiom *be able to* plus a base form is most often interchangeable with the modal *can* or *could:*

A:　I *can* (*am able to*) do anything that you can do.

B:　*Can* you (*are* you *able to*) stand on your head and juggle three balls at the same time?

A:　Oh, come on, you big bragger, you *can't* (*aren't able to*) do that, *can* (*are*) you?

A:　*Could* you (*were* you *able to*) attend yesterday's meeting?

B:　No, I *couldn't* (*wasn't able to*) get to it.

2.　The idiom *be able to* has a much greater scope than *can* or *could.* It may appear with all the verb tenses:

A:　I'm not going to *be able to* get out of here until late.

B:　Listen, I haven't *been able to* get out of this office on time since I started working here thirty years ago.

A:　Are you going to be in Europe next summer?

B:　Oh, no, never will I ever *be able to* save enough money.

A:　Why was she so upset when I saw her the other day?

B:　She was disappointed that she hadn't *been able to* do well on some test or other.

3.　*Be able to* can also appear with the modal auxiliaries *may, might, should, ought to* and *must:*

A:　What are your plans for tonight?

B:　Well, if you're not busy, I *might be able to* go out with you, but I'm not sure yet.

A:　I just can't lift this big stone, Daddy.

B:　Oh, come on, Danny, you *should be able to* do that. You're almost seven now, aren't you?

A:　His company produced three million units last year.

B:　A big plant like that *ought to have been able to* produce much more than that.

A:　A number of people didn't show up for the meeting.

B:　They *may not have been able to* get through the rather heavy traffic last night.

A:　Yes, they weren't carrying any credit cards while they were traveling.

B:　They *must not have been able to* rent any cars.

❑ 4.15 *Hardly*

We often use the adverb *hardly* in verb phrases with *can, could* or *be able to:*

A: How's your mother doing, Mrs. Cole?
B: Not well, I'm afraid, she*'s hardly able to* get out of bed.

A: What kind of singing voice do you have?
B: I *can hardly* carry a tune, but I can whistle quite well.

A: How was yesterday's meeting?
B: It was so boring that I *could hardly* stay awake.

❑ 4.16 Possibility and Impossibility Versus Conjecture

Supply in each blank an appropriate verb phrase using *could, may* or *might.*

Examples

a. A: Is that rain on the roof I hear? (*rain*) <u>*Could it be raining*</u> at this time of year?

B: Why, yes. Didn't you know this is the rainy season?

A: Oh, no, I've just arrived. (*pick*) I <u>*couldn't have picked*</u> a worse place for my vacation.

b. A: Your secretary was in a rather bad mood yesterday, wasn't he?

B: Yes, I don't know what was wrong. (*feel*) He <u>*may not have been feeling*</u> well. It's hard to tell about him.

1. A: Oh, how nice! A bottle of Mitsuko, my favorite perfume. (*give*) I _____ _____ a nicer present for my birthday. Thank you so much, Pedro. (*be*) Nobody in the world _____ happier than I am now, sitting here on my terrace with you. (*be*) The evening _____ more romantic, _____ _____?

B: (*be*) Yes, darling, we _____ happier, _____?

2. A: I'm afraid we're driving on the wrong road. Are you?

B: (*give*) Yes, do you think we _____ the wrong directions at the last gas station? That attendant didn't look very smart to me.

A: (*make*) Or, _____ the wrong turn at the last light?

3. **A:** Yesterday, I saw old Tom Brown sitting under the oak tree in front of City Hall.

    B: (*see*) Why, you _____ him there. Didn't you

    know he's been dead for almost five years?

    A: What? That's hard to believe. (*see*) _____ his

    ghost?

    B: Oh, don't be silly. You're too intelligent for that. (*never / believe in*)

    You _____ such things as

    ghosts, _____?

4. **A:** I tried to call James all weekend but never got an answer.

    B: (*work*) Do you think his phone _____?

    A: (*work*) Yes, it _____, but I don't think so; I

    always got a ring, the line wasn't dead.

    B: Well, it's exam time at the university. (*answer*) He _____

    _____ his calls because he was so busy studying.

    A: Well, there's one thing that I know for sure.

    B: What's that?

    A: (*be*) James _____ with his girlfriend all

    weekend.

    B: Why not?

    A: Because she was with me, that's why.

    B: You know, you're a bigger skunk than I thought you were.

5. **A:** What's wrong?

    B: I don't know where our traveler's checks are.

    A: (*put*) Oh, no! Where _____ them?

    B: (*steal*) Perhaps a better question is: _____?

    A: Oh, come on now, let's not jump to any drastic conclusions yet. We haven't

    investigated all the other possibilities. (*leave*) _____

    _____ them at the restaurant where we had dinner?

    B: (*leave*) No, I _____ them there; I had them

    later when we went to the theater.

    A: (*call*) We _____ the theater now to see if they

    have them.

    B: That's a good idea. Let's give it a try.

[A few minutes later]

B: Great news! The theater has our traveler's checks and is holding them for us.

A: Thank God we didn't lose them. (*be*) We _____

luckier. (*lose or steal*) They _____ so easily in

this big city. (*end up*) Our vacation _____ a

disaster, _____?

❑ 4.17 *Could* Versus *May* or *Might*

1. As we do with *may* or *might*, with affirmative verb phrases we frequently use *could* to express conjecture:

> A: I always get a busy signal when I call her.
> B: The receiver *could* (*may* or *might*) be off the hook.
>
> A: He didn't seem to notice me when he passed me in the hall.
> B: He *could* (*may* or *might*) have been avoiding you.

In this case, the three modal auxiliaries are essentially interchangeable.

2. With *may not* or *might not*, we express negative conjectures:

> A: Boy, Bobby, look at that snow coming down.
> B: Hey, great, Timmy, we *may not* be having school tomorrow.
>
> A: Why didn't they accept my offer?
> B: They *might not* have liked the conditions you'd set.

However, *could not* (*couldn't*) expresses **impossibility** or lack of ability:

> A: Why doesn't he enter the university?
> B: He *couldn't* do that; he doesn't speak English well enough.
>
> A: Yes, I did see Frank Chen walking along Madison Avenue the other day. I'm absolutely positive.
> B: You *couldn't* have seen him. That's impossible! He's in the hospital with a broken leg.

Note: In a rather literary and formal style, *cannot* may replace *could not:*

> The discovery *cannot* have been made at that time.

3. In affirmative phrases with *could*, we may express **a past opportunity not realized:**

> A: Why didn't you like the way I carried out the project?
> B: You *could have taken* a longer time; you certainly did have the opportunity.
>
> A: Well, do you think that decision was the right one?
> B: Yes, you know, I *could have married* the richest and the most beautiful woman in town, but I didn't. I married the most wonderful woman in the world instead.

We also sometimes use *might* to express a past opportunity not realized:

> A: Yes, I had some inside information, but I didn't invest any money in that project.
> B: Why, you *might have made* a million dollars.

4. Unlike *may*, which has no question form, and *might*, which occurs only in quite formal usage, *could* is often used to ask questions representing conjecture in the present or the past:

A: I don't know why, but they're not returning my calls.

B: *Could they* be discouraging you from calling again?

A: We waited for an hour, but they never showed up.

B: *Could you* have been waiting at the wrong corner?

5. In the present, negative questions with *could not* can express a suggestion:

A: Darn it! I don't have enough money to take a taxi.

B: *Couldn't* you take a bus?

A: We don't know what to do this weekend.

B: *Couldn't* you just take it easy?

6. In past time, we can use *could not* in questions to express an opportunity not realized:

A: *Couldn't* you have married that fellow? He's the richest man in town.

B: Yes, but I married the man I love instead.

A: Mom and Dad, I'm sorry I got such bad grades this semester.

B: Oh, son, *couldn't* you have paid more attention to your books?

7. In idiomatic usage, we often use adjectives and adverbs in the comparative degree in sentences expressing impossibility with *could not*. This usage is very emphatic:

A: Isn't she a lovely and wonderful person?

B: Oh, yes, she just *couldn't* be *nicer,* could she?

A: Are you enjoying yourselves at my party tonight?

B: Why, we *couldn't* be enjoying ourselves *more.*

A: The soup at dinner was wonderful.

B: Wasn't it? It *couldn't* have been *more delicious.*

❑ 4.18 *Have To* with Modal Auxiliaries

Supply in each blank an appropriate verb phrase using *should, ought to, may, might* or *must* with the idiom *have to.*

Example

A: That monster murdered his wife, but he was sent to prison for only two years.

B: (go) He ___*should have had to go*___ to jail for life, ___*shouldn't*___ ___*he*___?

1. A: Do you think you can go to the movies with me tonight?

B: Perhaps, but I'm not sure yet. (*do*) I _____

some chores for my mom and dad. But today's been a slow day at the store,

(*really / do*) so I _____ much today. I'm pretty

sure I can go with you. I'll give you a call as soon as I can.

2. A: Look! How odd! The Smiths across the street left their garage door open.

B: Yes, how unusual! They always close it when they go out. (*leave for*)

They _____ some place in a big hurry. I hope

nothing is wrong.

3. A: At the opening night of the opera, the king himself had to open the door of his car before he got in. (*do*) He _____ that, _____?

   B: Why not? He's just like everybody else, isn't he?

   A: Well, he *is* the king, isn't he?

   B: Listen, even kings have to open their car doors these days.

4. A: Isn't that Tad Jackson? Why isn't he at school?

   B: Oh, Tad goes to a Catholic school, and today's a religious holiday, isn't it? (*go*) He _____ to school.

5. A: They went to Tokyo, Riyadh, Paris and London on their last trip.

   B: (*spend*) They _____ a great deal of money. Those are just about the most expensive cities in the world, aren't they?

   A: Oh, no, the two of them work for the government; it was an official trip. (*spend*) They _____ a dime. (*spend*) They _____ a few dollars on things for themselves, but that was all.

   B: Nice job, huh?

6. A: Well, I think I'm going to go mop the floor now.

   B: My dear, you have two maids, a cook, a gardener and a chauffeur. (*surely / get down on*) You _____ your hands and knees and do such menial work, _____?

   A: Please don't be such a snob, Harriet. Hard physical work is good for one's soul as well as for one's body.

7. A: Our daughter didn't have to do any homework at all last semester.

   B: That's too bad. Homework is essential in any good educational program. (*do*) She _____ a lot. (*spend*) She _____ at least two hours a night on homework.

❑ 4.19 The Idiom *Have To* with *May* or *Might*, *Should* or *Ought To*, and *Must*

We frequently use the idiom *have to* plus a base form with the modals *may* or *might*, *should* or *ought to* and *must:*

1. *May* or *might* (meaning possibility or conjecture):

A: Aren't you going to be here tomorrow?

B: Perhaps not, I *may* **have to** *stay* home and look after the kids.

A: Was he able to leave the hospital earlier than planned?

B: Yes, and he *might not have* **had to** *have* an operation, but my information isn't too reliable.

2. *Should* or *ought to* (meaning expectation or obligation):

A: Everyone *should* **have to** *pay* his or her fair share of taxes.

B: I agree, it's only fair, isn't it?

A: You *ought not to have* **had to** *pay* so much for your car repairs. You were cheated.

B: Thanks for telling me now, pal.

3. *Must* (meaning deduction):

A: I drive to work every day; it takes me an hour and a half.

B: You *must* **have to** *spend* a lot on gas.

A: I worked hard on a farm for almost 25 years. I retired last year.

B: Let's see your hands. Why, you *must not have* **had to** *work* much with them; they're as smooth as silk.

☐ 4.20 Contrasting Verb Tenses with *Have To*

Supply in each blank a verb phrase using the idiom *have to* and an appropriate verb tense.

Example

A: I'm going to go to bed; I just can't keep my eyes open.

B: (*get up*) ___*Do you have to get up*___ early tomorrow?

A: I'm afraid so. (*get*) I ___*don't have to get*___ to the office any earlier than usual, (*do*) but I ___*do have to do*___ some things around the house before I leave for work.

1. A: Scott, what in the world are you doing now? (*make*) _____

    _____ so much noise? What a racket!

    B: (*use*) I'm putting up a shelf, Dad, and I _____

    _____ a hammer, _____?

    A: (*be*) You _____ so thoughtless,

    Scottie, _____? (*put up*) That

    shelf _____ tonight, _____

    _____? It's almost midnight. You're going to wake up all of

    the neighbors. (*always / begin*) Listen, son, why _____

    _____ one of your projects in the middle of the night? (*just /*

put off) You _____ your shelf

project until tomorrow morning.

2. A: When her husband suddenly died, all the people in town were very surprised,

    weren't they?

    B: You can say that again. (*never / go*) Why, when he died, he _____

    _____ to a doctor a day in his life.

    C: (*never / take*) Yes, and he _____ a single

    pill.

    D: (*always / listen to*) That's all true, but he _____

    _____ a nagging wife since the very first day of his marriage. That

    can kill any man, can't it?

3. A: (*do*) Yes, Dad, by the time I get out of medical school in about two years,

    I _____ a great deal of studying.

    B: (*pay*) And your mother and I _____ a lot

    of tuition, but it will have been worth it when you finally become a doctor and

    begin to pay us back.

4. A: Good morning, Mrs. Black, how do you do?

    B: Oh, good morning, Dr. Adikari. I'm doing just fine, thank you. How do you do?

    A: Now there are a few questions I'd like to ask you. (*ever / take*) At any time in

    your life, _____ any kind of medication?

    B: Not ever, except for a few aspirins here and there.

    A: (*ever / have*) _____ an operation?

    B: (*go into*) Doctor, fortunately, not once _____

    _____ the hospital.

5. A: What a stupid thing to do! (*put*) Just at the most important part of the meeting

    with the press, why _____ your foot in

    your mouth?

    B: (*pay for*) Well, I don't know why that remark came out of my mouth the way it

    did, but I now _____ the consequences.

❏ 4.21 *Have To* with Verb Tenses and *Be Going To*

In addition to the simple present and past tenses and certain modals, we can use the idiom
have to plus a base form in the other verb tenses and the idiom *be going to* plus a base form:

1. Future tense and *be going to:*

    A: Ma'am, here's a letter of rather great importance.
    B: Indeed it is, and it*'ll* **have to** *be answered* at once.
    A: All of us *are going to* **have to** *concentrate* very hard.
    B: Why? What do you have in mind? A test perhaps?

2. Present perfect tense:

    A: I *have* **had to** *have* three dental appointments this month, and I still have some cavities.
    B: Recently, three of my teeth *have* **had to** *be pulled out.*
    C: Not once *have* I ever **had to** *sit* in a dentist's chair.

3. Past perfect tense:

    A: Why were you so tired when I saw you the other day?
    B: It was because I *had* **had to** *work* so hard the night before.

4. Future perfect tense:

    A: You'll be able to pay your back taxes by the end of the year, won't you?
    B: Listen, I *will have* **had to** *pay* them by that time, or else I'll have to go to jail.

❑ 4.22 Contrasting Modal Auxiliaries: *Have To* and *Be Able To*

Supply in each blank an appropriate verb phrase using *should* or *ought to, may* or *might, can* or *could, must, have to* and *be able to.*

Example

    A: (*please / move over*) *Could you please move over* a bit?

    B: (*move*) I *can't move*.

    A: Why not?

    B: You're standing on my foot.

1. A: Ouch!

    B: What's wrong?

    A: I hit my knee on the piano leg.

    B: (*hurt*) That _____.

2. A: What are you looking for?

    B: An outlet for this plug. I want to listen to my radio.

    A: (*plug in*) You _____ your radio, _____

    _____? Doesn't it work on a battery?

    B: The battery is dead.

3. A: I wrote Bill Bailey almost four months ago, and I still haven't gotten an answer.

B: (*the letter / lose*) _____ in the mail?

A: That's not likely, is it? (*want*) He _____ to write to me. After all, it's been four months.

B: Frankly, I don't trust the mail that much. (*give*) _____ _____ him another chance? Why don't you write another letter? (*hurt*) It _____ anything, _____?

4. **A:** I think my neighbor is engaged in some kind of criminal activity.

   B: (*the police / tell*) _____?

   A: Not by me, I want to keep my nose clean.*

   B: That's not being a good citizen.

5. **A:** How was your weekend up in the mountains?

   B: Perfectly lovely. (*have*) We _____ better weather—not a drop of rain and endless sunshine.

6. **A:** Yes, I had to carry my luggage up to the room myself.

   B: (*carry*) You _____ your luggage up to the room yourself. This is a first-class hotel; there are porters who do that sort of thing.

   A: (*find*) I _____ one.

7. **A:** I've been trying to get this number for hours, but I always get a busy signal.

   B: (*punch*) _____ the wrong number?

   A: No, I'm absolutely sure this is the right one.

8. **A:** This toy is mine, Mommy. I don't want anybody else to play with it.

   B: (*be*) _____ so selfish, Teddy? (*share*) _____ your things with others? (*stop*) _____ thinking about yourself so much?

9. **A:** Madame Tosca, you are a splendid hostess. (*serve*) No one in Rome _____ _____ the dinner more graciously than you did last night.

   B: (*be*) Why, thank you, Countess, and you _____ a more charming guest. (*be*) You _____ *the* sensation of the party.

*Not get involved.

10. **A:** I spent about forty thousand for my car.

   B: That wasn't at all necessary, you know. (*buy*) You _____

   _____ a car for much less money than that, _____

   _____?

   A: (*pay*) Yes, but if you want luxury, you _____ for it.

   B: (*spend*) Yes, of course, but you _____ so

   much money on a car, _____? (*lose*) After

   all, you don't have a dime in the bank, and you _____

   _____ your job if business doesn't get any better.

❑ 4.23 *Have Got* and *Have Got To* Versus *Have, Have To* and *Must*

Using *have, have to, have got, have got to* or *must,* fill in the blanks with appropriate verb phrases. *Have (has)* or *have (has) got* will be required when no base form is given in parentheses.

   ### Example

   A: (*work*) <u>*Do you have to work*</u> very hard at your office?

   B: Very. I <u>*'ve got*</u> a difficult boss, (*take*) and
   I <u>*'ve got to take*</u> a great deal of stress.

   A: (*be*) That <u>*must be*</u> an unpleasant situation.

1. **A:** Because my stomach is empty, it's growling. (*just / eat*) I _____

   _____ something soon, or else I'll get sick.

   B: Well, we _____ a lot of fresh food in the fridge,

   (*go out*) so we _____ to a restaurant.

   A: (*do*) Yes, but we _____ the dishes.

2. **A:** _____ any problems in school last semester?

   B: Just one. I _____ a typewriter, (*type*) and all

   the papers for my courses _____.

   A: _____ enough money to buy a typewriter?

   B: (*borrow*) No, so I _____ my roommate's

   typewriter when she wasn't using it.

3. **A:** (*work*) My grandfather _____ ten hours at the

   store yesterday.

B: (*be*) Why, he's almost eighty. He _____ tired when he finally got home.

A: (*kid*) You _____. Despite his age, he's still as strong as an ox.

4. A: When I'm in London this spring, I'm going to meet the queen of England.

(*bow*) _____ when I do? (*my wife / curtsy*)

And _____?

B: (*do*) No, you _____ that, _____

_____? You're American citizens, aren't you? (*bow or curtsy*)

Neither of you _____. Just shake her hand. At least that's what I think the custom is.

5. A: Because of my appointment here in Los Angeles this morning, (*drive*)

I _____ more than seven hundred miles yesterday.

B: (*be*) You _____ exhausted when you finally got to your hotel.

A: No, I was on a four-lane highway all the way, and the traffic was light; (*do*)

I _____ any heavy driving.

6. A: I'm a little nervous today; tonight I'm going to a banquet at which I'll be the guest of honor.

B: (*give*) _____a speech?

A: (*speak*) Yes, but I _____ for very long; they want to keep the speeches short, thank goodness.

❏ 4.24 *Have Got*

1.   Informally, we use the verb phrase *have got* (or *has got*) to show possession in the same way that we use the verb *have*. The phrase may refer only to the present and the future. We generally use subject pronouns and *have* or *has* in a contracted form. Most often, *have got* appears in affirmative verb phrases:

A: I've *got* (*have*) a brilliant and clever idea.
B: Your wife *has got* (*has*) a lot of good ideas, too.

2.   For questions and negatives in North American English, we use *have got* less frequently than *have*, but we do use it from time to time:

A: What kind of car *has your dad got* (*does your dad have*)?
B: He *hasn't got* (*doesn't have*) one; he takes the subway.
A: Excuse me, Miss, *have you got* (*do you have*) a quarter?
B: Listen, I *haven't got* (*don't have*) enough money to feed myself.

❏ 4.25 *Have Got To*

1. Also for the present and the future only, we use the idiom *have got to* plus a base form, which has the same meaning of necessity as the modal auxiliary *must* or the idiom *have to*. It expresses very strong necessity. The idiom usually appears in affirmative verb phrases:

> A: They*'ve got to* (*must, have to*) think about the future.
> B: We*'ve all got to* (*must, have to*) do that.
>
> A: Their son *has got to* (*must, has to*) improve at school.
> B: But their daughter *has got to* (*must, has to*) have more physical recreation.

2. Questions with *have got to* occur less frequently in North American English:

> A: *Have you got to* (*must you, do you have to*) spend much time on your home-work?
> B: Oh, I've got to spend about two hours and a half.
>
> A: What time *has she got to* (*must she, does she have to*) get up?
> B: My roommate has got to get up at six.

3. Negative verb phrases are even less common than questions:

> A: What have you got to do tomorrow?
> B: I *haven't got to* (*don't have to*) do anything but loaf.

4. As with *must* and *have to*, in the present and the future only, we can make a deduction with *have got to:*

> A: Isn't it a lovely evening?
> B: Yes, it*'s got to* (*must, has to*) be the nicest we've had.
>
> A: Yeah, that's who I am, Superman himself.
> B: You*'ve got to* (*must, have to*) be kidding.

❏ 4.26 Warnings and Threats; Reviewing Articles and Prepositions

Compose a sentence using each set of given words as a cue. Supply an appropriate form of a verb. Use *had better* or *had best* when it is appropriate; then, when it is required, place in the sentence *a, an, the* or an appropriate preposition chosen from the following list. Transcribe any punctuation that is used. Do not add any words other than auxiliary verbs, modal auxiliaries, articles and prepositions.

about	between	for	into	on	to
at	down	in	of	out	with

Example

you / be / naughty, / or else / Santa / bring / you / any presents.

A: Christmas is coming soon, isn't it?

B: Yes, it is, sweetie. *You'd better not be naughty, or else Santa might not bring you any presents.*

1.   you / take / least / thousand dollars; / otherwise, / you / run / money / before / end / week.

A: I'm going to be staying in Paris for a week.

B: Paris is beautiful and exciting, but it's very expensive. _____

_____

2.   we / keep / it / secret / us, / we?

A: We don't want anyone to know about this information, do we?

B: In no way. _____

_____

3.   [At the dinner table]
     you / please / pass / butter / me?

A: _____

     you / cut / butter?   it / be / good / you, / it?   it / be / full / fat, / it?   also,
     you / get / least / hour / exercise / day?   you / put / weight / recently.

B: _____

_____

_____

4.   I / work / my desk / when / boss / come / office / this morning.   I / gossip /
     when / he / come/ .

A: Hi, Dave. Listen, I'd like to tell you a little story.

B: Sorry, Bill, but I have to get back to work. _____

_____

_____

5.   I / keep / my mouth shut, / I?   otherwise, / I / put / my foot / it.

A: _____

_____

     yeah, / you / shut / it, / or else / I / shut / it / you.

B: _____

_____

A: listen here, buddy, / you / get / so tough / me. _____

_____

❏ 4.27 *Had Better* and *Had Best*

1. For the present and the future only, we use the idiom *had better* plus a base form to
express advisability, similar to the way we use *should* or *ought to*. However, *had better* is
much stronger in force. It often conveys a kind of warning or threat. There is the added suggestion that an undesirable result will occur if we do not pay heed to the warning. *Otherwise*

and *or else* frequently accompany the idiom. *Had* is most often contracted with a subject pronoun.

A: You'*d better* slow down, or else you'll get a ticket.
B: Listen, you'*d better* stop criticizing my driving, or you'll end up walking.

A: You'*d better* be working at your desk when I get back to the office. This work *had better* be done by then, or else you'll be fired.
B: You'*d better* stop pushing me, or I'll quit. I'm tired of always being threatened.

A: The dog *had better* be tied up.
B: You bet, or else he'll go running after every cat in town.

2. *Not* follows *better* in negatives:

A: Kids, you'd *better not* be fooling around when I get home. You'd *better not* be watching TV. Or else!
B: Right, sure, Mom, we'll be working on our homework.

3. Questions using *had better* are always negative, and they emphasize the advisability or warning:

A: *Hadn't you* better keep your mouth closed for a while?
B: Right, or else I'll put my foot in it.

A: Wait, just a second. Isn't that gas I smell?
B: Right, and it's strong. *Hadn't we* better get out of here?

4. Negative tag endings with *had better* are quite common:

A: I'm thinking seriously about quitting my job. My boss is driving me nuts, and the pressure is killing me. I just can't take it anymore.
B: Well, you'*d better* find a new job first, *hadn't you?*

5. In North American English, the idiom *had best* occurs much less frequently than *had better.*

A: We'*d best* not take any chances.
B: Yes, if we do, we might lose our pants.

A: So long, I'm going to go out and play.
B: *Hadn't* you *best* put on a jacket, Jack? Or else you might catch a cold.

❑ 4.28 *Be Supposed To*

Supply in each blank an appropriate verb phrase using *be supposed to*. Use the verbs in the following list.

arrive	clean	have	set	use
be	do	present	sit	watch
bring	get	reach	smoke	

Example

A: Who *'s supposed to clean* _____ the apartment today?

B: *Aren't you supposed to do* _____ it? I did it last week, didn't I? Now

don't try to get out of it again.

1. A: Oh, yes, my roommate helps me with my homework all the time.

B: You _____ that, _____

_____?

A: Why not? I _____ it by

myself, _____? The teacher didn't

say that, did she?

B: Yes, weren't you in class when she did? She said that everyone _____

_____ his or her homework without the help of anyone

else.

2. **A:** What's the big hurry, Vito?

   B: We _____ at Bob's surprise birthday

   party before he does. So let's hurry up, shall we?

   [At the party]

   C: Hi, Vito, where's Bob's birthday present? You _____

   _____ it with you, _____?

   B: I _____ his present, _____

   _____?

   A: No, you weren't, I was, and here it is—a gold watch.

   C: Shall I present it to him when the right time comes?

   B: Hey, wait a minute, folks. I _____ it to

   him, _____? After all, I _____

   _____ one of Bob's best friends, _____

   _____?

3. **A:** I got angry with my kids last night.

   B: Why was that?

   A: Oh, they _____ TV when I got home last

   night; they _____ their chores.

4. **A:** I'm sorry, Professor, for the great number of typos in my paper. My eyes just

   seem to pass over them.

   B: Well, you know my rule, don't you? A student _____

   _____ more than two typos a page, and you have six or seven. Also,

   another rule is that you _____ any color

   ribbon other than dark blue or black. (*certainly*) You _____

   _____ a red ribbon.

5. A: Oh, good morning, what are you doing here now?

    B: _____ here at nine for my conference with

    Professor Miller?

    A: Yes, but it's ten. You must have forgotten that we went on daylight saving's time

    at two this morning. You _____ your clock

    an hour forward last night.

    B: Darn it! I always forget.

❏ 4.29 *Be Supposed To*

1. The idiom *be supposed to* plus a base form can mean the following:

    a. "It is believed that":

        A: French wine *is supposed to* be the best in the world.
        B: Yes, I know, but I really do prefer Italian.

        A: French trains aren't as fast as Japanese trains.
        B: That's not correct. French trains *are supposed to* be the fastest in the world, aren't they?

        A: I can't stand that restaurant.
        B: But it'*s supposed to* be the best in San Francisco.
        C: Oh, that's just advertising.

        Very often a supposition that we make with *be supposed to* is open to dispute.

    b. "Be required to":

        A: Nobody *is supposed to* smoke in this building.
        B: Then why do you see all the butts on the floor?

        A: Hey, *aren't* you *supposed to* be wearing seat belts?
        B: Yes, I'*m supposed to* wear them, but I hate them.

    c. "Be expected to" or "be scheduled to":

        A: *Isn't* the bus *supposed to* get here at seven?
        B: Yes, it'*s supposed to* get here then, but it never does.

        A: The dictator's wife *is supposed to* give a speech tomorrow.
        B: Yes, but everyone knows she's fleeing the country tonight.

2. In the present and the future, when we use *be supposed to* in order to express an expectation or a requirement, its meaning is similar to that expressed by the modal auxiliary *should* or *ought to:*

        A: Ladies and gentlemen, you *aren't supposed to* (*shouldn't*) smoke in the public rooms of this hotel.
        B: *Aren't* smokers *supposed to* (*Shouldn't* smokers) have rights, too?
        A: You'*re supposed to* (*ought to*) say thank you when somebody does a favor for you.
        B: I know, but I sometimes forget.

❑ **4.30** **Past Custom**

Fill in the blanks with appropriate verb phrases. Give your examples variety by using a combination of *used to*, *would* and the simple past tense for past custom. You will use the idiom *have to* frequently.

> ***Example***
>
> A: (*do*) When you were a child, what _____*did you use to do*_____ to
>
> entertain yourself in the summer?
>
> B: (*do*) Oh, I _____*would do*_____ all kinds of things. Just your
>
> question brings back all sorts of fond memories. I can be a rather nostalgic person
>
> at times, you know.

1. A: (*ever / do*) When you were a child, _____

    anything that was naughty?

    B: (*sometimes / play*) No, not really, but I _____

    tricks on kids in the neighborhood and at school.

    A: (*do*) Could you give me an example of how you _____

    _____ that?

    B: (*put*) Oh, I _____ a frog or a snake in some

    kid's desk, (*put*) or I _____ a dead mouse in

    some kid's lunch bag. Stupid things like that.

    A: (*ever / get into*) _____ trouble when you played

    tricks on kids like that?

    B: (*usually / get out of*) Oh, sure, but I _____ it. I

    was a pretty smart cookie.*

2. A: (*be / finally / retire*) Mr. Cole, what line of business _____

    _____ you in before you _____ some

    years ago?

    B: (*work*) I _____ for an international bank.

    A: (*your work / require*) _____ lots of travel?

    B: Oh, yes indeed, a great deal. (*go*) And in the early days of my career, when I

    _____ to Europe, South America or Asia on

    business, (*go*) I _____ by ship. (*be / be*) Getting

*Clever person, but cunning, like a fox.

somewhere _____ as easy as it _____

_____ today with jet travel. (*cross*) When I

_____ the Atlantic Ocean during the winter,

(*often / do*) which I _____, (*usually / be*)

it _____ a rough trip, (*nearly / freeze*) and

I _____ to death. (*go*) When I _____

_____ to the Far East in the summer, (*also / often / do*)

which I _____, (*be*) it _____

_____ unbelievably hot. (*enjoy*) But, all in all, I _____

_____ my business trips. I had a lot more fun than people do

today.

3. A: (*be*) Great-great-grandpa, please tell us about the days when you _____

_____ a young boy on a farm way out in the country.

B: (*be*) Oh, those _____ the good old days. (*want*)

I remember that when I _____ to go

somewhere, (*ride*) I _____ my horse or walk.

A: (*ever / go*) _____ on long trips on your horse?

B: (*sometimes / ride*) Oh, yes, in the summers we _____ twenty or

thirty miles in a single day.

A: (*get*) How _____ to school?

B: (*walk*) We _____. (*have*) We _____

_____ cars or buses in the old days, (*have*) and we

_____ many roads, either. (*be*) And

there _____ no electricity, (*read*) so at night

I _____ by the light of a kerosene lamp, (*run

out of*) and when we _____ kerosene, (*read*)

I _____ by candlelight.

A: (*do*) Besides reading, Grandpa, what else _____

for entertainment?

B: (*hunt*) Oh, I _____ a lot in the fall and spring,

(*fish*) and I _____ all summer long. (*always /

have*) We _____ a lot of delicious salmon and

trout to eat. Just the memory of it makes me hungry.

A: (*happen / get*) What _____ when somebody in

the family _____ sick?

B: (*be*) That _____ a serious matter. (*live*) The

nearest doctor _____ in a small town about

five miles away, (*ride*) so one of us in the family _____

_____ a horse there to get him. (*be*) Remember that when there

_____ an emergency, (*have*) we _____

_____ a telephone to call for help. (*be*) As you can see, the

good old days often _____ so good as we often

think they were.

❏ 4.31 *Used To* and *Would*

1.   We use the idiom *used to* plus a base form to express a condition that once existed but no longer does:

> A: Los Angeles, the second largest city in the United States, *used to* be a very small Mexican town.
> B: And New York City, the largest, *used to* be a collection of Indian villages.

2.   We sometimes employ *used to* for a condition that existed in past time and still does:

> A: When we were living in Paris, spring always *used to* be so lovely, and I imagine it still is.
> B: Yes, the air just *used to* be full of lovely fragrances and romance.

3.   We most frequently employ the idiom for expressing a past custom or habitual activity that occurred with regularity in the past but no longer does:

> A: All year long when I was a boy in California, we *used to* have all our meals outside on the patio.
> B: Well, all summer long when I was a girl in Connecticut, we *used to* have our meals outside, too, but on the terrace, not on a patio as you did in California.

4.   *Used to* becomes a base form in questions, negatives and emphatic forms:

> A: Didn't you *use to* live in Saudi Arabia?
> B: No, but I did *use to* live in Yemen, right next door.

> A: When you were living in Switzerland, did you ever *use to* go mountain climbing?
> B: No, I was too chicken.

5.   We also use the simple past tense to express a habitual activity or custom in the past:

> A: In the summer when I was a kid, my friends and I *went* fishing almost every day.
> B: During that time of year when I was young, I *worked* with my father on our farm every day.

6.   Often the modal auxiliary *would* replaces the simple past tense or *used to* for expressing a past custom:

> A: When they were still married, they'*d fight* (*used to fight, fought*) from morning to night, every day, year in and year out until they got sick of it.

B: Yes, and they *would fight over* (*used to fight over, fought over*) absolutely nothing.

7. However, we do not use *would* for a condition that once existed but no longer does:

A: My father *used to be* [never *would be*] a farmer, but now he's a park ranger.
B: Mine *used to* be an art teacher, but he now teaches English.
A: Istanbul *used to be called* [never *would be called*] Constantinople.
B: Yes, and Ho Chi Minh City *used to be called* Saigon, and it still is, isn't it?

8. We frequently use the idiom *have to* with *used to* and *would* to express a past custom:

A: When I was a kid, I always *used to* **have to** do a lot of chores around the yard when I got home from school.
B: What *would* you **have to** do?
A: Oh, I *used to* **have to** feed the ducks and chickens, and then I *would* **have to** help my father milk the cows.

❑ 4.32 *Would Like* Versus *Would Rather*

Supply in each blank an appropriate verb phrase using *would like* or *would rather*. When no base form appears in parentheses, use a form of *would like* (or *love*).

Examples

a. **A:** _____Would you like_____ another cup of coffee?

   B: (*have*) No thank you, I _'d rather have_____ a glass of milk.

b. **A:** (*go*) I _'d like to have gone_____ to the beach yesterday.

   B: But it was so cold. (*go*) _Wouldn't you rather have gone_ to your place in the country?

1. **A:** (*be*) _____ a dancer or an actor in the theater or movies?

   B: (*be*) I _____ either; my voice is too weak, and I'm rather clumsy and awkward on my feet.

   C: I wouldn't either. I _____ the life of a dancer or an actor. It's too insecure—too unstable.

   D: (*become*) Well, as you all know, I'm a dancer; I _____

   _____ an actor when I was younger, but I just didn't have the talent for it.

   A: Oh, I _____ a life on the stage or in the movies, too, but I was always too busy raising a family.

   B: Oh, I don't think so. You _____ all of that

pressure and frequent uncertainty. (*spend*) Also, you _____

_____ any time away from your family.

2. **A:** (*stay*) My husband and I _____ home last

    summer, but because of some business deals in Europe, we had to spend most of

    the summer there.

    B: Are you serious? I'm surprised. (*really / be*) _____

    _____ in hot and dirty New York City than in Europe?

    A: (*be*) Yes, there's no place in the world where we _____

    _____ than our little house and garden in Brooklyn, New York.

    C: Oh, yes, I've heard about your place. (*see*) I _____

    _____ it some time.

    A: (*have*) Why, we _____ you, come any time.

3. **A:** (*be*) I'm sure you _____ at the party I

    went to last night. Some outrageous things occurred.

    B: Like what? Tell us all about it.

    A: Well, at one point everybody jumped into the swimming pool with all of their

    fancy clothes on.

    C: Ha, ha, ha. (*see*) I _____ that.

    D: (*get*) Yes, I _____ a photograph of that.

4. **A:** Don't you think you should fire your secretary? He's quite incompetent, isn't he?

    B: (*really / do*) I _____ that. He's a great

    guy, even though his work can be a bit sloppy at times.

    C: (*have*) For a secretary, _____ an efficient

    person than a great guy?

    D: (*have*) Yes, _____ a more skilled person?

5. **A:** In the war I was fighting at the front lines during all the major battles.

    B: (*be*) I _____ in that situation.

    A: Oh, it wasn't so bad. It was better fighting in the trenches than sitting at some

    desk.

    C: What! (*really / fight*) _____ in the trenches

    than sitting at a desk?

    A: (*be*) Yes, I'm the sort of person who _____

    where the action is and not where it isn't.

6. A: In my job I have to do a lot of work on the phone.

B: (*do*) I _____ that; I dislike spending a lot

of time on the phone. (*have*) I _____ a job

where I meet people face to face. I _____

your job at all, I'm afraid.

A: Oh, really, wouldn't you? Well, just what kind of work do *you* do?

B: I work in the complaints department of a large Chicago department store.

A: Well, I would *hate* your job. (*certainly / listen to*) I _____

_____ complaints all day long.

❑ 4.33 *Would Like*

1.   The verb phrase *would like* means "want." The phrase, however, conveys a certain degree of politeness:

> A: May I have your order, please, ma'am?
> B: Yes, thank you, I'*d like* a banana split.
> A: And what *would* you *like*, sir?
> C: I'*d like* a strawberry soda, and would you please put some whipped cream on top?

2.   As with the verb *want*, we frequently follow *would like* with an infinitive:

> A: I wouldn't like *to be* in the president's shoes.
> B: Well, I certainly would.
> C: Why on earth would you like *to be?* He's facing a lot of hard criticism at this time.
> B: I wouldn't like the criticism, that's for sure, but I would like *to have* all that power.

3.   The idiom *have to* sometimes combines with *would like:*

> A: I have to spend a couple of days in a slaughterhouse for a research paper that I'm doing.
> B: I must confess I *wouldn't like to have to* do something like that.

4.   On occasion, we substitute *love* for *like;* however, we usually do not use *love* in negatives and questions:

> A: It's so hot, humid and sticky this afternoon, isn't it?
> B: Yes, I'*d* just *love* to be sitting in our swimming pool at home right now.

But we do use *love* for negative questions:

> A: *Wouldn't you love* to be riding the waves right now?
> B: Yes, and *wouldn't you just love* lying on the beach?

5.   For past time, we put perfect infinitives after the verb phrase *would like* (*love*):

> A: I'm disappointed that I wasn't able to get to that party in Hollywood. I'*d like to have been* there. I'*d love to have been introduced* to all those movie stars.
> B: Oh, I'*d like to have gone* to it, too. I'm a big movie fan.
> C: Of all the stars at the party, Barbara, whom *would* you *like to have met* the most?

D: I *wouldn't like to have met* any of them; I'm not particularly fond of actors. They're too egotistical.

6. We also use the construction *would have liked* (*loved*) plus a simple infinitive:

A: We *would have loved to go* skiing last weekend, but we had to entertain some customers from out of town.

B: Oh, no, you *wouldn't have liked to do* that at all last weekend. We did, and it was terrible. The snow was all slush.

7. This construction may also occur without an infinitive:

A: Yes, last year I traveled around the world three times.

B: I *would have* just *loved* that.

C: I *wouldn't have liked* it at all—too many hassles.

☐ 4.34 *Would Rather*

1. With the idiom *would rather* plus a base form, we express a preference for one choice or possibility instead of another. In conversation the idiom often appears together with the verb phrase *would like:*

A: I*'d like* to climb a mountain today.

B: Oh, I*'d rather explore* a cave than go mountain climbing.

C: What *would* you *like* to do, Bill?

D: Well, I'm afraid of heights, and I don't like cold and dark places. I*'d rather stay* home in front of the fire.

2. In statements we usually use *than* between the choices:

A: Would you like to be an engineer?

B: No, I'd rather be an architect *than* an engineer.

3. In questions we may replace *than* with *or:*

A: Would you rather be a lawyer *or* (*than*) a doctor?

B: Neither, I can't read or write very well, and I can't stand the sight of blood.

A: John, would you rather be single *or* (*than*) married?

B: What a foolish question! You know what I'd rather be without asking, don't you?

But in negative questions we may use only *than:*

A: I just love being married.

B: Come now, *wouldn't* you rather be single *than* married?

C: Yes, *wouldn't* you rather have freedom *than* security?

4. In past forms with *would rather,* affirmative verb phrases suggest the action did not take place:

A: How did you enjoy the game yesterday?

B: I*'d rather have been studying* at the library; I've got an important examination next week. I don't like football anyway.

A: I spent Christmas with my family.

B: You*'d rather have spent* it with your girlfriend, wouldn't you?

Negative verb phrases suggest the action took place:

A: I*'d rather not have spent* so much money yesterday.

B: Yes, and I*'d rather not have gone* shopping with you. You made me spend a lot of money.

5

Compound Sentences and Coordinate Conjunctions

❑ 5.1 Compound Sentences; Reviewing Articles and Prepositions

Compose a sentence using each set of given words as a cue. Supply an appropriate form of a verb; then, when it is required, place in the sentence *a, an, the* or an appropriate preposition chosen from the following list. Finally, punctuate each sentence with either a comma or a semicolon and a period at the end. Do not add any words other than articles, prepositions, auxiliary verbs, modal auxiliaries and related idioms.

about	at	during	in	on	to	with
above	below	for	of	out	under	

Example

time / go / quickly / I sleep / flight

A: I have to fly down to Rio once a month.

B: Doesn't it take a long time to fly all that way?

A: *Time goes quickly; I sleep during the flight.*

1. one / my roommates / always / worry / thieves / she / hide / her purse / pillow / her bed

A: _____

_____

B: Really? Isn't the dormitory safe?

2. never / I / ever / be / Belgium / nor / I / ever / be / Netherlands

A: I'm going to Amsterdam and Brussels next month. You know a lot about those two cities, don't you?

B: Why, where did you get that idea? _____

_____

3.   most / South America / be / equator / all / Central America / be / it

A: _____

_____

B: Would you please show me on the map?

4.   I / study / hard / this semester / or else / I / kick / school

A: You're spending a lot of time at the library, aren't you?

B: _____

_____

5.   owl / sleep / day / it / hunt / night

A: _____

B: Well, I like that schedule; I'm a night person.

C: So am I, I'm a real night owl.*

6.   I / spend / few hours / my grandchildren / or / I / go shopping / department stores / mall / Highway 80

A: Well, Gabriela, now that lunch is over, what are your plans for the afternoon?

B: I haven't made up my mind yet. _____

_____

7.   Union / South Africa / be / wealthy country / it / have / huge deposits / gold / and / other / minerals

A: _____

_____

B: They also have huge social and political problems.

8.   something / do / problem / or else / world / become / too small / size / its population

A: Could you give a comment, sir, concerning overpopulation?

B: _____

_____

9.   I / never / forget / my classmates / grammar class / nor / I / forget / all / good / times / my other classes

A: Well, on this, the last day of school, how do you feel?

B: Rather sad. _____

_____

*Person who likes to stay up late.

10.   United States / produce / huge amount / wheat / and / Soviet Union / buy / great deal / it

A: _____

_____

B: Oh? That's not still true, is it? I just can't keep up with the world, can you?

11.   lab test results / be / positive / patient / enter / hospital / once / operation / lower intestine

A: Well, Doctor, what's your opinion?

B: _____

_____

12.   citizens / nation / desire / end / crime and corruption / public / as well as / private / sectors / society / for / they / get / sick / it

A: Just what is your opinion of this situation, Ambassador?

B: _____

_____

_____

❑ 5.2   The Comma and the Semicolon; Coordinate Conjunctions: *And, But and Others*

1. A **simple sentence** always contains a subject and a verb:

Subject	Verb	Balance of Sentence
The moon	*reflects*	the light of the sun.
The sun	*is*	the source of life.

2. Two sentences that are closely related to each other may be combined to form a **compound sentence**. We can join the two sentences with a **semicolon** (;); each sentence is called an **independent clause** (or **main clause**):

> They have a boat. They love to sail.
> *They have a boat; they love to sail.*
>
> They've studied hard. They should do well on the test.
> *They've studied hard; they should do well on the test.*

3. Two independent clauses may be joined together with the following **coordinate conjunctions**; we usually separate the two clauses with a **comma** (,):

a. *And* shows addition:

> She has a lovely daughter, *and* I've got a lovely son.

It also sometimes shows result:

> Our company has a good product, *and* we make a lot of money.

b. *But* and *yet* express contrast:

He's a good secretary, *but* he doesn't type well.
She studies hard, *yet* she receives poor grades.

c. *So* expresses result:

The cost of living is high, *so* expectations for the future are low.

d. *For* (meaning "because") introduces clauses of reason:

The child was crying, *for* she had lost her way.
The nation is grieved, *for* they've lost their leader.

For in this use occurs in rather literary English.

e. *Or* expresses an alternative or a choice:

In the afternoon she goes shopping, *or* she visits her friends and relatives.
We could have gone to Yellowstone last summer, *or* we could have gone to Yosemite.

On occasion, we express a condition with *or:*

You'd better deal with this problem now, *or* it'll get worse.
You must take better care of yourself, *or* you might get sick.

f. *Or else* expresses a stronger condition than *or:*

She absolutely must lose weight, *or else* her blood pressure won't go down.
I'd better write that number down, *or else* I'll forget it.

g. Like *or, nor* expresses an alternative or a choice. However, *nor* makes a negative opening, and an emphatic form must follow:

They hadn't called the fire department by that time, *nor had they* called the police.
He doesn't want money, *nor does he* want success.
They've never been in that country, *nor have they* ever wanted to be.

4. A comma or a semicolon in writing usually indicates a pause in speech. Very often, we breathe in slightly when we make the pause:

The crowd is cheering; [pause] the dictator has fallen.

The people of the nation demand peace, [pause] yet the government still refuses to put an end to the war.

When two independent clauses are short, we are less likely to use a pause in speech. Similarly, we may omit the comma in writing:

She's tired and he's sick.
The moon is cold and the sun is hot.

❏ 5.3 Coordinate Conjunctions and Elements; Reviewing Articles and Prepositions

Follow the directions for section 5.1. This time, however, the sentences will be longer and will sometimes require more punctuation, and you will supply prepositions of your own choice.

Example

we / rarely / speak / each other / I / like / her / and / she / like /
me / yet / we / just / get

A: What's your neighbor next door like?

B: *We rarely speak to each other; I like her, and she likes me, yet we just don't get along.*

1.   I / make / cake / we / have / flour / milk / and / sugar / but / we / have / eggs

A: Would you please make a cake for dinner, Dad?

B: _____

_____

2.   we / plan / to spend / week / Netherlands / two weeks / Alps / and / week / and / half / Lake Como / Italy / we / spend / great deal / money

A: What are your plans for your vacation this summer?

B: _____

_____

_____

3.   apartment / be / hot / and / stuffy / so / I / open / all / windows / turn / radiator / and / turn / fan

A: What did you do first when you got home last night?

B: _____

_____

4.   there / be / few reasons / I / be / very high / company / and / make / much money / but / I / enjoy / my job / and / want / to quit / and / go / looking / another one

A: You stayed with that company for a long time before you finally quit. Why is that?

B: _____

_____

_____

5.   he / have / million / dollars / bank / Switzerland / great many friends / all / world / and / absolutely beautiful family / yet / poor / fellow / be / happy / man

A: I just cannot figure out that guy, can you?

B: No, I really can't. _____

_____

_____

6.   weekends / his girlfriend / like / to play tennis / or / go / swimming / but / he / fish / hunt / or / go / sailing / they / have / much / common*

Much in common means "mutual interests."

A: _____

_____

_____

yes / they / have / much / common / but / they / be / very much / love / each other / this / keep / them happy

B: _____

_____

7.   oh / I / suddenly feel / little sleepy / I / just / keep / my eyes / open

A: _____

_____

why / you / go / upstairs / lie / your bed / and / take / little nap?   you / rest / while / or else / you / be / too tired to go / circus tonight / me / and / kids   short nap / refresh / you / it?

B: _____

_____

_____

_____

❑ 5.4 Coordinate Elements

1.   Besides independent clauses, we use coordinate conjunctions to connect **coordinate elements** such as the following:

a. Nouns and pronouns:

Ladies and gentlemen, would you all please take your seats?
Hadn't we best keep this a secret between *you and me*?

b. Adjectives and adverbs:

He isn't *rich or famous.*
Our cashier always works very *quickly but accurately.*

c. Verbs and verb phrases:

The children *lay down and took* a long and refreshing nap.

I*'m thinking about* your proposal *and will give* you a straightforward answer tomorrow.

She *was reading* the book *but (was) not understanding it.*

The guests *have come and (have) gone.*

We*'re working* hard *and (are) making* very good money.

Note: A second auxiliary may be omitted if it is the same as the first auxiliary.

d. Objects:

These drinks are for *the adults but not the children.*
Would you please give these memos to *your boss and mine*?

e. Infinitives:

I definitely need *to get* to bed *and* (*to*) *rest*.
Would you like *to watch* TV *or* (*to*) *listen to* the radio?

Note: The second *to* is optional.

f. Prepositional phrases:

There are economic problems *in the towns and on the farms*.
Elephants live *in the jungles and on the plains*.

2. When two coordinate elements occur in a compound, we do not use a comma:

We *have seen and done* many marvelous and interesting things.
A hammer and a sickle appear on the Soviet flag.

When three or more items occur, we call the compound a **coordinate series**. We use commas to separate the items, but the comma preceding the conjunction is frequently omitted by writers nowadays, even though we often retain the pause when we are speaking:

Mr. and Mrs. Brown, Dr. and Mrs. Jackson(,) *and Prince and Princess Von Belsen* will be at the tea.

The hostess suddenly *stood up from* the table, *faced* the door(,) *and marched out of* the room in a military style.

3. For the sake of clarity, a coordinate series does not usually exceed four items, except in a sentence such as the following:

On our shopping trip this afternoon, we purchased a stepladder for the kitchen, some towels for the bathroom, a few things for the garden, two steaks for dinner, a sweet bonnet for our new baby(,) and a bottle of champagne to celebrate our first wedding anniversary.

4. When we combine more than two sentences, we must often make certain changes in the sentences so that they will flow more smoothly:

My grandmother wasn't feeling well.
My grandmother hadn't been taking her medicine.
My grandmother hadn't been getting enough rest.

Connected

My grandmother wasn't feeling well, for she hadn't been taking her medicine or getting enough rest.

She was depressed. She was unhappy.
The weather was cold. It was raining all the time.
She wasn't able to work in the garden.

Connected

She was depressed and unhappy; the weather was cold and rainy, and she wasn't able to work in the garden.

5. In writing, a run-on sentence—in other words, an overconnected sentence—is considered poor style:

Overconnected

I didn't enjoy the cocktail party, nor did I enjoy the dinner party, and I hated the movie, but I loved the party later, and I loved the ride home with my friends.

Better

I didn't enjoy the cocktail party, the dinner party, or the movie, but I loved the party later and the ride home with my friends.

❑ 5.5 One or the Other of Two

With *either . . . or,* connect each set of sentences or coordinate elements. Some independent clauses may be abridged.

Example

Their food is superb. It is dreadful.

A: Hey, by the way, how is that restaurant?

B: It's always a gamble; it's never just ordinary. _Either their food is_
superb, or it's dreadful.

1. He's a devil. He's a saint.

   A: Just what kind of person is he?

   B: Oh, a very complicated person, indeed. You could never call him Mr. Average.

   _____

2. My roommates help me. My boyfriend helps me.

   A: Your homework is always excellent. Do you do it by yourself?

   B: Well, not always, sometimes, on occasion _____

   _____

3. She's gambling in Las Vegas. She's gambling at some racetrack.

   A: You never see much of his wife, do you?

   B: She's addicted to gambling. _____

   _____

   He's running after women. He's getting drunk.

   A: What a sad pair they are!

   B: Yes, _____

4. I'll have made a billion. I'll have lost my pants.

   A: Well, it's a terrific gamble I'm taking. That's for sure. _____

   _____

   B: I certainly wish you the best of luck.

5. We have them on the porch. We have them in the garden.

   A: In the summer, where do you usually have your meals?

   B: It depends on whether it's raining or not. _____

   _____

My sons cook. My husband cooks.

A: Who does the cooking in your house?

B: It depends on who's home. _____

_____

6.   I've been dancing. I've been swimming.

A: Well, I haven't seen you since the plane. How have you been enjoying yourself here in Miami Beach?

B: They can't keep me away from the beach, nor can they keep me out of the discos and clubs. _____

7.   A man picked my pocket. A woman picked my pocket.

A: Who picked your pocket?

B: _____, I don't know which; I was jammed into a crowded subway car.

8.   It's a feast. It's a famine.

A: How do you like running a hotel at a beach resort like this?

B: Well, you know, everything depends on the weather and the conditions of the ocean. _____

9.   His friends are responsible for it. Bobby is responsible for it.

A: My! Have you seen the mess in the kitchen yet?

B: Yes, and I know who made it. _____

_____

And they are going to clean it up. He's going to clean it up.

A: _____

10.   You should have gone to India. You should have gone to China.

A: Why do you think I didn't plan my trip very well?

B: _____,
but not both in only three weeks. You didn't get to know either country in much depth.

11.   He's being given money. He's being given presents.

A: Your neighbors' child can be rather a brat, can't he?

B: You can say that again. They're spoiling that poor kid. _____

_____

❑ 5.6 *Either . . . Or*

1. **Paired conjunctions**, traditionally called **correlative conjunctions**, consist of two parts. The paired conjunction *either . . . or* indicates a choice; it means "one or the other of two." It may connect two independent clauses; when it does, we use a comma:

> He spends it. He loses it.
> A: Why doesn't your roommate ever have any money?
> B: *Either* he spends it, *or* he loses it.
>
> I tend to it. My son takes care of it.
> A: How do you manage to keep your garden so beautiful?
> B: *Either* I tend to it, *or* my son takes care of it.
>
> He will marry Jane. He will marry her sister.
> A: Who do you think he'll eventually take to the altar?
> B: *Either* he will marry Jane, *or* he'll marry her sister.

2. When we connect two independent clauses with *either . . . or*, we may abridge the second clause by using an auxiliary verb after the subject:

> A: How do you manage to keep your house looking so beautiful?
> B: *Either* I do the housework, *or* my sweet husband *does*.
>
> A: Who's going to wait on me? I want service now.
> B: Yes, sir, yes, sir. *Either* the owner of the store will serve you, sir, *or* the manager *will*.

We frequently abridge both clauses:

> A: Who gave you this message?
> B: *Either* your wife *did*, *or* your daughter *did*, I can't remember which.
>
> A: Who's going to get to sit in the best seat at the restaurant this evening?
> B: Is there any question? *Either* I *am*, *or* nobody *is*. It's my birthday, isn't it?

3. We do not use a comma when we connect two coordinate elements; *either* precedes the first element, and *or* precedes the second:

> He *either spends* money *or loses* it.   [two verbs]
>
> *Either my son or I* tend to the garden.   [two subjects]
>
> He will marry *either Jane or her sister.*   [two objects]
>
> They'll have *either success or failure.*   [two adjectives]
>
> We'll have a picnic *either in the country or at the beach.*   [two prepositional phrases]

4. When we connect two verb phrases that have auxiliaries, we place *either* after the auxiliary and omit the auxiliary after *or:*

> She has told the truth. She has lied.
> A: Well, Your Honor, what do you think of her testimony?
> B: She *has either* lied *or told* the truth.

If there are two auxiliaries, we put *either* after the second one:

> She has been telling the truth. She has been lying.
> A: And what do the jurors think?
> B: She *has been either* lying or telling the truth.

5. In compound subjects with *either . . . or*, the subject that is closer to the verb determines whether the verb is singular or plural:

> A: When is the best time for me to come to your office?

B: Either my boss or *I am* there at all times of the day and night, 24 hours a day, 7 days a week.

A: And when is the best time to visit your store?

B: Either my sister or my *brothers are* at the store all day.

A: And when is the best time to visit your home?

B: Either my brothers or my *sister is* always there in the evenings.

❑ 5.7 Not One or the Other

With *neither . . . nor,* connect each set of independent clauses or coordinate elements.

Example

He isn't studying. He isn't working.

A: Chris isn't studying this semester, is he?

B: [two verb phrases] No, he's sick. *He's neither studying nor working.*

1.   Veronica won't be there. Her sister Laura won't be coming.

   A: Gloria, Sandra and Wanda won't be at your Christmas party this year, will they?

   B: [two independent clauses] No, _____

   _____

   I've got to invite some more women; I've got too many men.

2.   My parents aren't going to attend. I'm not going to attend.

   A: I won't be at the wedding; I'm going to be away for the weekend.

   B: [two subjects] So are we. _____

   _____

3.   We don't need your help. We don't need your money.

   A: Isn't there anything that I can do for you? Just anything?

   B: [two noun objects] Listen, you big crook, _____

   _____

4.   She hasn't got any money. She hasn't got any friends.

   A: I feel very sorry for her; she's in a terrible situation.

   B: [two noun objects] Yes, _____

   _____

5.   He doesn't want love. He doesn't want money.

   A: Doesn't your friend want love in his life?

B: [two noun objects] No, _____

_____

He doesn't seek fame. He doesn't need success.

A: Doesn't he have a desire for fame?

B: [two independent clauses] No, _____

_____

A: Well, just what *does* he want?

6.   They're not inside. They're not outside.

A: [two adverbs] Where are the children? _____

_____

B: Oh, they're most probably down at the school playground.

7.   It isn't downstairs. It isn't in the basement.

A: Where did you hide the Easter basket, Daddy? It's not upstairs, because I've

looked everywhere and can't find it.

B: [two independent clauses] You're right. _____

_____

It isn't in the garage. It isn't in the tool shed.

A: Is it up in the attic?

B: [two independent clauses] No, _____

_____

It isn't anywhere. The Easter bunny hasn't come yet.

I don't believe in Santa Claus. I don't believe in the tooth fairy.

A: Oh, Daddy, ha, ha, ha.

B: What! Don't you *believe* in the Easter bunny?

A: [two independent clauses] Oh, come on, Dad. _____

_____. You know that.

8.   You're not making a mistake. I'm not making a mistake.

A: I think we're making a mistake.

B: [two subjects] I don't think so. _____

_____. The boss is.

9.   You shouldn't drink coffee. You shouldn't drink tea.

A: Well, Doctor, what do you recommend?

B: [two noun objects] _____

You shouldn't drink milk. You shouldn't drink cola.

A: Can I drink alcohol?

B: [two independent clauses] Never. _____

_____

A: Listen, Doc, just what *am* I supposed to drink?

B: Well, a good glass of water won't hurt you, will it?

10.   You can't stop me. Your friends can't stop me.

A: My friends and I will not allow you to start a new business in this town. This is *our* territory.

B: [two subjects] Listen, and listen hard. I'm going to do what I want. _____

_____

11.   She hasn't written in months. She hasn't called in months.

A: [two verb phrases] I'm worried about my grandmother. _____

_____

B: Well, have you written to or called her?

12.   I haven't been working much. I haven't been going out much.

A: How are things going with you?

B: [two verb phrases] Well, _____

_____. I haven't been feeling well lately.

13.   I'm not happy. I'm not sad.

A: I'm in a strange mood this evening.

B: How's that?

A: [two adjectives] _____. I'm just somewhere in between.

❑ 5.8 *Neither . . . Nor*

1. The paired conjunction *neither . . . nor* means "not one or the other." A statement with two independent clauses connected by *neither . . . nor* expresses a negative choice of two things; it is always made in response to a statement or question that contains a third choice or more choices. Because *neither* and *nor* make negative openings, we must use the emphatic form, and we always set off two independent clauses with a comma:

A: That employee *isn't ever late* in the mornings, and he *doesn't ever take off* early in the afternoons.
B: *Neither* does he ever steal, *nor* does he ever lie.
A: At least let me give you *some financial support* during this crisis.
B: No, thank you, *neither* do we need your moral support, *nor* do we need any of your advice.

A: Would you like to go to *Asia* on our vacation this year?

B: I don't think so. *Neither* would I like to go to Europe, *nor* would I like to go to South America. I just don't want to go anywhere; I'd rather stay home. Wouldn't you?

2. We do not use a comma when we connect two coordinate elements:

A: Why do you think she would be a good worker?

B: She *neither steals nor lies.*   [two verbs]

A: Where are all those important tax papers?

B: They're *neither here nor there.*   [two adverbs]

A: He's got a great deal of money in the bank, hasn't he?

B: He's loaded. He's got *neither worries nor cares* in this world.   [two noun objects]

A: Now is that a promise?

B: Why, yes, of course, *neither my companion nor I* will ever reveal this information to anyone.   [two subjects]

A: Just where did you put my ice skates, Mom? They're *neither up in the attic nor down in the basement.*   [two prepositional phrases]

B: Look out in the garage, dear.

3. When we connect verb phrases that have auxiliaries, we put *neither* after the auxiliary:

A: Have you ever seen that singer?

B: No, I've *neither* seen nor heard her.

If there are two auxiliaries, we put *neither* after the second one:

A: She's just loafing and taking it easy, isn't she?

B: Yes, she*'s been neither* working nor studying.

4. In compound subjects, the subject that is closer to the verb determines whether the verb is singular or plural:

A: Just who is responsible for the mess in the kitchen?

B: Neither my brother nor *I am* responsible for it.

A: How's everyone in your family?

B: Neither my parents nor *my sister is* well.

A: Well, just who is going to join this committee?

B: Neither my father nor *my brothers are* going to do it.

❏ 5.9 *Not Only . . . (But) (Also)*

Using *not only . . . (but) (also)*, connect each set of independent clauses and coordinate elements.

Example

He has many friends. He has many enemies.

A: *Not only does he have many friends, he has many enemies.*

B: That's a problem the rich and famous sometimes have.

1.   She hides her money. She hides her toothpaste.

A: My roommate in the dormitory is so cheap. _____

_____

B: Why don't you move out if you dislike her so much?

2.   I'm tired. I'm depressed.

A: What's wrong?

B: _____

You work too hard. You take life too seriously.

A: Listen, let me tell you something. _____

_____

3.   She doesn't like you. She hates you.

A: Yes, I suppose that your sister doesn't like me much.

B: You can't be serious, can you? _____

_____

You are one of my friends. You are my best friend.

A: How can you tell me something like that? _____

_____

B: Well, I'm just telling you the truth, aren't I?

4.   She loves him. She worships him.

A: Have you ever seen anyone as crazy about her husband as she is?

B: Too much so, I think. _____

_____

5.   You're laughing at me. You're making a fool of me.

A: Ha, ha, ha.

B: How dare you do that? _____

_____

You should leave me now. You should leave me for good.

A: I'm sorry, I was just kidding. I suppose it's best that I leave you now, since
you're losing your temper.

B: Listen, and listen hard. _____

_____

6.   He designs clothes. He manufactures them.

A: I hear he's quite talented and successful in the fashion world.

B: Oh, yes. _____

7.   I've met her. I've been married to her.

A: Oh, by the way, have you ever met Marguerite Manet?

B: Why, yes. _____

A: Why, I didn't know that. Why on earth haven't you ever told me?

8.   She married the richest man in town. She married the nicest man in town.

A: _____

_____

They've got a house in the city. They've got a house in the country.

B: And they live very well, don't they? _____

_____

❑ 5.10 *Not Only . . . But Also*

1. We use the paired conjunction *not only . . . but also* to connect two independent clauses. We can omit *also* or can separate it from *but*. *Not only* makes a negative opening, and we must use the emphatic form; a comma separates the two independent clauses:

    a. *But (also)* together:

    She has a fine mind. She has a wonderful personality.
    Not only does she have a fine mind, *but (also)* she has a wonderful personality.

    b. *But (also)* separated by a subject:

    Not only does she have a fine mind, *but* she *(also)* has a wonderful personality.

    c. *But (also)* separated by a subject plus a verb:

    She is an intelligent woman. She is an interesting woman.
    Not only is she an intelligent woman, *but* she is *(also)* an interesting one.

    d. *But (also)* separated by a complete clause:

    Not only is she an intelligent woman, *but* she is an interesting one *(also)*.

2. When connecting independent clauses, we may omit *but also* entirely:

    A: I heard one of your neighbors is in the hospital with a broken leg.
    B: Worse than that. *Not only* did he break his leg, *he broke his neck.*

    A: Yes, I suppose I should have told him I was sorry.
    B: *Not only* should you have told him you were sorry, *you should have gotten down on your hands and knees and begged for forgiveness.*

3. When connecting coordinate elements, we do not usually omit *also,* nor do we use a comma. *Not only* precedes the structure:

    A: Kids just love Disney movies, don't they?
    B: *Not only children but also adults* love them.   [two subjects]

    A: Yes, I must say he's a rather talented writer.
    B: You know, he *not only writes but also paints.*   [two verbs]

    A: She's one of the most brilliant women I have ever met.
    B: And she is *not only intelligent but also charming.*   [two adjectives]

A: They're very well off, aren't they? They've got a Lincoln.

B: They're loaded with money. They've got *not only a Lincoln but also a Cadillac limousine.*   [two noun objects]

A: Yes, I'm just afraid of living in the cities. All that crime and violence frightens me.

B: Listen, these days there's crime *not only in the cities but also in the towns.* [two prepositional phrases]

4. A negative verb phrase may sometimes follow *not only:*

> She doesn't have a job. She doesn't have a home.

A: Yes, she's lost her job, but she'll find another one, won't she? She doesn't have to worry.

B: Listen, *not only* does she *not* have a job, she doesn't have a home.

> He didn't pay all those bills. He didn't pay the rent.

A: He didn't pay the water, gas, phone or electric bills.

B: More than that. *Not only* did he *not* pay all those bills, he didn't pay the rent. Now his family is out on the street.

❑ 5.11   *Both . . . And* Versus *Either . . . Or, Neither . . . Nor* and *Not Only . . . (But) (Also)*

Using the four paired conjunctions discussed in this chapter, connect each set of independent clauses or coordinate elements.

Example

She can play the harp. She can play the piano.

A: *She can play both the harp and the piano.*

B: Do her neighbors ever complain?

1.   We're going to visit London. We're going to visit Paris.

A: Where are you two going on your next vacation?

B: _____

2.   Men require love and affection. Women require love and affection.

A: _____

B: I agree, and *that's* what I want from you, but I don't get it.

3.   English is spoken there. French is spoken there.

A: Canada is a bilingual nation, isn't it?

B: Oh, yes. _____

4.   Articles aren't easy to use. Prepositions aren't easy to use.

A: _____

B: Man, you can say that again; they're driving me nuts.

5.   My roommate has an exam tomorrow. I have an exam tomorrow.

A: _____

B: Well, I wish both of you lots of luck.

6.   Time goes fast. Money goes fast.

A: Time is so fleeting, isn't it? Life is just flying by.

B: Yes, _____

7.   I speak Spanish. I speak English.

A: What language do you speak at work?

B: Well, it usually depends on the customer I'm waiting on. _____

_____

8.   I don't like whiskey. I don't like beer.

A: Do you like vodka, gin, tequila, rum or brandy?

B: I can't stand them. _____

_____

9.   He's complaining about something. He's flirting with the clerks.

A: That guy coming into the store now is a tough customer.

B: You're telling me? I know from experience. _____

_____

10.   My brothers are champions. I am a champion.

A: _____

B: O.K., champ, let's see you put this ball in the basket.

11.   They've got a beautiful apartment. They've got a fantastic view.

A: Just what's their place like?

B: _____

_____

12.   You didn't wash your face. You forgot to comb your hair.

A: Jimmy, _____

_____

You're too formal at times. You're too fussy.

B: Mom, _____

_____

13.   It's raining. It's snowing.

A: How's the weather in this part of the country during March?

B: Terrible. _____

14.   I hate strawberries. I am allergic to them.

A: Ech! They served strawberries at the luncheon yesterday.

B: Don't tell me you hate strawberries. I just adore them.

A: _____

B: We certainly do have very little in common.

15.   I'm hungry. I'm starving.

A: Let's have another drink, shall we? I'm not really ready to eat yet. Are you?

B: Oh, please, let's not. I had neither breakfast nor lunch. _____

_____

16.   I had to go to a doctor about that problem. I had to go into a hospital.

A: Did you have to go to a doctor about that problem?

B: _____

_____

❑ 5.12 *Both . . . And*

Unlike other paired conjunctions, we almost never use *both . . . and* to connect independent clauses. We do frequently use it, however, to connect the following:

a. Two verbs:

He lives in his apartment. He works in his apartment.
He *both lives and works* in his apartment.

She drinks the best. She eats the best.
She *both drinks and eats* the best.

b. Two noun objects:

My neighbor has a Chevrolet. My neighbor has a Ford.
My neighbor has *both a Chevrolet and a Ford.*

c. Two subjects:

February is a good month in Florida. March is a good month in Florida.
Both February and March are good months in Florida.

Apples are good for you. Oranges are good for you.
Both apples and oranges are good for you.

My wife is going to be there. I'm going to be there.
Both my wife and I are going to be there.

Note: Subjects with *both . . . and* always take a plural verb. Also, *both . . . and* does not usually appear with negative verb phrases.

❑ 5.13 Abridged Independent Clauses

In the first blank of each exercise, supply an appropriate verb phrase. Supply in the second blank an abridged independent clause using *and, but, too, so, neither, either* or *nor* with an appropriate subject and auxiliary. Use a noun subject or pronoun subject when it is given in parentheses. Use a pronoun subject of your choice when it is needed.

> ### Example
>
> A: How are you and your wife doing?
>
> B: (*work*) Just fine, I _have been working_ my head off,*
>   _and so has she_____.

1. A: (*never / drink*) Yes, my wife and I are teetotalers,† and we _____
    _____ alcohol, (*our friends*) _____.

    B: Well, neither my wife nor I am a teetotaler. (*enjoy*)
    I _____ a cocktail before dinner from time to
    time, _____.

    A: We've also noticed that you smoke.

    B: (*take*) Yes, on occasion I _____ pleasure in a cigar after
    dinner, (*my wife*) _____.

    A: (*be*) Yes, but alcohol _____ any good for you,
    (*tobacco*) _____.

    B: (*practice*) Moderation is the key word, sir, and my wife
    _____ moderation in everything that she
    does, _____.

    A: (*believe in*) I must say that I _____ that kind of
    moderation, (*my wife*) _____.

2. A: Both my husband and I absolutely hate housework. (*never / do*)
    I _____ any of the cleaning, _____
    _____. We've got a cleaning person. (*ever / do*) Also, he _____
    _____ anything in the garden, _____.

    B: Well, we just love to do things around the house and in the garden. (*always / work
    on*) My husband _____ some kind of project in the

---

*Working hard.

†People who never drink alcohol.

house, _____. And we both love gardening.

(*always / work in*) Why, all last summer I _____ the

garden, _____.

3. **A:** How did you and your brother like that movie last night?

    B: Well, the two of us must not be very smart. (*understand*) I _____

_____ a word of it, _____.

4. **A:** Both my sister and I each consume at least five or six candy bars a day.

    B: That's very foolish of you, young man. (*eat*) You _____ so

much candy, _____. (*eat*) For snacks, your

sister _____ things like nuts, raisins and

fruit, _____.

5. **A:** My companion and I, I'm afraid, don't have much in common. (*love*)

I _____ Mexican food, _____

_____.

    B: My companion and I don't have much in common, either. (*care for**)

I _____ Chinese food, _____

_____. (*like*) I _____ classical

music, _____.

6. **A:** I hear you've just published a new novel. How's it doing?

    B: Well, it's received excellent reviews, fortunately, and sales have been quite brisk.

The public reaction to the book has been rather strange, however.

    A: How's that?

    B: (*buy*) I wrote the book keeping a female audience in mind, but ever since the book

came out a month ago, men _____ the book,

(*women*) _____. (*respond*) For some reason or

other, men _____ to the theme of the novel,

(*women*) _____.

    A: What's the theme?

    B: Trying to juggle both a career and a marriage.

    A: How strange! (*be / usually*) Men _____ interested in such

books, (*women*) _____.

Care for usually occurs in a negative verb phrase.

7. **A:** Why weren't you and your sister in school yesterday, Timmy?

    B: (*go*) I _____ to the dentist, _____.

Now you will most often need to abridge both independent clauses.

> ***Example***
>
> **A:** Did you have any cavities?
>
> **B:** No, ____*I didn't*____, ____*and she didn't either*____.

8. **A:** I'm 5 feet 10 inches tall and weigh 230 pounds; my wife is about 5 feet 4 inches tall and weighs 180 pounds. Should we go on a diet?

    B: Yes, _____, _____.

9. **A:** Kids, would you please try not to make so much noise? You've got to quiet down.

    (*do / your mother*) I _____ my homework,

    _____.

    B: Do you have to go to evening school tonight, Daddy?

    A: (*your mother*) Yes, _____, _____.

10. **A:** Why are you going to Hawaii, but your brother is going to Switzerland?

    B: (*like*) I _____ surfing, _____.

    A: Don't you like mountain climbing?

    B: No, _____, _____.

❑ 5.14 Abridged Independent Clauses with *And, But, Too, Nor, So, Neither* and *Either*

1. To avoid repetition, we may abridge the second independent clause in a compound sentence. An auxiliary can represent the omitted words in a clause with *but:*

> **A:** Are you going to be at the game tomorrow?
> **B:** No, I'm not going to be able to go, *but* my roommate *is.*
> **A:** Everything on my plate is bland. Has your food been salted?
> **B:** The meat has been salted, *but* the vegetables *haven't.*

2. We can use an auxiliary plus the adverb *too* in an abridged clause with *and* to substitute for a second independent clause with an affirmative verb. We usually put a comma before *too:*

> **A:** Bolivia is a landlocked country, *and* Nepal *is, too.*
> **B:** Let's see. What other countries are?
> **A:** Christians have a belief in one God, and Jews and Muslims *do, too.*
> **B:** How about Buddhists and Hindus?

3. The adverb *so* (meaning "also") plus an auxiliary may also act as an affirmative substitute. In this case, the subject is inverted and follows the auxiliary:

> A: What do you think, Ambassador?
> B: Both the president and the government want peace, *and so do the people.*
> A: Yet the war continues, ma'am, *and so do the casualties.*

4. A negative auxiliary plus *either* may occur as a substitute for a second independent clause with a negative verb:

> A: The Republicans don't have a good candidate, *and* the Democrats *don't either.*
> B: Well, the Liberals certainly haven't come up with any good ideas lately, *and* the Conservatives *haven't either.*

5. *Neither* plus an auxiliary also occurs as a negative substitute. As with *so,* the subject follows the auxiliary:

> A: But the other students cheat. Why can't I?
> B: Your classmates don't have any excuse for cheating, *and neither do you.*
> A: I'll be seeing you tomorrow.
> B: I'm afraid not. I won't be here, *and neither will anyone else.* Didn't you know it's a holiday?

6. Remember that we also use *nor* plus an auxiliary as a negative substitute:

> A: The king doesn't know much about the real world, *nor does the queen.*
> B: Well, you don't know much more about it, *nor do I.*

7. We frequently use an abridged independent clause as a response to a statement made by someone else. We usually omit *and* or *but:*

> A: I don't really care for going to the movies tonight.
> B: (*And*) *I don't either.* I'd rather watch something on TV.
> A: I wasn't right in that last answer.
> B: (*But*) *I was.*

8. We often abridge both independent clauses when we respond to a yes/no question:

> A: Have you ever gone around the world by ship?
> B: No, I *haven't, and* not one of my friends *has either.*
> A: Should I get shots for malaria and cholera?
> B: Yes, you *should, and so should your wife.*

9. Informally, we frequently use *me, too* and *me, neither* as responses:

> A: I'm just dying to go out with that guy; I've got a big crush on him.
> B: *Me, too.* He's so cute, isn't he?
> A: Darling! Those hazel eyes! I don't think I'll ever have again as big a crush as I do on him.
> B: *Me, neither.*

❑ 5.15 Conjunctive Adverbs

Fill in each blank with an appropriate conjunctive adverb chosen from the following list; then supply any needed punctuation. Circle the punctuation so that it can easily be seen.

afterward	later (on)	nonetheless	then
consequently	moreover	otherwise	therefore
furthermore	nevertheless	still	thus
however			

Example

A: The thieves stole my coat and all my shirts and pants, and they even
took my belts and my last pair of old shoes. I've got nothing at all to
wear ⊙ *therefore* ____.

B: You'd better call the police. ____ *Otherwise* ⊙ ____ you won't be able to make
an insurance claim.

1. **A:** How are things going on your project at VacuClean?

   B: We've put together some of the most expensive talent in the world, taken
   over a whole research center and done a terrific amount of research and
   development _____ we haven't come up with a design for a
   vacuum cleaner that is better than the designs we already have.

2. **A:** Not only has our company done well in producing new and exciting products, but
   also we have managed to keep our prices competitive with those of other
   manufacturers. Our labor relations _____ have been excellent.

   B: Your relations with our company _____ have not been
   excellent. We've been supplying you, but you people just haven't been paying
   your bills. _____ we have decided to consult with our lawyers
   and perhaps take some kind of legal action. You'd better pay those bills,
   sir. _____ you might end up with a lawsuit on your hands.

3. **A:** No, I'd rather not, I just don't want to talk about it.

   B: Why not? Why don't you? Please don't hesitate to tell me
   everything _____ you will feel better. You can confide in me.
   I'm your best friend, aren't I?

   A: It's my girlfriend. Not only is she cruel to me, but she is unfaithful also. I can't
   live without her _____.

4. **A:** Well, Ambassador, what do you think?

   B: Relations between your country and mine have improved a great deal in recent
   months _____ we are discussing the possibilities of a
   negotiated settlement.

   A: Mustn't we make this settlement, sir? _____ this terrible
   bloodshed and carnage will continue.

5. **A:** Just why hasn't this trial come to an end yet? What's holding things up?

B: Much of the evidence that both sides have introduced during the trial

has been contradictory; the jury can't come to any kind of

consensus _____.

A: What do you think is going to happen?

B: Well, both sides had better come up with some new and good

evidence _____ we'll have a hung jury* on our hands.

6. **A:** How do you like *Desire Me Again*?

B: The author's not a genius, nor is he a Hemingway or a Faulkner.

He _____ has written a very fine novel, and we think it would

appeal to a very wide and mixed audience. We see the possibility of some very big

sales _____ we here at Mountain Press have decided to

publish the book in the fall.

A: Why in the fall?

B: We'd better bring it out then. _____ we would miss Christmas

sales. *Desire Me Again* has a theme centered around Christmas. Mountain

Press _____ wants to take advantage of those sales.

A: What a strange title for a book about Christmas!

7.   [Two passengers on a plane]

A: Just what is the situation with the drought in your part of the country? Things

have gotten quite bad in Missouri. We haven't had any rain for almost four

months now, and everything in the fields is all dried up. _____

the waters of the Mississippi have gone down so much in the past few weeks that

all shipping has stopped. The economies of the communities along the

river _____ have been deeply affected.

B: Well, in our neck of the woods,† we couldn't have had more rain than we have had

in the past few months. In fact, we've had so much rain that we haven't been able

to do our spring planting. Everyone up in the Northwest _____

is praying for the rain to stop. It had better stop fairly soon. We'll have a lot of

landslides and property damaged by floods _____.

8. **A:** Before you were married, Grandpa, where would you take Grandma when you

went out on a date?

---

*Jury whose members cannot come to a consensus.
†Part of the country.

B: I'd always take her to the movies; they were much better in the old days.

_____ we'd go to a soda fountain, and we always

used to have banana splits. I'd have to get your grandmother home by nine

o'clock. _____ your great-grandfather would give me a hard

time. In fact, he was always giving me a hard time; he didn't want me to

marry your grandmother. He thought I was a lazy good-for-nothing guy.

_____ I was finally able to convince him to give me his

daughter's hand in marriage. _____ young lady, you are

sitting here today and talking with me.

❑ 5.16 Conjunctive Adverbs: *However, Furthermore* and Others

1. Besides coordinate and paired conjunctions, we can connect two independent clauses with a **conjunctive adverb**. These are the most common conjunctive adverbs:

afterward	later (on)	nonetheless	then
consequently	moreover	otherwise	therefore
furthermore	nevertheless	still	thus
however			

2. We can put a conjunctive adverb in the following places:

   a. Between two independent clauses; a semicolon precedes the word, and a comma usually follows:

   I did my exercises; *however,* my roommate didn't do his.

   b. In the initial position of a second sentence followed by a comma:

   I did my exercises. *However,* my roommate didn't do his.

   c. In the final position of a second sentence preceded by a comma:

   I did my exercises. My roommate didn't do his, *however.*

   d. Within a second sentence following a noun subject preceded and followed by a comma:

   I did my exercises. My roommate, *however,* didn't do his.

3. We use *however,* the most common of the conjunctive adverbs, to show contrast:

   A: Did you turn in the last assignment?
   B: Yes, I did. Only a few of the other students, *however,* turned in theirs.
   A: Yes, your answer is certainly relevant to the situation.
   B: Your question was completely irrelevant, *however.*

4. *Nevertheless (nonetheless)* is similar in meaning to *however,* but the word also has the meaning of concession, similar to that of *although* and *despite:*

   A: You're very proud of your husband, aren't you?
   B: Yes, it was very difficult for him. My husband, *nevertheless (nonetheless),* was

finally able to give up smoking.   [Although it was very difficult for him, he gave it up.]

A: Not only does she humiliate you in public, she makes you look like a fool to your family. And she takes advantage of you so; she's just plain cruel to you.

B: I worship her and adore the ground she walks on, *nevertheless* (*nonetheless*). [Despite all these things, I adore and worship her.]

5. We use *moreover* and *furthermore* when we wish to add some information to a relatively large amount of information that has already been given:

A: Well, tell us what was said at the meeting.

B: The major focus of the meeting was the problem of housing in the city. We discussed how some new tax laws would enable the poor to get affordable housing. The mayor was opposed to any such taxes, and she said she would always oppose them in the future. *Furthermore* (*moreover*), she demanded that we not discuss the problem with the press, which, of course, is what I am doing right now.

Note: As in the preceding examples, a conjunctive adverb is often related to more than one sentence or clause.

6. *Therefore* and *consequently* appear in a second sentence or clause that expresses result. The first sentence or clause expresses a situation:

A: There are four feet of snow on the ground.

B: Nobody is going to go anywhere today, *therefore*.

A: The children have been running a high fever.

B: *Consequently*, they have been sent to bed.

A: All of the teachers have walked out on a strike; *consequently*, no classes are being held.

B: And none of us has to do any homework, *consequently*.

7. *Then*, *afterward* and *later* (*on*) express time:

A: Well, what are your plans?

B: I'm going home and eat; *then* I'm going bowling. What are you doing?

A: My date and I are going to the movies; *afterward** we're going to go dancing until dawn.

A: I'll be at Yale for my undergraduate studies; *later on* I'll be at Harvard for my graduate studies.

B: I'll be doing just the opposite; I'll be at Yale *later*.

Then may also express result:

A: Doesn't the lawn look brown and dry?

B: You should water and fertilize it; *then* it will get green.

Note: We do not use a comma with these words.

8. *Still* as a conjunctive adverb is similar in meaning to *nevertheless*:

A: The patient is being given the best medication available; *still*, her condition isn't improving.

B: All that we can do now is pray.

9. *Otherwise* expresses a condition in the same way that *if* does:

A: Something had better be done about this dreadful situation right away.

B: Yes, both you and I will be in some hot water, *otherwise*.

---

*In less formal usage, *afterward* sometimes appears as *afterwards*.

10. *Thus,* which can be rather formal in tone, is similar in meaning to *therefore*. It does not appear in final position:

>A: The government has drastically reduced taxes; *thus,* there are no available funds for social programs.
>
>B: The people of the nation are demanding reform. *Thus,* our intelligence sources expect a change to take place in the government soon.

☐ 5.17 Coordinate Conjunctions with Conjunctive Adverbs

Supply in each blank an appropriate combination of coordinate conjunctions and conjunctive adverbs. Provide a comma when it is needed.

>*Example*
>
>A: What did you guys do last night?
>
>B: We went to a pizza joint ⓐ *and then* _____ we went roller-skating.

1. A: I've never met such a fanatic for cars, have you?

   B: He's got three antique Cadillacs, a 1932 Buick and a fantastic 1954 Chevrolet Impala convertible _____ he has a 1938 Rolls-Royce that is so beautiful, it takes your breath away.

   A: You sound like a car fanatic yourself.

2. A: He's almost ninety now _____ my father runs in the park five miles a day. I can't even do one.

   B: He must be in a fine state of health.

   A: It just couldn't be better. Why, he's never had to go into any kind of hospital or clinic a day in his life, and neither has he ever had to visit a doctor's office. Not even once! _____ he's never had to take any kind of medication, either, not even an aspirin. And you know, he's eaten three eggs a day ever since he was a little boy, and he's drunk a fair amount of hard liquor. _____ he's been addicted to tobacco since the age of sixteen _____ he's in a state of perfect health. He's always joking that when he dies, people will say his vices have finally killed him.

3. A: What are your plans for this evening?

   B: We're going to take in a movie* _____ we're going down to Chinatown and have a big feast with some of our friends.

*See a movie.

A: Don't you have to go to work tomorrow?

B: No, I don't, and neither does my wife. My company is going through a big inventory tomorrow, and I don't have to be there _____ I can sleep late. And my wife doesn't have to work, either _____ _____ both of us can stay up late tonight.

A: And what are you going to do after dinner?

B: We're going to visit some friends of ours _____ we're going to go dancing.

A: Listen, you'd better get some rest _____ you won't be able to go into work the day after tomorrow.

4. **A:** Why on earth did he flunk* you? I got an "A" in that course without any trouble at all. It couldn't have been easier.

   B: I rarely attended class, I did almost none of the homework and I had a rather fresh attitude _____ he didn't pass me.

   A: Well, you failed his course _____ you have to take the same course again by a different teacher, don't you?

5. **A:** How was your vacation?

   B: On the very first day I arrived on Magic Island, I developed a bad toothache _____ the next day I hurt my back diving into the swimming pool. My toothache went away, and my back got better _____ I started having trouble with my eyes. Not only did I have all these problems, but also I was slowly running out of money _____ I had to come home quite a bit earlier than I'd planned. My vacation turned out to be a disaster.

6. **A:** We'd best stop at the next gas station _____ we may be running out of gas. _____ we might need to get some oil.

   B: We're in kind of a hurry. We don't have to have the tires checked, do we?

   A: Oh, let's go ahead and have them checked _____ we won't have to worry about them later.

7. **A:** Why are you working so hard at this time of your life?

   B: Well, I'm not getting any younger, am I? I've got to put aside some money for a

*Fail.

rainy day. I'm going to make sure I have some savings _____

_____ I won't have to worry about myself and my family.

8. **A:** Don't you like the theater? You never go. And you don't ever go to the movies or watch TV. Just what do you like to do?

   B: You're right; those things don't interest me much, _____

   I do like to read _____.

9. **A:** Let's get going, come on _____ we'll miss the beginning of the movie, which is supposed to be the best part.

   B: O.K., let's go. Oh, wait, I should turn a light on _____ we won't have to come home to a dark apartment, or thieves.

10. **A:** Do you really find English a challenge?

    B: Yes, a very big challenge. I find pronunciation extremely hard, and punctuation confuses me to no end. I just hate articles and prepositions _____

    _____ I'm going to master this language one day in the future.

☐ 5.18 Coordinate Conjunctions with Conjunctive Adverbs

1. These are the coordinate conjunctions and their corresponding conjunctive adverbs:

But	And	So	Or
however	afterward	consequently	otherwise
nevertheless	furthermore	then [for result]	
nonetheless	later (on)	therefore	
still	moreover		
then [for time]	then [for time]		
	thus		

2. In a free and informal style, a conjunctive adverb may follow a coordinate conjunction. The second word conveys the meaning; the first word is used only to connect. We use these combinations for emphasis; they often occur in conversation:

   > **A:** Why should he retire? He's only sixty.
   > **B:** He's worked very hard, *so therefore* he's ready to retire.
   > **A:** How's the baby?
   > **B:** She's napped for two hours, *but still* she's sleepy.

Note: We use a comma to separate two independent clauses, but we do not use a comma if a combination appears in the initial position of a sentence:

   > **A:** I'd better check this out with my lawyers before I do anything, hadn't I?
   > **B:** *Or otherwise* you might lose your shirt as well as your pants.

These combinations do not appear in final position.

3. A clause usually separates *however* from *but:*

A: What! You didn't go out on New Year's Eve?

B: We didn't go out, *but* all of our friends came over, *however.*

❑ 5.19 Transition Words

Supply in each blank an appropriate transition word chosen from the following list. Supply any needed punctuation.

also	on the contrary
besides	on the other hand
in addition	on the one hand . . . on the other (hand)
in addition to	then
for example (for instance)	first . . . then
such as	after this
in fact	after this . . . then
as a result	

Example

A: There are a great many social and economic problems in our cities

today (;) *for example* (,) _____ we have poverty, crime on the

streets and a lack of affordable housing. _____ *Besides* _____

these problems, we find drug abuse, poor nutrition and female and child abuse.

B: _____ *In addition* (,) _____ there has been an increase in gang violence

as well as organized crime.

1.   A: Do you know Monica Moore at all well?

B: Oh, yes, quite well. Poor Monica, she's not at all happy. _____

_____ she's terribly miserable. _____

her inability to find a good and interesting job, she cannot find a decent

apartment, nor can she afford to buy a car. _____

all of this, her husband has left her. _____

she has to face all of her problems alone.

A: What do you think she should do?

B: _____ she must find a good job _____

_____ she must find a decent apartment. _____

_____ she should buy a car (so she can get

around) _____ she should find a new boyfriend,

husband, lover or companion, whatever best suits her needs at the time. Do you

think I have the right order of priorities for her?

A: Well, not really. I think she should find the man first _____

_____ she won't have to do everything else by herself.

B: You've certainly got a point there, but I don't agree with you.

2. A: Just who *is* J. W. Powers? Is he some big shot?

B: You've got to be kidding. Why, he's the biggest man in this town; he's *the* biggest

man in the state _____.

C: Yes, _____ his ranch, which is one of the largest

in Texas, he has _____ things _____

_____oil wells, radio stations and packing plants.

_____ all these businesses, he has a big ski resort

in Colorado. Some people think he's a man greedy for wealth and power.

D: Yes, they do, but old man Powers is a pretty good guy.

E: _____ he has a lot of power in this state, and he

uses it when he wants to, that's for sure. Many people call him

ruthless _____. _____

_____ he has done a great deal of philanthropy; he's contributed lots of

money _____ he's built hospitals, stadiums and

museums for the people of the great state of Texas.

3. A: We've been having quite a few problems in our company lately.

B: _____?

A: Well, _____ we have dedicated and hard workers

who would give their right arm for the welfare of this factory _____

_____ we cannot afford to pay them as much as we once did when

business was better. _____ the workers' union has

just recently demanded more generous health benefits and retirement

pensions. _____ the problems with our workers

and their union, we find that we cannot compete in price with our foreign

competition _____ our sales have gone down

dramatically this past year.

4. A: I'd like you to meet Tom Katz, a good friend of mine.

B: Oh? What sort of person is he?

A: Oh, he's the sort of guy who tries to keep abreast of the news. _____

_____ magazines _____ *Newsweek,*

The Economist and *The New Republic* are always lying on his coffee table. You'll

also see _____ literary magazines _____

_____ *The New Yorker*, *The Atlantic Monthly* and *Harpers*

scattered about his apartment, which is in Georgetown, by the way. Oh,

_____   _____

magazines, Tom reads *The New York Times* and *The Washington Post* every day.

_____ he listens to National Public Radio and

watches all kinds of programs on PBS.

B: You've got to be kidding! Why do you want *me* to meet *him*? I'm not a very

literary person, am I? Why, we would have absolutely nothing in common.

A: _____ you would have a *great* deal in

common. _____ literature and affairs of the

world, he's very interested in art _____ he's

considered almost an expert in the field of art history. He teaches the subject at

Georgetown University _____.

B: Oh, does he?

A: Yes, and _____ art, he has a keen interest in all

kinds of music, including _____ classical

composers _____ Bach and Gluck to the latest

exponents of rock and roll. Aren't you interested in both art and music?

_____   _____

his many sterling qualities, he's one of the best-looking men in Washington, D.C.,

and he's single. He's just about the most eligible bachelor around. Do you still *not*

want to meet him?

B: _____ I'm dying to meet him. Can you set up a

date for me?

A: I'd love to. You know how I love being a matchmaker.

Now in a few blanks, use the conjunctive adverb *however*.

5. **A:** In recent years many new high-rise office buildings have gone up in our part of

the city. _____ companies _____

_____ Consolidated Insurance, Nationwide Bank and MiniMax

have moved in. _____ we have lost a great deal of

residential property that was torn down to make room for the high-rises.

B: The same thing has been going on in our part of town. It's become very hard to

find a rental apartment _____ it's almost next to

impossible to find one. You have to buy an apartment, and they cost a small

fortune. _____ an apartment _____

_____ mine, which I bought for $100,000 twenty years ago, would

go for $500,000 today. _____ the housing

problem, public transportation cannot handle all of the new people coming into

the area, and other public services have become overburdened. _____

_____ we have a great many new jobs around, the economy is

booming, and everyone these days seems to have some extra money in his or her

wallet. Everyone is flying high. I hope the balloon doesn't burst.

6. **A:** You certainly don't have any complaints about various members of your family,

do you?

B: _____ I have many, but I usually try to keep

them to myself. I don't want to be a complainer.

A: That's hard to believe; all of you seem to get along so well.

B: Listen, I've got a wonderful family: a lovely and kind wife, a wonderful son and a

darling daughter. _____ there are a few things

that my wife and children do that can get on my nerves.*

A: _____?

B: Well, my wife _____ never puts the cap back on

the toothpaste _____ she always squeezes the

toothpaste out in the middle of the tube.

A: Oh, that's nothing, my husband does the same thing.

B: _____ my wife, my son helps to mess up the

bathroom. _____ when he comes into the house

after playing, he has to wash up, so he goes to the bathroom. I don't know why,

but _____ he wipes his hands on a clean

towel _____ he washes his hands in the sink.

Does he leave the sink clean? No, of course not, he leaves it to someone else,

usually me, to clean up his mess.

A: Oh, he's just a kid. He'll eventually become more thoughtful.

*Can annoy me.

B: Yes, I suppose so. That's what I keep telling myself.

A: What's your daughter like? Does *she* ever mess up the bathroom, too?

B: No, not at all. She's very good about being neat and tidy in the bathroom

_____. But her bedroom _____

_____ looks just like a junk shop. _____

_____ things _____ toys, comic

books, art projects and all other kinds of things are strewn about.

A: Oh, that's not so bad. Most kids that age are that way, aren't they?

B: But wait a minute, you haven't heard it all. _____

all the stuff she keeps, she keeps two cats and three birds in her bedroom.

_____ the place stinks.

A: Ha, ha, ha. Don't worry, she'll grow up, and then she'll go away, and you will

miss her so much.

☐ 5.20 Transition Words: *Also, Besides* and Others

Besides coordinate conjunctions, paired conjunctions and conjunctive adverbs, we can join clauses and sentences with transition words. These are the most common ones (study the punctuation carefully):

1. *Also:*

   A: What does the midwestern state of Kansas produce?
   B: Kansas produces a great deal of wheat; *also,* its farmers grow a lot of corn.
   A: How about the northeastern state of Maine?
   B: Maine produces a large amount of lumber. *Also,* its fishing industry catches thousands of tons of fish a year.
   A: And how about the southern state of Kentucky?
   B: Kentucky produces some of the finest horses in the world. It produces excellent sour-mash whiskey *also.*

2. *In addition* (meaning "also"):

   A: What's the latest news from that country?
   B: They've declared war against their neighbor; *in addition,* they've declared martial law throughout the country.

   A: Why don't you want to go out tonight?
   B: I've got a wicked headache. *In addition,* a wisdom tooth is killing me.

   A: How are you handling your finances on your trip?
   B: I'll be carrying credit cards, letters of credit and checks. I'll be carrying a million in cash *in addition.*

3. *In addition to,* a prepositional phrase, which must always be followed by an object:

   A: How do you get to work?
   B: *In addition to a car,* I've got a bike and a motorcycle. I also sometimes take a bus to work *in addition to **the subway.***

4. *Besides* used as conjunctive adverb (meaning "also"):

    A: Why do I have to drink orange juice, Dad?
    B: Orange juice is delicious; *besides,* it's good for you. It has a lot of vitamin C in it *besides.*

5. *Besides* used as a preposition, which must always take an object:

    A: *Besides an apartment in town,* they have a house in the country.
    B: And they have a lot of money in the bank *besides their property.*

    Note: The preposition *beside* means "next to." For example: His dog is always *beside* him.

6. *For example* and *for instance:*

    A: How are prices now in your native country?
    B: They're sky high; *for example,* a good pair of shoes can cost more than three hundred dollars.
    A: And could you tell us a bit about the political situation?
    B: Things haven't been going at all well. The president, *for example,* has recently been forced to resign.
    A: And human rights?
    B: Very bad. Recently, some rightist group was found guilty of torturing a number of leftists, *for instance.*

7. *Such as* (meaning "for example"):

    A: I prefer to play easy games *such as* checkers, canasta and hearts.
    B: I prefer board games *such as* Scrabble, Trivial Pursuit and Monopoly.
    C: Games *such as* poker and whist are fun.
    D: *Such games as* chess and bridge require a great deal of concentration.

    We use *such as* most frequently with compounds and coordinate series.

8. *In fact* (meaning a very emphatic "furthermore" or "moreover"):

    A: Could you tell us a little bit about the man?
    B: P. D. Ames is a powerful and influential man. He's got more money than he knows what to do with. He has billions, *in fact.*
    A: What are the reasons for social unrest in your country?
    B: There are very few problems in the nation. The average man or woman on the street is quite happy; *in fact,* people have never been happier than they are now under the present government. There's no social unrest. *In fact,* everything you've heard and read is just pure propaganda.

9. *As a result* (meaning "therefore"):

    A: Well, what's happening in your country now?
    B: There's rioting and looting in the streets, the military is about to take over and many citizens are fleeing the country. *As a result,* I'm not going back until things cool down a bit.
    A: The spring rains have been good; *as a result,* the countryside is lush, green and fertile.
    B: And our incomes are going to go up *as a result.*

10. *On the contrary* means "directly opposite." It also has the meaning of the conjunctive adverb *however,* but the transition words *on the contrary* almost always follow a sentence or clause containing a negative verb phrase; therefore, it is rarely interchangeable with *however.* Compare the following:

Not Interchangeable

A: The dinner *wasn't* any good, was it?

B: *On the contrary,* it was delicious.

A: I *wasn't* at the last meeting, and you weren't either.

B: *On the contrary,* I was the main speaker.

A: I must have millions, or otherwise I won't be happy.

B: Money isn't everything; *on the contrary,* it means very little if you're not happy.

Interchangeable

A: A good worker *makes* a lot of money; *on the contrary* (*however*), a poor worker makes very little.

B: Yes, that's the way it is when you're doing piece work.

11. *On the other hand* (meaning "look at something in another way"):

A: World War II was a catastrophe for millions and millions of people.

B: *On the other hand,* it was the cause of a great deal of technological development.

A: Women still very much suffer from discrimination in the business world. They are not paid as well as men for doing the same kind of work, nor are a woman's chances for promotion as good as a man's.

B: The woman of today, *on the other hand,* has more opportunities placed before her than she has ever had before.

12. *On the one hand . . . on the other* (*hand*) (meaning "look at something in two ways"):

A: *On the one hand,* my children have all the comforts of a lovely home and everything that money can buy.

B: *On the other,* they have no father to love and respect.

A: Just what's going on in that country?

B: Well, *on the one hand,* they have a large military government that is greedy for power and prevents any kind of social or economic reform; *on the other hand,* they have a selfish and spoiled class of aristocrats and plutocrats who want to have everything for themselves.

13. *First . . . then* (meaning "afterward"):

A: What did you do last Sunday?

B: *First,* my wife and I took a drive in the country; *then* we had dinner at one of our favorite restaurants in town.

A: How shall I prepare this fish?

B: *First,* you dip it in flour; *then* you fry it in hot butter.

14. *After this* (meaning "then"):

A: Well, what are your plans for the evening?

B: I'm going to have a little snack, and then I'm going to write a letter home; *after this,* I'm going to go right to bed. I've got an early class tomorrow.

A: Yesterday I spent a couple of hours at the library; *after this,* I spent a few hours in the park.

B: Good! Creation versus recreation.

15. *After this . . . then:*

A: What are your plans for tomorrow morning?

B: First, we're going to have breakfast at the St. Francis Hotel; then we're going to go walking around Chinatown and North Beach. *After this,* we're going to go for a quick look at the collection at the Palace Legion of Honor; *then* we're going to have lunch in the Clift Hotel's Redwood Room, which is supposedly one of the most beautiful restaurants in San Francisco.

6

Complex Sentences: Subordinate Conjunctions and Adverb Clauses

❑ 6.1 Contrasting Subordinate Conjunctions

Supply in each blank a subordinate conjunction chosen from the following list.

when	before	until	because	even though
whenever	after	till	since	although
while	once	as	now that	while
as	by the time (that)	as (so) long as	though	whereas
as soon as	since			

Example

A: _____*Although*_____ they're twins, they've got nothing in common.

B: Yes, she's so refined, _____*while*_____ he's so coarse.

1. A: What a perfectly lovely apartment!

   B: Thank you, we really do love it. _____ we looked at this

   place—just last year at this time, in fact—we rented it immediately. _____

   _____ we saw the view of Honolulu and the Pacific Ocean, we just had to

   have it. Also, _____ we are on the fortieth floor, we don't have

   to worry about insects; they don't come up this high. In addition, _____

   _____ we are so high up, we don't get much noise from the street.

   A: It's just so nice. Everything looks just perfect.

B: Well, not everything. _____ it rains, for example, the doors

leading out to the terrace always leak. And, _____ the

building is only four years old, the air conditioning is always breaking down.

_____ we have complained and complained, nothing has been

done about it yet.

2. A: How's the situation in your native country now?

B: Fortunately, things are getting a bit better, but we have a long, long way to go.

The industrial growth of the nation, for example, has been fantastic, _____

_____ the agricultural sector has gone into a serious decline. _____

_____ life in the country has improved a great deal in recent years, people

still want to come to live in the big cities. _____ they are

leaving the countryside, there are not enough people to work on the farms. Worst

of all, _____ the present government came into power ten

years ago, there has been a tremendous amount of corruption.

3. A: _____ the female lion is energetic and active, the male is

relatively lazy and passive.

B: The peacock is one of the most beautiful of all birds, _____ the

peahen is a rather plain-looking bird.

4. A: You don't seem to expect a great deal out of life. You just take

things _____ they come, don't you?

B: Isn't that the best way? _____ I have a place to hang my hat,

I'm happy. _____ I have gotten older, I think this is the best

philosophy to have.

5. A: Why do you say your husband is lazy?

B: Listen, we're both lazy. _____ our garden looks like a jungle,

and our house is a mess, we just sit around and take it easy. However, _____

_____ we must be two of the laziest people in the world, we still love

each other very much. _____ we have one another, we'll be

happy.

6. A: Where's Roger? He hasn't been in class for a few days.

B: He's been sick in bed ever _____ he ate some bad lobster in a

seafood restaurant uptown. _____ I'd told him not to eat

shellfish at this time of year, he ate some anyway. And he got food poisoning.

7. **A:** _____ our daughter finally graduates from law school, she'll

have been in school for eighteen years.

B: Yes, _____ she has graduated, you and your husband can

finally stop worrying about finances.

A: Oh, no. _____ she graduates, our son will be entering Cornell

University, and _____ he graduates, our baby will be entering

Smith College. We'll be having financial problems _____ they

all graduate.

8. **A:** Why don't you like soy sauce on your food?

B: _____ I use it in food, I always get very thirsty. Also, I think

I might be allergic to it or something. _____ I smell it, I start

sneezing. I like soy sauce, actually, but it just doesn't like me.

9. **A:** Can you give this message to your boss?

B: I won't be seeing him _____ we meet at the airport tomorrow

afternoon. He's already left for the day.

A: Well, _____ you meet him at the airport tomorrow, please give

it to him. He can call me from there. Please don't forget. It's important.

B: Listen, _____ I leave today, I'll give him a call at home.

❑ 6.2 Types of Adverb Clauses; Subordinate Conjunctions

1. A **complex sentence** always contains an independent clause and a **dependent clause** (or **subordinate clause**):

INDEPENDENT CLAUSE   DEPENDENT CLAUSE

Rainbows appear everywhere   *when it rains.*

2. We usually use a comma to separate the two clauses when the dependent clause comes first:

Before the monsoon comes, farmers do their planting.

When the two clauses are very short, we may omit the comma:

When it rains it pours.   *Before it arrives* they plant.

3. A dependent clause has little meaning when it stands alone; it is not a complete thought:

When it rains   *Before it arrives*

However, a dependent clause may occur by itself when the independent clause is understood:

A: When do rainbows appear?
B: *When it rains.*

A: When do farmers do their planting?
B: *Before the monsoon comes.*

4. An **adverb clause,** a type of dependent clause, modifies the verb in an independent clause. Adverbial **time clauses** are introduced in a sentence by **subordinate conjunctions of time:**

a. *When* (a specific point in time):

A: The class begins *when* the bell rings.
B: *When* it rings again, the children are ready for recess.

b. *Whenever* (any point in time):

A: They go by Air France *whenever* they go to Europe.
B: *Whenever* I go anywhere overseas, I always go by freighter.

c. *While* (a period of time; duration):

A: *While* he was juggling twelve tennis balls, he was standing on the top of a flag-pole.
B: And he was whistling "Dixie" *while* he was doing it.

d. *As* (meaning "while" or "when"):

A: I could hear the ticking of the clock *as* I fell asleep.
B: *As* I was falling asleep, old memories were racing through my mind.

e. *As soon as* (emphasizing a specific point in time):

A: *As soon as* the teacher arrives at nine, the class begins.
B: And it always ends *as soon as* both hands on the clock hit twelve.

f. *Before* (prior to a specific point in time):

A: *Before* you have woken up, I'll have left the house.
B: I'll have gone to bed *before* you've gotten home.

g. *After* (following a specific point in time):

A: *After* the ball game, the stadium was a mess.
B: The players were exhausted *after* they played their game of defeat.

h. *Once* (meaning "after"):

A: *Once* I've mastered English, I'm going to study Chinese.
B: I'm giving my brain a rest *once* I've mastered English.

i. *By the time* (that) (meaning "before"):

A: *By the time that* our children have grown up, we'll be ready to take it easy for a while.
B: Listen, we'll most probably be ready to retire *by the time* they're ready to leave the nest.

j. *Since* (meaning "from a time in the past until now"):

A: *Since* I bought my car, I've had a new and exciting life.
B: Yes, and you've also had four accidents *since* you bought the darned thing.

k. *Until* (a specific point in future time):

A: *Until* I find an apartment, I'll be living in a hotel.
B: You'll be spending lots of money *until* you find one.

l. *Till* (meaning "until"):

A: *Till* we meet again, I shall be thinking only of you.
B: I'll be writing every day *till* we're together once more.

Note: Till usually occurs either in conversation or in the poetic language.

m. *As (so) long as* (expressing duration):

A: Our little boy is happy *as long as* he has his little security blanket.
B: *So long as* our baby girl has her pacifier, she is quite contented.

5. Dependent **clauses of reason,** which answer *why,* are introduced by the subordinate conjunctions:

a. *Because:*

A: Why on earth are you going to do it?
B: *Because* I need the money, I'm going to cut off my beautiful hair and sell it.
A: Why are you limping?
B: I'm walking this way *because* I've got a corn on my right foot.

b. *As* (meaning "because"):

A: *As* I was full of pep and energy, I stayed out almost all night last night.
B: I went to bed at eight *as* I was completely exhausted.

c. *As (so) long as* (expressing reason):

A: *As long as* you've got your health, you've got everything.
B: Yes, *so long as* you've got that, you don't have to worry.

d. *Since* (meaning "because"):

A: *Since* there's not going to be any school tomorrow, I'll be able to sleep in for a change.
B: However, *since* it's snowing so hard now, you'd better get up early tomorrow morning and shovel the sidewalk.

We usually do not use a comma when a clause of reason with *because* appears in second position:

A: Why do you think you're not feeling well?
B: I'm feeling weak and tired *because* I haven't been taking my vitamins.
A: No, that's not it. You're feeling poorly *because* you haven't been eating right.

However, when *since* or *as* occurs in second position, we usually use a comma, as the meaning of the clause is similar to that expressed by an independent clause introduced by the coordinate conjunction *for:*

A: The times are hard and difficult, *since (for)* we are having this terrible drought.
B: We haven't been able to plant anything, *as (for)* the earth is nothing but dust.

On occasion, we use a comma with *because* in second position:

A: The troops are worn out, discouraged and ready to surrender, *because (for)* the battle has been long and hard.
B: They want to go home *because* they've had enough.

e. *Now that* (meaning "because now"):

A: *Now that* the sun has finally come out, let's go for a tramp in the woods.
B: Yes, let's get out of the house fast *now that* it's so nice.

6. Essentially, the subordinate concessive conjunctions *though, even though* and *although* have the same meaning; however, *even though* is more emphatic. We use these conjunctions to introduce **clauses of concession** (or **contrast**). The adverbs *still, anyway* and *anyhow* frequently occur in independent clauses that accompany such sentences:

a. *Though:*

> A: *Though* I've been looking day and night for weeks, I still don't have a full-time job.
> B: Yes, *though* times are good, dancers still can't find jobs.

b. *Even though:*

> A: *Even though* I have a fear of flying, I fly everywhere anyway.
> B: I rarely fly *even though* I love it.

c. *Although:*

> A: *Although* they're difficult, I still do the exercises.
> B: Just try your best, and you will do well.

When such clauses appear in second position and are closely related to the independent clause, we do not use a comma:

> A: We are twins *even though* we don't look like it.
> B: Our attitudes are different *though* we're twins.

However, very often a clause of concession is more loosely related to the independent clause; then we need to put a comma. *Although* most often appears in this type of clause:

> A: The garden looks brown, grim and gray, *although* spring has come and brought with it rain.
> B: Yes, and neither the birds nor the bees have returned, *even though* it's the season.

7. We use the subordinate concessive conjunctions *whereas* and *while* (meaning *whereas*) to show direct opposition; in other words, one is exactly the opposite of the other. Whether the dependent clause appears in first or second position, we usually use a comma:

a. *Whereas:*

> A: The rich are getting richer, *whereas* the poor are getting poorer.
> B: Yes, and *whereas* the people want freedom, the government wants suppression of human rights.

b. *While:*

> A: *While* a giraffe's neck is extremely long, its tail is relatively short.
> B: A female lion is always busy hunting, *while* the male of the species is always taking it easy.

☐ 6.3 Contrasting Dependent Clauses and Prepositional Phrases

Supply in each blank a subordinate conjunction or a prepositional phrase.

when	once	because	despite
whenever	by the time (that)	now that	in spite of
while	since	though	on account of
as	until	even though	owing to
as soon as	till	although	because of
before	as	while	due to
after	as (so) long as	whereas	(the fact that)

Example

A: _____*Because*_____ I'm so tired, I'm turning in* early tonight.

B: Well, I'm tired, too, but ____*in spite of*____ my tiredness, I'm still going

out.

1. A: _____ I go to Acapulco, _____ the water in

Acapulco Bay isn't very clear, I always go skin and scuba diving.

B: Gee, I haven't gone skin diving _____ I was a

girl _____ I was living in Hawaii.

2. A: You've lived a long life, Grandma.

B: Yes, but _____ my great age, I still remember the good old

days. _____ I'm almost ninety now, my memory is still fairly

good. However, _____ my mind is still good, my body is

giving out.†

3. A: Just why are you selling your house?

B: _____ our children are no longer with us (they've all finally

moved out of the nest), we don't need such a big house anymore. You know how it

is. _____ your children have grown up, you want to make

some kind of change. _____ our great love for this house and

its beautiful garden, we still want to put it on the market.

4. A: What's the political situation in your country?

B: The people in the west want a capitalist society, _____ those

in the east desire socialism. The people in the north are Royalists, _____

_____ those in the south are Fascists. _____ we have

this kind of political situation, the country will exist in a state of chaos.

5. A: Professor Hansen, _____ your project finally comes to an end,

what will have been accomplished?

B: Well, _____ we reach the end of this project, the largest

computer system in this country will have been installed in our research center

here at the National University.

*Going to bed.
†Weakening.

A: Has it been a difficult project, ma'am?

B: Yes, very. _____ this country is one of the richest nations in this part of the world, the citizens aren't willing to support education. However, _____ this negative attitude on the part of the public, we have realized success on this project. _____ everything, we have succeeded.

6. A: Congratulations, Wayne, on your new job. I'm jealous. _____ you've become the president of International Motors, you must be making tons of money. On the other hand, you must have lots of headaches.

B: On the contrary, Alex, I don't have any headaches at all. _____ you become the president of a big company such as mine, your subordinates are the ones who get the headaches. _____ my very responsible position, I've never worked so little in my life. Ever _____ I started my job, it's not been hard at all, in fact.

A: Really? _____ you are the president?

7. A: Well, how did you do in Chemistry 9000?

B: _____ I was rarely at the lab sessions, I flunked the course.

A: How did that happen? _____ I'm no genius, I got a good grade in that course.

B: Oh, it was silly, really. _____ all the other kids in the lab liked her, I just couldn't get along with the lab assistant.

A: Why not?

B: _____ her negative attitude, I just couldn't stand her.

A: Are you serious? Just _____ you didn't like your lab assistant, you flunked that course?

8. A: What are your twins like?

B: Oh, they're like night and day. Their names are Mary and Meredith. Everyone calls them the M and Ms.

A: Ha, ha, ha, that's cute.

B: Meredith is a very active girl; she likes to be outside all the time, _____ _____ Mary is a reader. She's always got her head in a book. Meredith is the classic extrovert, _____ Mary is the classic introvert. _____ they are twins, they are two completely different people. _____ Meredith can't wait to get outside and experience the real world, Mary just prefers to bury her head in some book or other.

9. **A:** _____ her great charm, beauty and wit, she's able to capture men's hearts easily. _____ a man meets her, he just can't resist her charms.

   B: You're not talking from experience, are you?

   A: Yes, I'm afraid so. _____ I first met her some years ago, _____ I laid my eyes on her,* I fell in love with her. You know, love at first sight. We started going out together, and we had a lot of good times. However, there was one thing wrong. _____ she got her own way, things would be O.K. But _____ she didn't get her own way, life could be hell.

   B: All her charms had spoiled her, hadn't they?

10. **A:** Good morning, Captain.

   B: Good morning, ma'am. Have you been enjoying your voyage?

   A: Very much, sir. When do we arrive in Singapore?

   B: Well, _____ the bad weather, we should be there by Friday. How long are you going to be with us? _____ we get to Bangkok?

   A: No, I'll be on this ship _____ she gets to Yokohama.

❑ 6.4 *Despite* and *In Spite of;* Prepositional Phrases and *The Fact That*

  1. The concessive prepositions *despite* and *in spite of* may be combined with a noun to form a phrase of concession:

    A: *Despite* the great depth of the ocean [Though the ocean is very deep], many shipwrecks are found.

    B: Yes, even the *Titanic* was eventually found.

    A: *In spite of* the small size of their house [Although their house is very small], a great many people live in it.

    B: I hope they all get along with each other.

  2. We can combine *despite* or *in spite of* with *the fact that* to form a dependent clause of concession:

    A: *In spite of the fact that* [Even though] he has three degrees, he's driving a taxi at night to make ends meet.

*I saw her.

B: Yes, *despite the fact that* [Although] he's gone to Princeton, Brown and Columbia, he still can't make a decent living for some reason.

3.   We sometimes make subordinate conjunctions of reason by combining *the fact that* with the prepositional phrases *because of, due to, on account of* and *owing to:*

A: Just why is it so difficult to do business with that company? Is it because of politics?

B: Yes, *on account of the fact that* there's so much corruption in the government, you just can't depend on the company's honesty.

A: The game has been canceled *owing to the fact that* it's raining so hard.

B: Why don't we play in the rain? It would be fun.

A: Just why do you think he's jealous of you?

B: Simple. He's jealous *because of the fact that* I am better looking, more intelligent and more successful.

A: You know, *due to the fact that* you are so egotistical, quite a few people don't like you.

4.   Dependent clauses made out of prepositional phrases and *the fact that* can look wordy and are often avoided by writers. However, they can be quite effective for emphasis, particularly in conversation. Note how we may avoid wordiness by using a prepositional phrase and a noun object:

. . . *on account of* so much corruption in the government.
. . . *owing to* the heavy rain.
. . . *because of* my better looks, greater intelligence and greater success.
. . . *due to* your egotism.

❑ 6.5 *So . . . (That)* and *Such . . . (That)*; Reviewing Articles and Prepositions

Using no words other than auxiliaries, prepositions, articles and *so . . . (that)* or *such . . . (that),* compose a sentence using each set of given words as a cue. Follow the procedure shown in the examples, or do the exercise on a separate sheet of paper. Omit *that* in approximately half of your sentences and replace it with a comma.

Examples

a. **A:** I / be / just / angry / my landlord / I / scream⊙

with handwritten corrections: *am* (above be, be crossed out), *so* (above just), *with* (above the caret before my landlord), *could* (above before scream)

B: Hey, wait a minute. Let me get my earplugs.

b. **A:** this* / be / lovely champagne / I / like / another glass⊙

with handwritten corrections: *is such* (above be, be crossed out), *that would* (above before like)

B: Don't you think you'd better not? You're getting a bit tipsy.

1. **A:** you / act / funny way / I / believe / it

B: Why do you say that? I'm just behaving in my usual manner.

*Three lines drawn below a letter indicate that it should be a capital letter.

A: No, I don't think so. You're up to something.   you / have / funny / smile / your

face / you / have / some sort / unusual / idea / your head

2. A: our troops / have / much courage / they / be / afraid / nothing   they / be /

brave / they / never / surrender / enemy

B: That's what our enemy says about its own troops.

3. A: you / have / fascinating fish / your aquarium / I / just / stop watching /

them   they / be / beautiful / they / take / my breath

B: Yes, but I'm getting tired of them.   they / require / great amount / work / I /

give / them / some friends / mine

4. A: there / be / many people / Columbus Day Parade / yesterday / Fifth Avenue /

police / count / them

B: yes / and / it / rain / hard / my feet / get soaked

5. A: Just what are you giggling about?

B: you / have / funny-looking hat / I / stop laughing

6. A: Why don't you like to play catch with your brother, Jackie?

B: he / always / throw / ball / fast / I / catch / it

7. A: what / be / your plans / this coming weekend?

B: we / have / many things / our attic / and / our basement / we / have / tag sale /

Saturday   fact / we / have / much junk / our house / and / our garage / we /

also / have / auction / Sunday   I / be / busy / I / have / minute / to sit / nor / I /

have / any time to do my homework.

8. A: I / go / shopping / now / there / be / little food / fridge / we / have / enough /

dinner   our family / have / big appetite / we / keep / anything / fridge / long

B: well / all / us / work / hard / we / need / lots / food / to keep us going

9. A: your roommate / certainly / need / to go / special diet

B: yes / she / lose / much weight / recently / she / wear / any / her clothes   she /

eat / little food / I / worry / her

10. A: Dear, I've prepared this lovely dinner, and you're not eating.

    B: I / be / sorry / honey / but / I / have / big lunch / I / have / much / appetite / now

11. **A:** Describe your new boyfriend to me. Is he handsome?

    B: very / example / when / I / walk / street / him / he / be / good-looking / women /

        just / keep their eyes / him

❏ 6.6 Result Clauses; *So . . . That* and *Such . . . That*

1. Another type of adverb clause is a **result clause,** which is used as a dependent clause to show the result of a situation or a condition expressed in an independent clause:

    A: India is *so* large and varied [situation] *that it's difficult to govern effectively* [result].
    B: Well, China is in very much the same situation, isn't it?
    C: And doesn't the Soviet Union face the same situation?

2. The subordinate conjunction *so . . . that* frequently occurs in a sentence containing a result clause. However, *so . . . that* is split by the following:

  a. Adjectives:

    A: I'm *so tired that* I can hardly stand up.
    B: Well, I'm *so nervous that* I can hardly sit down.

    A: Love is *so wonderful that* it can cure all ailments.
    B: Hate is *so terrible that* it can make one sick.

  b. Adverbs:

    A: I'm sorry, you're speaking *so fast that* I can't keep up with you.
    B: Excuse me, my mind is operating *so quickly that* I can hardly keep up with myself.

    A: Speed up. You're driving *so slowly that* we'll never get where we're going.
    B: You're criticizing my driving *so frequently that* you'd better stop it. Otherwise, you might end up walking.

  c. *Many, few, much* and *little* plus countable or uncountable noun:

    A: How's your vegetable garden doing this year?
    B: We've got *so many tomatoes that* we're giving them away.

    A: Just what's her problem?
    B: She's got *so few friends that* she's extremely lonely.

    A: I hear that couple is called Mr. and Mrs. Moneybags.
    B: Yes, they've got *so much money that* they can't count it.

    A: How's school going this semester?
    B: I have *so little time that* I can't fit everything in.

3. Adjectives, adverbs and nouns are often accompanied by prepositional phrases and/or adverbial expressions of time:

    A: He's **so** *tired now* **that** he can hardly move a muscle.
    B: Listen, I've been **so** *tired for the past few weeks* **that** I haven't been able to work at all.

    A: She spoke **so** *fast during the meeting the other day* **that** I couldn't understand a word she had to say.

B: And she was digressing **so** *often from the main topic of the speech* **that** nobody else could understand her either.

A: They have **so** *little money these days, in fact,* **that** they've been begging on the streets.

B: Do they have **so** *little pride in themselves* **that** they can do that?

4. We may omit *that* and replace it with a comma in writing and a pause in speech:

A: This ice cream is so cold, [pause] it hurts my teeth.
B: It's got so much sugar in it, [pause] it's going to make me thirsty.

5. The subordinate conjunction *such . . . that* also occurs in sentences containing result clauses; it is split by the following:

a. A *(an)* plus an adjective plus a singular noun (plus a prepositional phrase):

A: He's *such a good player* [*on the team*] *that* all the fans love him.
B: He's *such a good hitter* [*during a game*] *that* all the pitchers are afraid of him.

A: That's *such an ugly painting* [*on the wall*] *that* I can't even look at it.
B: However, there's *such an unusual theme* [*in the painting*] *that* I'm quite intrigued.

b. An adjective plus a plural countable noun or an uncountable noun (plus a prepositional phrase):

A: He tells *such fantastic stories* [*to everyone*] *that* nobody believes him anymore.
B: Yes, he talks about *such unbelievable characters* [*in his stories*] *that* they aren't credible.

A: They have *such ancient furniture* [*in their house*] *that* I'm afraid to sit down.
B: Well, you have *such new furniture* [*in your house*] *that* I am also afraid to sit down.

6. As with *so . . . that,* with *such . . . that* we may omit *that* and replace it with a comma in writing and a pause in speech.

A: I have such a bad headache, [pause] I can't think straight.
B: She's got such a bad backache, [pause] she can't bend over.

A: He's got such an odd name, [pause] I can't pronounce it.
B: She's got such a long one, [pause] I can't spell it.

❏ 6.7 Purpose Versus Result; Reviewing Articles and Prepositions

Follow the directions for section 6.5. This time, use purpose clauses with *so (that)*.

Example

A: this / ̶b̶e̶ *is a* / terrible thing⊙   why / you / ̶l̶a̶u̶g̶h̶? *are laughing?*

B: I / ̶l̶a̶u̶g̶h̶ ̶/̶ ̶I̶ ̶/̶ ̶c̶r̶y̶ *am laughing so that I won't cry⊙*

1. A: I / now / look / part-time job / I / save / little bit / money / my tuition / university

B: there / be / lot / them / but / they / pay / much / however

2. A: why / you / go / last night?

B: I / stay / home / I / watch / my favorite program / TV / but / unfortunately / I /

fall / asleep / my chair / before / it / come

3. A: what / you / do / ice cream?

B: it / melt / I / put / it / refrigerator

4. A: well / what / be / your / plans / this / coming spring vacation?

B: I / lose / least / five pounds / I / go / strict diet

5. A: you / look / pale   you / feel / well / today / you?

B: I / feel / worse   when / I / go / yesterday morning / I / wear / heavy coat / I /

catch / cold / but / I / still / catch / one / anyhow

6. A: young man / you / do / more physical exercise / you / get / yourself / better

shape   also / you / get / haircut / you / look / more presentable / when / you /

be / school / and / when / you / walk / street

B: ah / Uncle George / you / always / pick / me

7. A: gosh / you / be / stingy   you / spend / nickel / anything

B: I / have / money / my old age / I / save / some / now / I?

8. A: when / we / go / California / last summer / we / drive / way / Arizona / we / see /

Grand Canyon   while / we / be / Los Angeles / we / rent / limousine / we / do /

any driving / since / traffic / be / just terrible there   our stay / northern

California / we / rent / motorcycles / we / go riding / mountain roads

B: you / have / fabulous trip

Now you will need to add an independent result clause with *so* to some sentences.

> *Example*
> Aren't going to go out
> A: ~~be~~ / you / ~~go~~ / tonight?
>   am   so am going to
> B: no / I / ~~be~~ / tired / I / ~~go~~ / bed / early.

9. A: dear / we / go / tonight?

B: it / snow / hard / and / it / be / very cold / I / stay / home / and / play / chess / you /

front / fire

10. A: we / talk / this meeting / almost three hours now

     B: we / take / break / we / rest / our brains / bit / we?

11. A: well / it / be / almost tax time again   I / pay / lot / darn it

     B: unfortunately / I / make / much money / last year / fortunately / I / pay / many

       taxes this year

     A: yes / there / certainly / be / two ways / looking / it

12. A: why / you / take so much cash / you / your last trip?

     B: I / want / to have some extra money / me / I / run

13. A: why / you / go / Rome / last summer?

     B: we / want / to go / Rome / we / pay / visit / Vatican / and / see / pope / person

       addition / we / want / to spend / few days / relative / ours

14. A: why / you / finish / all / this / work / today? why / be / it / so important?

     B: tomorrow / be / busy day / I / try to finish this project today / I / worry / it /

       tomorrow

❑ 6.8 Purpose Clauses; *So That*

1.   We use the subordinate conjunction *so that* to introduce a **purpose clause,** which usually answers a question with *why.* A verb phrase in a purpose clause most often contains the modal auxiliaries *can, may* and *will* for the present and the future and *could, might* and *would* for the past:

   a. *Can* and *could* appear most frequently:

     A: Why have you decided to dye your hair?
     B: I want to do it *so that* I *can* have a new image.

     A: Why weren't you at the concert last night?
     B: I had to go to the library *so that* I *could* do some research.

   b. *May* and *might* occur less often:

     A: Why would you like to meet the president?
     B: I'd like to meet him *so that* I *may* shake his hand and share with him my concerns.

     A: Why did that man steal? Does he have no sense of right and wrong?
     B: He stole *so that* he *might* buy food for his starving family.

   c. *Will* and *would* show a determination to achieve result:

     A: Why are you working so hard now?
     B: I'm doing it *so that* I *won't* have to work hard in the future.

     A: Why did their forces attack at five in the morning?
     B: They did it *so that* the enemy forces *would* be caught by surprise.

2.   We may omit *that;* however, we do not usually replace it with a comma, nor do we use a pause in speech:

> A: Are you going to be going to that concert tonight? It's going to be classic rock-and-roll.
>
> B: Yes, we'll be standing in line early *so* (*that*) we can get tickets.
>
> A: I'm going to buy some headphones *so* (*that*) I won't disturb my roommates while I'm listening to music.
>
> B: I'm going to have to buy some earplugs *so* (*that*) I won't have to listen to my roommate's constant practicing on her guitar.

3.   On occasion a purpose clause with *so* (*that*) occurs in initial position; it is followed by a comma in writing and a pause in speech:

> A: *So* we won't run out of money in the future, [pause] we're trying to spend very little now.
>
> B: You see, *so that* our children can get their education, [pause] my husband and I have had to make many personal sacrifices.

4.   We often use the modals *should, must* and others in independent clauses that accompany purpose clauses:

> A: *So that* we won't burn much gas, we *shouldn't* drive over fifty, nor should we do much passing.
>
> B: Yeah, we*'d better not* go any faster *so* we can make it to the next gas station.
>
> A: I *have to* study as hard as I can *so that* I'll get into college.
>
> B: *So that* I may be able to find a girlfriend, I *must* go to a dance studio and learn all the new dances.

5.   We frequently respond to a statement or a question with just a purpose clause:

> A: Hey, kids, why do you have to use those headphones? You'll hurt your eardrums.
>
> B: *So that* we won't disturb you and Dad, Mom.
>
> A: Tell me why you are making so many compromises.
>
> B: *So* we might come to some kind of satisfactory agreement with you.

6.   When we do not use *that*, it is easy to confuse the coordinate conjunction *so*, which expresses *result* and introduces an independent clause, with the subordinate conjunction *so* (*that*), which expresses *purpose* and introduces a dependent adverb clause. Compare the following:

> A: We have good jobs, *so* we're not worried.   [coordinate]
>
> B: We're going to go to a bigger town *so* we can find better-paying jobs.   [subordinate]
>
> A: She has perfect skin, *so* she doesn't have to use makeup.   [result]
>
> B: I must wear makeup *so* I can hide all of my imperfections.   [purpose]

Note: A comma precedes the coordinate conjunction.

❑ 6.9   *In Order That* and (*In Order*); Reviewing Articles and Prepositions

Follow the directions for section 6.5. This time, use *in order that* and (*in order*) plus an infinitive.

Example

A: On our way / home, we / stop / at the store / in order / to buy / groceries.

B: good. not only / am be / I / hungry, I / am starving.

1. **A:** I / go / my lawyer / yesterday / talk / her / problem / I / have / my landlord / but / order / get / her office / I / wait / more than / hour / waiting room   addition / she / even / have / any magazines / me / read

   B: well / order that / I / see / my doctor / last week / I / wait / least / hour / and / half   and / while / ago / I / wait / more than / month / order / get / appointment / my dentist

   C: doctors / dentists / and / lawyers / make / tons / money

2. **A:** you / make / comment / press / this time / Mr. President?

   B: yes / order that / we / make / more progress / our society / we / have / equal rights / all members / society / otherwise / there / be / revolution

3. **A:** these days / I / rarely / see / you / either / town / or / campus   where / you / be?   you / be / sick / you?

   B: no / I / be / sick   order / save / money / trip next summer / I / now / work / part-time job / evenings   as / result / I / see / much / my friends   also / neither / I / do / very well / my school work / nor / I / go / my girlfriend very much   I / have / much fun / I?

4. **A:** that period / crisis / Ambassador / what / your government / do / establish / peace and order?

   B: well / they / be / very difficult times   order that / we / maintain / peace and order / that country / my government / deploy / all / its military might / suppress / revolutionary forces that / be / threat / government / then / power   we / do / this / order / save / people / cruel domination / large and powerful neighbor   unfortunately / we / underestimate / strength / revolutionary forces / and / we / know / corruption / government that / we / try / to protect   consequently / order that / we / prevent / further bloodshed and slaughter / we / withdraw / our troops /

country   we / force / to leave / country / shame

❑ 6.10 *In Order That* and *In Order*

1. The subordinate conjunction *in order that,* which introduces a purpose clause, has the same meaning as *so that.* But it usually appears in somewhat formal usage. It is most often followed by *may* or *might:*

   A: Yes, Ambassador, what do you think?
   B: *In order that* we *may* find peace, we must negotiate, but we mustn't capitulate.
   A: And what did your company do at that time?
   B: We increased production substantially *in order that* we *might* eventually control the market.

2. Less formally, the phrase *in order* plus an infinitive also expresses purpose:

   A: I've got to stop at the bank *in order to get* some cash.
   B: *In order to make* a deposit so that none of my checks bounce, I have to make a stop there, too.
   A: What do you have to do *in order to* enter that club?
   B: *In order to get into* that club, you must be a first-class snob.

3. We may omit *in order* and express purpose with just the infinitive:

   A: Here in Hawaii I get up early in the mornings (*in order*) *to see* the magnificent sunrises.
   B: I often go up to the mountains (*in order*) *to watch* the sun set. It's always an inspiration.

❑ 6.11 Future Conditionals

Fill in each blank with an appropriate conditional subordinate conjunction or the expression *what if.*

if	provided (that)	only if
even if	providing (that)	only unless
unless	as (so) long as	only in the event (that)
in the event (that)	suppose (that)	only in case
in case	supposing (that)	what if

Example

A: _____*If*_____ I am ever broke at any time in the future, will I be able to depend on you for a loan?

B: ___*Providing that*___ you pay it back with interest.

1. A: _____ it rains, we're going on a picnic tomorrow.

   B: _____ it rains? What will you do then?

A: Well, _____ that happens, and I hope it doesn't, we'll

have lunch at my house or at a restaurant.

2. A: What are you doing these days?

   B: I'm in business for myself, and _____ some bank will

   give me a loan, I might make a million within a year. _____

   _____ I can get that loan, I'll make a mint.

   A: _____ no bank gives you a loan, what will you do

   then? _____ they think you're too much of a risk?

   B: Well, I'll have to go out of business _____ I get it.

3. A: General, I have a question. _____ our forces are defeated

   in tomorrow's battle, what will be the final outcome of the war?

   B: _____ we lose the battle tomorrow, we'll still win the war.

   No matter what! _____ we are down to our last soldier,

   we shall never surrender to our enemy.

4. A: When I go to China next summer, I'm taking some travelers checks with

   me _____ I run out of money.

   B: _____ you have cash, you'll be much, much better off.

   Travelers checks aren't always so easy to cash in China.

   A: Well, _____ I lose my cash, what should I do then?

5. A: Do you think you'll ever marry your boyfriend?

   B: _____ he changes his political views, will I ever become

   his wife. Serious Democrats and Republicans don't make good marriage

   mates.

   A: Well, _____ he does come over to your way of thinking?

   B: Ha, ha, ha. _____ that happens, it'll be a miracle. He's a

   staunch believer in his party.

6. A: Are we always going to be happy together?

   B: Darling, _____ we respect each other's views, we won't

   have any problems. _____ we lose respect for one

   another, will our marriage ever fall apart.

   A: Will you always remain faithful?

   B: Yes, of course, _____ you will remain faithful to me.

   A: Why, that will be an easy provision to keep.

B: Oh? Really? _____ on one day you meet walking down
the street the most exciting and glamorous person in the world?

7. **A:** So, Bobby, today will be the first day of your life that you ride the subway to
school by yourself. Excited?

   B: Yeah, but I'm a little scared, too.

   A: Oh, you won't have any problems _____ you ask for
   them. _____ you mind your own business, nobody will
   bother you.

   B: _____ I get lost, should I call 911?*

   A: Ha, ha, ha, of course not. _____ someone tries to rob you,
   should you call 911. _____ you lose your way, honey, just
   call home.

Now supply in each blank an appropriate verb phrase.

   Example

   A: This is quite a climb. Do you think we'll ever reach the summit of this mountain?

   B: (*break*) Yes, provided that we ___*don't break*___ our necks, (*make*)
   we ___*will make*___ it.

8. **A:** (*slow down*) Have you got a lead foot? If you _____,
   (*have*) we _____ an accident. You're driving like a maniac.

   B: Why, I'm an excellent driver; you don't have to worry about a thing. I've been
   driving for 25 years.

   A: (*want to live*) Well, if you _____ another 25 years, (*let up
   on*) you _____ the gas, _____?

9. **A:** I'd like to visit you at your place in the country. How do I get there?

   B: (*have*) Only if you _____ a car, (*get*) _____
   _____ to my place. (*have*) I'm in a very isolated spot high up in the
   mountains, and even if you _____ good directions, (*still /
   lose*) you _____ your way.

   A: I'll give it a try. I'm pretty good at finding places that are hard to find. (*have*)

---

*In the United States, 911 is the emergency telephone number.

Providing that I _____ a good map, (*find*) I _____

_____ your place, I'm sure.

B: (*get*) Well, if you _____ lost, (*blame*) _____

_____ me. I've warned you.

10. A: (*do*) Only if the governments of the world _____

something about overpopulation, (*the earth / support*) _____

_____ the size of its population.

B: (*do*) Yes, if it _____ soon, (*have*) people _____

_____ neither enough air to breathe nor enough space in which to live.

(*have*) Only if we _____ population control in the

future, (*there / be*) _____ enough room for everyone

in the human race.

❏ 6.12 Future-Possible Real Conditions

1. A **future-possible conditional statement** expresses a possibility that can be realized in future time:

> A: *If* we have love for our fellow man and woman, we *will have* peace in the world.
> B: Love *will conquer* all *if* we give it a chance.

2. We most often use the subordinate conjunction *if* to introduce a dependent conditional clause. The simple present tense or its continuous form after *if* can express future time:

> A: *If* it's pleasant tomorrow, we'll take a stroll in the park.
> B: Yes, we'll go for a nice walk *if* it *isn't raining*.

3. We sometimes use *will* after *if* to make a polite request, a suggestion or a strong command:

> A: *If* you *will* stand up, sir, I'll take your measurements.
> B: Shall I stand at attention?
> A: *If* you *will* please turn to page 292, we can begin the lesson.
> B: We've already done that exercise, Mrs. DiGaetano.
> A: Tom! *If* you *will* please raise your hand when you wish to catch my attention, I will appreciate it.
> B: Yes, ma'am. I'll raise my hand next time.

On rather rare occasions we put *will* after *if* to express strong determination or willingness:

> A: *If* the government *will* declare war, the people will suffer.
> B: *If* the people *will* demand peace, they will have it.

4. We occasionally use the present perfect tense after *if* when we wish to emphasize an event being completed before the event in the independent clause:

> A: If I *have finished* (or *finish*) this project by the end of the semester, both my teacher and I will be very surprised.
> B: All of us will be.

5. *Can, must, have to* and *be able to* frequently follow *if*:

> **A:** *If* you *must* go out on a cold day like this, kids, will you please put on some warm jackets?
> **B:** O.K., Mom, *if* we *have to* wear jackets, we'll do it.
>
> **A:** *If* we*'re able to* get a loan from the bank, I'll be relieved.
> **B:** Well, we'll be in some hot water *if* we *can't* get one.

6. The independent clause in such sentences is called a result clause, since it expresses the result of a condition expressed in the dependent conditional clause. All future forms, modal auxiliaries and related idioms can appear in result clauses:

> **A:** If it's snowing hard tomorrow, we *might* not go to work.
> **B:** Well, if it snows tonight, we*'re going* skiing tomorrow.
>
> **A:** Oh, I'm going to do this job later.
> **B:** Don't put it off. If you do it now, you won't *have to* worry about it later.

7. The verb in a result clause may often be in the imperative mood; in this case, the subject [*you*] is not expressed but is understood:

> **A:** If your feet get wet in the playground, *come* home right away and change into some dry sneakers, boys.
> **B:** Please *come* and *watch* us play, Dad, if you're not too busy.
>
> **A:** If you must smoke, *don't blow* the smoke my way, please.
> **B:** If you don't mind, please *stop* complaining about my smoking.

8. We frequently abridge conditional and result clauses:

> **A:** Do you think she's going to say yes to your proposal of marriage?
> **B:** If she *doesn't,* one of her sisters *will.*
>
> **A:** Is your boss going to be at the holiday party?
> **B:** Well, if he *is,* I*'m not.*

9. The following subordinate conjunctions also introduce dependent conditional clauses:

a. *Even if* expresses contrast:

> **A:** You won't remain a bachelor if you fall in love.
> **B:** Listen, I'm going to stay single *even if* I fall in love.
>
> **A:** *Even if* they don't give their permission, I'm going to elope.
> **B:** When you elope, you don't ask your parents for permission to do it, do you?

b. *Unless* means "if not":

> **A:** The patient isn't going to get better *unless* a miracle occurs [*if* a miracle doesn*'t* occur].
> **B:** *Unless* God intervenes [*If* God doesn*'t* intervene], the patient will die.
>
> **A:** *Unless* taxes are raised, the poor will suffer from a lack of social and medical programs.
> **B:** However, business will not be able to invest in new enterprises *unless* taxes are lowered.

c. *In the event* (*that*) shows that the condition is open to chance, luck or fate:

> **A:** *In the event that* there is a hurricane, all ships will remain offshore.
> **B:** *In the event* there is one, shouldn't all ships come back to port?
>
> **A:** What are you going to do *in the event that* there's an earthquake?
> **B:** I've got no idea. What should I do *in the event* there is? Run outside? Stay inside? Get under the bed? Stand in a doorway? *In the event that* there is one, just how can we prepare for an earthquake?

d. *In case,* which is somewhat similar in meaning to *in the event* (*that*), usually appears in sentences in which we give instructions in the independent result clause:

A: *In case* there is a fire, please walk to the nearest exit.
B: And please keep a fire extinguisher in your kitchen *in case* a fire breaks out.

A: *In case* you lose your passport, you must notify your embassy at once.
B: Here's your embassy's number. Give them a call right away *in case* you have any problems.

Note: We frequently use *in case of* plus a noun or a pronoun:

A: *In case of* an emergency, punch 911.
B: *In case of* anything serious, punch that number.

e. *Provided* (*that*) or *providing* (*that*) shows that there is a provision in the condition. This conjunction most often occurs in initial position:

A: May I use your bicycle, Dad?
B: *Provided that* you ride it carefully and safely, you can ride it anytime, son.

A: Do you think we're going to be able to make it to the Desert Inn?
B: *Providing* we can find a gas station, we're going to make it. Otherwise, we're going to be sleeping in the desert.

A: Do you think you're going to get a passing grade in the course?
B: *Providing that* I do the final paper, I will pass. Otherwise, I'll have to repeat the course.

f. *As* (*so*) *long as* has the meaning of *if* but also expresses duration:

A: *So long as* we have each other, we'll have happiness.
B: Yes, we'll be happy *as long as* we are together as one.

g. *Suppose* (*that*) or *supposing* (*that*) expresses a supposition. It usually appears in initial position. The independent clause is most often a question:

A: I get paid every Friday morning, and on the following Friday morning, I'm almost always flat broke.
B: *Suppose that* you get sick, *supposing that* you lose a week's work, what on earth will you do?
A: Oh, I do get sick leave; the company isn't that cheap.

A: Fred and I are getting married tomorrow at the little church around the corner.
B: *Supposing* he doesn't show up? *Suppose that* he leaves you standing alone at the altar, what will you do?
A: Ha, ha, ha. You've got to be joking.

A: *Suppose that* there's a revolution in the near future, how will this affect you and your family?
B: *Supposing* there is one, my family will have nothing to fear from either side, will it? Haven't we been neutral?

h. *Only if* makes a negative opening; however, we use the usual word order in the conditional clause, but we use the emphatic form in the independent clause:

A: Oh, why are you going to rent a car for yourself?
B: *Only if* I have a car, *will I be* able to enjoy my summer vacation to the fullest.

A: I'd really rather stay home; I don't want to go to that old and boring party.
B: Oh, please, pretty please. *Only if* you go, *will I go*.
A: Oh, come on, honey, don't try to make me feel guilty.

When *only if* appears in second position, we use the usual word order in the independent clause:

A: He'll move to California *only if* his wife is able to go with him.
B: And she'll go with him *only if* she can find a job in L.A. as good as the one she has in Chicago.

i. In addition to *if,* several other conditional subordinate conjunctions can be preceded by the adverb *only:*

A: *Only unless* our army has food, *will our men and women be* able to fight.
B: *Only so long as* they have bread, *will they have* strength.
A: *Only in the event that* I win the lottery, *can I* ever have all the things I want.
B: That's silly! Why don't you work harder?

Note: Only unless and *only if* have the same meaning.

10. The expression *what if* has the meaning of *suppose* (*that*) or *supposing* (*that*). *What if,* however, does not occur as a subordinate conjunction. It always appears in a one-clause question:

A: *What if, General, there is a revolution?*
B: Yes, supposing that there's an uprising and an eventual revolution, just what will happen?
C: Ladies and gentlemen, suppose that this does happen, all of us will be the first ones to be put up against the wall and shot.
A: *What if we run out of gas?*
B: Yes, supposing we do, what should we do then?
C: Listen, suppose we do run out of gas, you two had better start walking. I was the one who wanted to stop at the last gas station, wasn't I?

11. When speaking, we often respond with just a dependent clause:

A: Are you going to use your credit cards on your trip?
B: No, *unless* I run out of money.
C: *Only if* I run out of cash, or *if* I lose it.
D: I feel the same way. *As long as* I don't have to use them, I won't.

❑ 6.13 Generalizations

Supply in each blank an appropriate verb phrase.

Example

A: Do you usually get to school on time?

B: (*be*) Only unless there _____ *is* _____ some kind of transportation problem, which is rare, (*get*) _____ *do I get* _____ to class late. I'm quite a punctual person.

1. A: Why are you always knitting?

B: (*do*) If I _____ anything with my hands, (*get*) I _____

_____ very nervous. (*watch*) Even if I _____ TV, (*knit*)

I _____ something. (*read*) Only if I _____ a

book or a newspaper, (*knit*) _____.

A: My grandmother used to be the same way, but she was always darning or sewing.

2. A: I don't understand how the boiler in the basement works. (*put in*) What if

    I _____ too much water?

    B: (*put in*) If you _____ too much, (*turn*) the boiler _____

    _____ itself off automatically, (*put in*) and if you _____

    _____ enough water, (*do*) it _____ the same thing.

3. A: Our little girl lies down and takes a nap in the afternoons. (*take*) If

    she _____ one, (*be*) she _____ a little

    cranky in the evenings.

    B: Well, you know, I'm the same way. (*take*) When I _____ my

    little siesta* in the afternoon, (*be*) I _____ quite cranky in the

    evenings.

4. A: How often do your parents give a party?

    B: (*celebrate*) Only when someone in the family _____ his or her

    birthday, (*entertain*) _____.

5. A: You've got a beautiful dog. Is he a good pal?

    B: (*be / bark*) Yes, he _____ excellent company when he _____

    _____, (*chase*) and if he _____ the mail carrier.

    A: I wouldn't like to have the responsibility of a dog.

    B: Oh, I must have one; I've had at least ten. (*have*) Only if I _____

    _____ a good dog around me, (*be*) _____ a happy person.

6. A: (*goes away*) If my father _____ on a business trip, (*always /*

    go) he _____ alone.

    B: My mother and father are just the opposite. (*go along*) Only unless my mother

    _____, (*go away*) _____ on a business trip.

    He just can't bear to go anywhere without her, nor can she bear to be without

    him. They're like two teenagers in love.

7. A: How's your neighbor old Pat O'Rourke doing?

    B: Old Pat is getting on now; he's almost 98. (*pay*) Only when he _____

    _____ a visit to his doctor (*ever / leave*) _____ the house.

    A: It must be terrible to be so old.

    B: Oh, you just think that because you're so young. (*confine*) Even if old Pat

---

*Nap.

_____ to his bed most of the time, (*manage*) he _____

_____ to keep himself busy with different types of hobbies. He's enjoying life.

When I'm 98, if I live that long, and if I'm doing as well as old Pat is doing now,

I won't complain to anyone. No, sir, I'll be darned happy to be alive.

8. A: Do you have to do much homework for that class?

    B: (*have*) Oh, no, it's an easy class, only if we _____ a quiz the

        next day, which isn't very often, (*do*) _____ any—a real easy

        teacher.

    A: How about your other classes? Lots of homework?

    B: A lot—tough teachers. (*enter / do*) In one class, the students _____

        _____ the classroom unless they _____ their homework.

        That teacher is very strict. (*do*) In another class, if you _____

        your homework, (*humiliate*) the teacher _____ you in front of

        the whole class.

    A: I think that's terrible.

❑ 6.14 Present-Real Conditions

1. We use **present-real conditions** to make generalizations about events and conditions in the general present. When we do, the simple present tense or its continuous form indicates present time in both conditional and result clauses:

> A: My grandmother has few demands. So long as she *has* her little house, she *is* happy and contented.
> B: My grandmother is just the opposite. Only as long as she *has* excitement and glamour in her life, *is* she a happy woman.
> A: That fellow *is* hungry for power. He's not satisfied unless he's running every-thing.
> B: Yes, only if he's *running* the show, *does* he *function* well.

2. In generalizations about the present, *if* has the meaning of *when* or *whenever:*

> A: *If* (*when*) it's raining, I rarely seem to have an umbrella.
> B: And you're never wearing the right kind of clothes *if* (*whenever*) it's cold.

3. The future tense also occurs in present-real conditional statements. When it does, it may express willingness, strong determination or inevitability. It is usually interchangeable with the simple present tense:

> A: While the cat's away, the mice *will* play (or *play*).
> B: I just love that old saying. Whenever I hear it or say it, I *laugh* (or *will laugh*).
> A: If you don't put yeast in the dough, Mommy, what *happens* (or *will* happen)?
> B: It *won't rise* (or *doesn't rise*).

❑ 6.15 *Happen To*

Fill in the blanks with appropriate verb phrases. Wherever you can, use *should* in conditional and independent clauses. You will often use the imperative mood.

> ### Example
>
> **A:** How long will it take for my order to be delivered?
>
> **B:** (*be*) Approximately ten days. If there ___*should be*___ a delay, due to the fact that this is the holiday season, (*notify*) you ___*will*___ ___*be notified*___ at once.

1. **A:** I'll be at your house at about five. Will you be there?

    B: (*be / be*) Most likely I _____, but _____ _____ there when you get there, (*find*) you _____ _____ the key under the doormat.

2. **A:** (*be*) When I'm in Florida this coming September, and if there _____ _____ a hurricane, (*do*) what _____?

    B: (*there / be / go*) Oh, this is important, _____ one, you _____ outside. Never! There can be a lot of debris flying about during a hurricane.

3. **A:** Ambassador, Washington says you ought to attend the reception at the National Presidential Palace tomorrow evening.

    B: (*be*) Yes, _____ there, (*notice*) my absence _____ by everyone in high government circles, (*make*) and our situation in this country and in this part of the world _____ _____ worse than it already is.

4. **A:** (*have*) Ladies and gentlemen, after my lecture this morning, _____ _____ any questions, (*hesitate to ask*) _____ _____ them, please. (*ask*) I must say at this point that _____ any questions, (*be*) I _____ _____ disappointed.

    B: (*understand*) Excuse me, Professor, _____ your lecture, (*ask*) how _____ questions?

    A: Good question, that's exactly the point I'm trying to make.

5. **A:** (*ever / fall in*) Darling, _____ love with

someone else, (*tell*) _____ me, please, I don't

want to know.

B: (*the same thing / ever / happen*) Well, _____

to you, (*tell*) _____ me, please, I would like to

know.

6. **A:** Valentine's Day is coming. I wonder if I'll get any valentines.

B: (*get*) Well, _____ any, (*be*) I _____

_____ *very* disappointed.

A: Oh, are you expecting one? Is something going on that I know nothing about?

B: (*get*) Yes, I *am* expecting one from someone, and _____

_____ it, (*never / speak*) I _____ to

that person again.

A: Oh, come on, who is it? Who are you talking about? Let me know.

B: (*tell*) _____ you, (*promise*) _____

_____ not to tell anyone else?

7. **A:** Are you going to work this coming weekend?

B: I'm not sure, but I might have to. Why?

A: (*work*) Well, _____, (*go*) _____

_____ with me up to the mountains? It'll be fun.

B: I'd love to go. (*my boss / ask*) _____ me to work

overtime, (*just / tell*) I _____ him a little white

lie, that my parents are sick or something like that.

❑ 6.16 *Should* in Conditional Clauses

1. In future-possible real conditions, the modal auxiliary *should* means *happen to* when it appears in an *if* clause. Such clauses usually appear in initial position:

   A: If it *should* (*happens to*) rain tomorrow, we'll still have the reception in the garden. We've put up a large tent.
   B: The reception should be lovely even if it rains.
   A: If there *should* be an earthquake, what can we do?
   B: And what should we do if there *should* be a tornado?

2. We may drop the *if* and put *should* before the subject as in a question form:

   A: What are your plans for tomorrow? The forecast predicts a fifty percent chance of rain.
   B: *Should it* be a rainy day, we'll just stay home.
   C: *Should the day* be nice and sunny, we'll still stay home, but we'll be working in the garden.

3. We use *not* after the subject in negative verb phrases:

> A: Should *I not* be promoted, I'm going to have to go out and look for a better-paying job.
>
> B: Yes, should *the company not* give me a raise, I'll have to do the same thing.

Note: Shouldn't never occurs in this pattern.

4. When we use *should* in this manner in a conditional clause, the verb in the independent clause is often in the imperative mood:

> A: *Should* someone ask for me, please *call* me at once.
>
> B: *Should* there be anyone asking for you, would you please *give* me your extension so that I can?

❑ 6.17 Hypothetical Result

Supply in each blank an appropriate verb phrase.

> ### Example
>
> A: Well, tell me, how would you like to have a billion dollars?
>
> B: (*ever / work / have*) There's one thing for sure. I *wouldn't ever have to work*
> again if I _____ *had* _____ that kind of money, *would*
> _____ *I* _____?

1. A: Let's do a little pretending, shall we?

> B: Oh, let's, that sounds like fun.
>
> A: (*do / make*) What _____ if you _____
> _____ yourself invisible?
>
> B: Ha, ha, ha. The possibilities are endless. (*do*) If I _____
> that, (*become*) I _____ the most powerful person in the
> world. (*never / work*) Also, I _____ again, (*listen to*)
> nor _____ my nagging boss anymore.

2. A: (*do / be*) What _____ if you _____
> _____ the president of the United States, (*have*) and if
> you _____ unlimited power in your hands?
>
> B: That's a tough question, but I know one thing for sure, however. (*try to improve /
> be*) I _____ the educational system in this country if
> I _____ he. (*establish*) Also, I _____
> _____ a four-day work week.
>
> A: Hey, that sounds great. (*have*) If I _____ a three-day

weekend, (*do*) I _____ some more moonlighting.

(*raise*) _____ taxes?

B: (*try*) I don't know about that, but I _____ to make

every single person in the country pay his or her fair share.

3. **A:** (*suddenly / find*) What if you _____ a wallet lying on

the sidewalk with a thousand dollars in it? And if the wallet had identification in

it.

B: (*take*) I _____ the money and drop the wallet in a

mailbox.

A: (*do*) You _____ that, _____?

B: (*do / have*) No, I'm just kidding, but I _____ it if

I _____ any money in my own wallet.

4. **A:** (*return*) What if you _____ to your native country

today? (*take*) What or who _____ with you?

B: (*take*) Besides my American wife, I _____ my two

American kids, (*take*) and I _____ tons of presents.

5. **A:** I'm trying to make a decision. I've already had three interviews with a company,

and they're interested in me. They're offering seventy thousand a year.

B: But you're tops in the field. (*be*) If I _____ you, (*ask

for*) I _____ at least a hundred thousand. (*offer*) Only if

I _____ that much, (*take*) _____

_____ the job.

A: Goodness! You must think I'm some kind of genius.

6. **A:** (*probably / do / live*) What _____ if you _____

_____ in your native country right now?

B: (*be*) If I _____ back home now, (*study*)

I _____ at the university, but I'm not really sure.

A: (*live*) You _____ with your parents,

_____?

B: Oh, yes, back home you live with your family until you get married, at least

that's the way it is in my family.

7. **A:** (*be*) Supposing that suddenly there _____ a cheap

substitute for oil on the world market, (*happen*) what _____?

    B: (*change*) The economy of the world _____ overnight;

        (*affect*) everyone _____ .

8. **A:** Excuse me, are you single?

    B: (*be / be*) Well, I _____ here unless I _____

        _____ . Isn't this a party for singles?

    A: Oh, yes, you just don't look single, somehow.

    B: (*be*) Well, if I _____ married, (*look*) I _____

        _____ any different, _____ ?

9. **A:** I have to work in order to make a living.

    B: (*do*) Suppose you _____ that, (*change*)

        how _____ your life?

    A: (*pack up*) I _____ and go to some lovely island in the

        South Pacific and just sit under a palm tree and take it easy.

    B: (*get / do*) You _____ bored if you _____

        _____ something like that, _____ ?

❑ 6.18 Present-Unreal Conditions; Reality Versus Hypothetical Result

  1. In a **present-unreal conditional statement,** a dependent conditional clause introduced by *if* expresses a situation that is unreal—in other words, contrary to fact or reality. The independent clause expresses a hypothetical result. Compare the following:

    REALITY Not everyone speaks English. There's confusion in the office.

    HYPOTHETICAL RESULT If everyone *spoke* it, there *would be* less confusion.

    REALITY I'm able to talk to the outside world. I have a phone.

    HYPOTHETICAL RESULT I *wouldn't* be able to talk to the outside world if I *didn't* have one.

A past form usually occurs in the *if* clause to express present time, and *would* appears in the result clause. We do not use *should* often in North American English.

  2. The verb *be* has a special form in a present-unreal conditional clause; we use *were* in all persons:

    I'm not able to work miracles. I'm not making millions.
    If I *were* able to work them, I'd be making millions.

    Her work is going fast. She's using a computer.
    Her work wouldn't be going fast if she *were* not using one.

  3. In addition to *would*, the modals *could* and *might* and the idioms *have to* and *be able to* often appear in the result clause:

I can't drive to work. I don't have a car.
I *could* drive to work if I had one.

I don't have any money. I don't really want to go on a trip anyway.
If I had some money, I *might* go on one, but I don't think so.

I have to worry about transportation. I'm not Superman.
I wouldn't *have to* worry about it if I were he.

There's an excellent medication for the patient's condition. He's able to walk.
If this medication weren't available, he wouldn't *be able to* walk.

4. *Could, have to* and *be able to* also appear in present-unreal conditional clauses:

The teacher can't work miracles. We're not able to speak fluently.
If she *could* work them, we'd be able to speak fluently.

I'm not happy. I have to wear a uniform every day.
I'd be happier if I didn't *have to* wear one.

I'm not able to speak English as well as you. I'm not winning this debate.
If I *were* able to speak the language as well as you, I'd be winning it.

5. To introduce present-unreal conditional clauses, we may also use *only if, even if, unless, suppose (that)* and *supposing (that)*:

I don't have a very big salary. I can't afford to live in Paris.
Only if I had a very big salary, *could I* afford to live in Paris.

I don't know the secret. I don't tell secrets anyway.
Even if I knew it, I wouldn't tell you.

You can live in a penthouse. You must be well off.
Well, you couldn't live in a penthouse *unless* you were well off, could you?

You're not the president. You're not doing what he's doing.
Supposing that you were he, just what would you be doing?

6. We frequently abridge clauses:

A: You don't understand my feelings. I love her. I'm not going to leave her.
B: I *would* if I were you.

A: Can't you please come with me? It'll be fun.
B: I'm sorry, I'm not able to. I *would* if I *could*, but I can't.

7. When the result clause is understood, we often use result clauses alone as one-clause responses:

A: Supposing you won the lottery, how would you spend the money?
B: *I'd jump off the rooftops for joy.*
C: *My wife and I would buy a jet of our own.*

8. Frequently, we use the expression *what if* with present-unreal conditions:

A: Frank, *what if* you gradually lost your hair?
B: I certainly wouldn't worry about it.

A: *What if* I went out with your boyfriend?
B: I wouldn't do that if I were you.

❑ 6.19 Wishes: *If Only* and *Would Only*

Supply in each blank an appropriate verb phrase. If no verb is given in parentheses, use an appropriate auxiliary word. Use *only* when it is appropriate.

Example

A: Can you join us for a cup of coffee?

B: No, sorry, I'm in a rush. If only I _____ *could* _____ .

1. A: What are you so unhappy about today?

   B: Oh, it's the same old story—my girlfriend again. She says she doesn't want to be

   tied down. (*marry*) If she _____ me, (*be*)

   I _____ so much happier. If only

   she _____ .

2. A: Bang! Crash! Bam!

   B: (*you / stop*) Class! If _____ making so much noise

   and racket, (*get*) we _____ something

   accomplished today. (*you / quiet down*) If _____

   just a little bit, (*much / appreciate*) it _____ .

3.   [On the phone]

   A: Well, darling, I've just got to get off the line now. (*be*) If only long

   distance _____ so expensive, (*talk*)

   we _____ forever.

Now, when required, supply a subject pronoun of your choice.

   B: (*be*) If _____ together now. How I miss you! Why

   aren't you here? (*be*) If _____ ! (*travel*)

   If _____ through space and time, (*rush*)

   I _____ to you right now.

4. A: Let's go to the movies, Robbie. There's a good thriller at the CineMar.

   B: I can't, if only I _____ . (*have*)

   If _____ this darned stomachache. (*go away*)

   If _____ .

5. A: Yes, father is failing quickly; he's already in a coma. It's only a matter of time,

   the doctors say. (*work*) If _____ a miracle.

   B: Pray, my dear.

   A: (*pray / believe in*) I _____ if _____

   _____ prayer.

6. A: Ha, ha, ha. That was a cute story.

   B: Yes, I heard another cute story the other day. Let's see now, how did it go? Boy, is my memory getting bad.' (*tell*) I _____ it to

you, (*remember*) if _____ it.

A: That's O.K., Grandma, it'll come back to you.

7. A: (*win*) Just think, honey, if _____ the lottery,

(*change*) our lives _____ overnight.

B: (*move into*) Yes, we _____ a large and beautiful

house, (*have / ride around*) we _____ servants

and _____ in a chauffeured limousine.

8. A: Oh, Mr. White, here's a phone message for you.

B: (*please / read*) If _____ it to me, (*appreciate*)

I _____ it. I left my reading glasses on my desk.

(*get*) If _____ so forgetful.

9. A: Excuse me, I'm looking for the executive editor's office.

B: I'm going that way. (*please / come*) If _____ with

me, (*be*) I _____ glad to show you where her

office is.

A: Thank you.

B: You're being interviewed today for that job as assistant to the executive editor,

aren't you?

A: Yes, I am. (*be*) If _____ so nervous.

B: Why, you don't appear nervous at all. You look as cool as a cucumber, in fact. I'm

sure everything will go smoothly, except for one thing, however.

A: Oh, what's that?

B: (*chew / be*) Well, it's just a little tip, but I _____

gum during the interview if I _____ you. The

executive editor is very fussy about things like that.

10. A: Our neighbors' son is entering MIT this coming fall.

B: (*be*) Oh, if only my son _____ as smart as that

boy.

C: Oh, he doesn't seem so smart to me.

D: You must be kidding. (*be*) Only if he _____ very

smart, (*get into*) _____ MIT. He's a real brain.

He's got brains to spare, in fact.

❑ 6.20 *If Only* and *Would Only*

1. We often use *if only* to introduce a present-unreal conditional clause:

   REALITY   I don't have much free time. I'm not able to pursue my hobbies much.

   HYPOTHETICAL RESULT   *If only* I had more free time, I'd be able to pursue them more.

   REALITY   You can't speak English well. You can't matriculate at the university.

   HYPOTHETICAL RESULT   *If only* you could speak English better, you could matriculate.

Compare *if only* with *only if:*

   Only if I had more free time, *would I* be able to pursue my hobbies.
   Only if you could speak English better, *could you* matriculate.

2. An *if only* conditional clause appearing by itself can express a wish:

   A: Yes, I'm leaving for the south of France tomorrow.
   B: *If only* I could go with you.

   A: You're having a hard time at the university, aren't you?
   B: Oh, yes, *if only* I were a genius.

   A: Some friends of mine and I are going skiing this afternoon. How would you like to come along?
   B: Darn it! *If only* I didn't have to work today.

Only may follow a verb or a modal:

   A: I'm sorry, but I must leave you now, I just must.
   B: *If* I *could only* go with you. *If only* you could stay.

   A: Who are you traveling with on this trip?
   B: No one. *If* my wife *were only* with me. I'm so lonely when I get back to the empty hotel room at night. *If only* she were here.

3. *Would* (*only*) may occur in an *if* clause. It is a kind of command:

   A: Dear, *if* you *would* stop smoking, you would feel a thousand times better.
   B: *If* you *would only* stop pestering me about my smoking, I'd appreciate it.

   A: Class, *if* you *would* pay a little bit of attention, you'd be getting a lot more out of this history lesson.
   B: *If* you *would only* explain things more clearly, Mr. Akona, the lesson would be much easier to understand.

4. We may also make a wish with *would only;* we often split it:

   A: Oh, shucks! Look at that rain! It's spoiling our day.
   B: *If only* the sun *would* come out. I want to play outside.
   C: Yes, if the sun *would only* come out; then I could get my housework done.

   A: I practice and practice, but I'm still not playing the guitar well. *If* my playing *would only* get better.
   B: *If only* you *would take* lessons, your technique would improve.

5. *Would* (*please*) occurs after *if* in a very polite request:

   A: Which way is it to the bank's vault?
   B: *If* you *would please* come with me, ma'am, I'd be glad to show you the way.

   A: *If* you *would* take hold of my arm, I'd feel more secure.
   B: Why, yes, of course.

❑ 6.21   Past-Unreal Conditions; Past Condition Versus Present Result

Supply in each blank an appropriate verb phrase.

Example

A: Why did you go to Dr. Kumar last week? She doesn't have a very good

reputation, does she?

B: (know) _____ *Had I known* _____ that, (go)

I _____ *wouldn't have gone* _____ to her. Why didn't you tell me?

1.   A: (*get / study*) You know, Dave, you _____ better

grades last semester if you _____.

B: Why, I was always at my desk.

A: But you were always talking on the phone. (*spend*) Perhaps, if you _____

_____ more time at the library, (*concentrate on*) you _____

_____ your studies more. (*have*) You _____

_____ so many distractions, (*talk*) nor _____

_____ on the phone all the time.

2.   A: Danny, what's the answer to number seven in the exercise?

B: I'm afraid I don't know, sir.

A: (*do*) _____ your homework last night, young man,

(*give*) you _____ me an answer now.

B: (*stay*) But if I _____ home last night to do it, sir,

(*go*) I _____ to the movies with my girlfriend.

A: Oh, Danny, I give up. Why on earth are you going to school?

3.   A: Where did you grow up?

B: In California. I was born in Los Angeles, but I was raised on a farm about 175

miles north of there.

A: (*bring up*) _____ on a farm, (*have*) I _____

_____ a happier childhood, I think.

B: No, I don't think so. (*like*) You _____ the isolation

on a farm far away from people, (*like*) nor _____

all the hard work.

A: (*live*) Yes, but I _____ in the fresh air.

4. **A:** Class, let us continue our discussion about the American Revolution. (*win*)

   Suppose that the British _____, (*happen*) what

   _____? (*the United States / be*) What _____

   _____ like today? (*still / belong*) _____

   _____ to the British? Raise your hands, please. Yes, John Williams.

   B: I don't think so, Mrs. Jackson. (*win*) Even if Britain _____

   _____, (*eventually / gain*) the Americans _____

   _____ their independence.

   A: Why do you say that, John?

   B: Doesn't everyone have the desire to be free of foreign domination?

5. **A:** How I hate being in prison!

   B: Let this be a lesson to you. (*cheat*) _____ on your

   income taxes for so many years, (*sit*) you _____ in

   this prison right now. (*live*) You _____ a normal

   life on the outside.

   A: (*be*) Oh, if only I _____ such a greedy fool.

6. **A:** I went up to Mt. Washington last week; I took Highway 60 all the way.

   B: (*take*) _____ Highway 80, (*be*)

   it _____ such a long drive.

   A: I know 80 is much faster, but 60 is much more scenic.

7. **A:** I had so much studying to do yesterday, I couldn't get out of the library for even

   an hour. (*be*) _____ so loaded down with

   homework, (*go*) I _____ shopping.

   B: You'd better hurry up; Christmas is almost here.

   [Two days later]

   B: Well, did you finally go shopping?

   A: (*afford*) Yes, if I _____ it, (*buy*) I _____

   _____ a gift for each of my friends, but I just bought a few things

   for my family. (*afford to buy*) If only I _____

   more.

8. **A:** We had to pay four hundred dollars a night for our hotel room in London.

   B: You didn't have to pay that much, did you?

A: (*pay*) Oh, yes, only if we _____ at least that

much, (*find*) _____ a nice room.

B: My, you must be very fussy.

9.   A: Dad, did you fight in that war?

B: No, I didn't, son, I was too young at the time. (*be / draft*) But even if I

_____ old enough to fight and even if I

_____, (*still / go*) I _____

_____ into the army.

A: (*fight*) But, Dad, _____?

B: (*go*) Perhaps, but I _____ to prison first. That

war was morally wrong.

❑ 6.22   Past-Unreal Conditions

1.   As with the present-unreal, in a **past-unreal conditional statement,** we use the dependent conditional clause introduced by *if* to express a condition that is contrary to fact or reality. The independent clause expresses a hypothetical result. Compare the following:

REALITY   We didn't stop at the station. We ran out of gas.

HYPOTHETICAL RESULT   If we *had stopped* there, we *wouldn't have run* out.

REALITY   I wasn't carrying travelers checks last summer. I wasn't traveling.

HYPOTHETICAL RESULT   I *would have been carrying* them if I *had been traveling.*

REALITY   They didn't have any money at that time. The roof of their house wasn't repaired.

HYPOTHETICAL RESULT   If they *had had* money then, it *would have been repaired.*

To express past time, we use the past perfect (continuous) tense in the *if* clause, and we use *would have* (*been*) plus a present or a past participle in the independent clause. The use of *should* is chiefly British.

2.   Verb phrases with *could* sometimes occur in *if* clauses:

They didn't send their children to college. They couldn't afford it.
They would have sent them to college if they *could have afforded* it.

The idiom *be able to* also occurs in *if* clauses:

I wasn't able to vote. I didn't vote for him.
If I had *been able to* vote, I still wouldn't have voted for him.

And we also use the idiom *have to:*

He had to work overtime last night. He didn't go to the show.
If he hadn't *had to* work, he would have gone to it.

3.   Frequently, we use *could, might, have to* and *be able to* in independent result clauses:

We didn't have a car. We couldn't drive out to the desert.

If we'd had a car, we *could have driven* out to the desert.

I didn't have much money, so I didn't go on that skiing trip, but I didn't want to go anyway.

If I'*d had* more money, I *might have gone* on it, but I doubt it.

She didn't have to go to the doctor. She was feeling well.

She would have *had to* go to him if she hadn't been feeling well.

He had to take care of his baby sister. He wasn't able to go out with his friends.

If he hadn't had to take care of his baby sister, he would have *been able to* go out with them.

4.   We often employ *even if, only if, suppose* (*that*) and *supposing* (*that*) to introduce past-unreal conditional clauses:

A: Too bad you didn't have an invitation to that cocktail party. It was quite an affair.
B: *Even if* I'd had one, I wouldn't have gone. I can't stand cocktail parties—all that small talk.*

A: Professor, just why was the steam engine such an important invention?
B: *Only if* the steam engine had been invented, could there have been the industrial revolution.

We also often employ *if only:*

A: What's your roommate so upset about this morning?
B: *If only* he had stayed sober last night, he wouldn't have made such a big fool out of himself.

5.   In both formal and informal usage, we sometimes drop the *if* in a conditional clause and put the auxiliary verb *had* before the subject, as in a question form:

A: When you told that little story at the dinner table yesterday evening, everyone had already heard it.
B: Well, *had I* known that, I certainly wouldn't have told it.

A: Why didn't you help your neighbors out?
B: I would have been glad to help them out *had I* been able to do so.

In negative verb phrases, *not* follows the subject:

A: I'm so glad I was able to make it to the meeting this evening.
B: Had *you not* been able to get here, we would all have been disappointed.

A: What a terrible storm it was last night!
B: Yes, we just stayed home. Had *it not* been raining so hard, we could have gone out.

6.   An independent result clause most often appears in a complex sentence combined with a dependent conditional clause. However, it may occur by itself if the conditional clause is understood:

A: Several years ago a friend of mine inherited a hundred thousand dollars, and he took all the money and started traveling around the world. After a couple of years, he ran out of money and had to come back home flat broke. Would you have done the same thing *if you had been he*?
B: No, I *would have invested* the money in some business or other.
C: Well, I *might have bought* a condo or a co-op.
D: I *would have done* the same thing. If your friend hadn't taken that trip, he would always have regretted it.

*Insignificant conversation.

7. We frequently abridge both the conditional and the result clauses:

    A: Did you attend that meeting yesterday?
    B: No, I couldn't, I wasn't feeling very well. Of course, I *would have* if I *could have,* but I just couldn't get myself out of bed.

    A: Did you ever invest in IBM in the early days, Grandma?
    B: No, I didn't have any money then. If I *had,* I *would have.*

8. A past-unreal conditional clause often appears with a result clause expressing present time:

Past-Unreal Condition	Present Result
If I'd slept well last night,	*I wouldn't be so tired now.*
Had you taken your medicine,	*you might be feeling better now.*
If you'd saved your money,	*you'd have money in the bank now.*

9. The expression *what if* frequently occurs in a past-unreal conditional clause:

    A: *What if* your mother and father had never met?
    B: I wouldn't have been born, and I wouldn't be sitting in this classroom today.

    A: *What if* you had studied English more when you were younger?
    B: I would already have been in the university for a couple of years, and I wouldn't be doing this exercise right now.

10. As in present-unreal conditions, we often make wishes with *if only* in past-unreal conditions:

    A: Darn it! *If only* I *had done* my homework last night.
    B: Yes, you wouldn't be so confused now.

    A: *If only* I hadn't been caught cheating on that test.
    B: Yes, had you not, you wouldn't have been kicked out of school.

❑ 6.23 Contrasting Conditional Statements: Future-Possible, Present and Past, Real Versus Unreal

Supply in each blank an appropriate verb phrase.

Example

A: (*be*) During our motor trip down to Mexico last summer, if I _____was_____ tired, (*drive*) my wife _____drove_____.

B: (*be*) And if both of us _____were_____ tired, (*drive*) our son _____would drive_____.

1. A: (*be*) When I was a young man and in love the first time, if

    I _____ out on a date with my girlfriend, (*pay*)

    I _____ all the bills.

    B: That was fifty years ago, Grandpa. Things have changed.

2. A: What's going to happen in that country?

B: (*give*) If the people _____ more freedom, (*be*)

there _____ a bloody revolution.

3. **A:** What does that sign say? I forgot to bring my glasses.

   B: (*there / be*) It says, "_____ a fire, don't panic and

   walk to the nearest exit."

4. **A:** Ouch!

   B: What's wrong, Timmy?

   A: Oh, I cut my finger on my Boy Scout knife.

   B: (*be*) If you _____ more careful with that knife,

   young man, (*cut*) you _____ yourself.

5. **A:** Do you think you'll quit your job soon?

   B: (*give*) Only unless I _____ a raise in pay and an

   office with a window, (*stay*) _____.

6. **A:** I know your neighbor is poor and has little money, but why did she steal all that

   food from the supermarket?

   B: Her children had nothing to eat. (*do / be*) _____

   the same thing if you _____ she?

   A: Yes, I suppose so.

7. **A:** Professor, I have a question. (*never / take place*) What if World War II _____

   _____? (*the British / still / have*)

   _____ an empire today?

   B: I don't believe so. (*never / occur*) Even if the war _____

   _____, (*still / lose*) they _____ their empire.

   The war only speeded up its dissolution.

   A: (*enter*) Suppose that, Professor, the United States _____

   the war, (*Germany / win*) _____?

   B: It's not likely. (*never / give up*) The Soviet Union _____

   _____, (*Britain / ever / surrender*) nor _____

   _____ to the Nazis.

8. **A:** Mommy, tell me again about the time when you and Daddy were going together

   and hadn't gotten married yet.

   B: (*be*) Well, every Saturday night, if your Daddy _____

   on duty at the army base, (*go*) we _____

to the movies. (*have*) After this, if we _____

enough money, (*have*) we _____ a nice dinner

somewhere.

9.   A: Sometimes Milo Vince can be so self-centered.

     B: He certainly can be. (*only / be*) If he _____ less

selfish and interested in himself, (*be*) he _____ so

much easier to get along with.

10.   A: I think we should have done this exercise at the beginning of the course.

     B: We weren't prepared. (*do*) We _____ very well,

_____?

11.   A: Dad, when you were in the army, did you ever wear civilian clothes?

     B: Oh, sure, all the time. (*be*) If I _____ on duty,

(*wear*) I _____ a uniform.

     A: Did you ever have to carry a gun?

     B: (*fight*) Yes, if I _____ at the front lines, (*carry*) I

_____ one.

12.   A: Well, is your team going to have a victory celebration tomorrow night?

     B: (*beat*) If we _____ by the champions.

13.   A: I am a self-made man. Only I am responsible for my great success in the business

world.

     B: (*have*) Perhaps, but _____ the help of your rich

father when you were starting out, (*be*) you _____

in the very good position you're in today.

     A: Why, that's not true. My father never gave me a dime in the early stages of my

career.

❑ 6.24 Past-Real Conditions

  1.   We use **past-real conditions** for making generalizations about events in the past. The past (continuous) tense appears in both the conditional and the result clauses. In this case, *if* means *when:*

     A: During the Great Depression, *if* (*when*) we *didn't* have meat to eat, we *had to have* an extra helping of potatoes.

     B: And *if* (*when*) my father *wasn't working*, we *didn't have* much to eat at all.

  2.   In addition to using the past (continuous) tense in the result clause, we also use *would* or *used to* plus a base form:

A: When I was a child during the thirties, *if* we wanted some entertainment, we *would listen to* the radio, or we *used to go* to the movies. There was no TV in those days.

B: My, that was such a long time ago.

A: It seems like yesterday to me.

❑ 6.25 Real Versus Unreal

Supply in each blank an appropriate verb phrase.

Example

A: How arrogant Manuela Molina is!

B: Isn't she? (*be*) When she walks into a room full of people, she acts as if she _____*were*_____ the queen of England.

1. **A:** Why are you sneezing so much, Freddie?

   B: I must be allergic to something in this room.

   A: Oh, no, honey, you don't have any allergies. (*catch*) It sounds as if you _____ a cold.

2. **A:** Were you nervous at the job interview last week?

   B: I couldn't have been more so. (*just / faint*) I felt as though I _____ any minute.

3. **A:** Those are rain clouds on the horizon, aren't they?

   B: (*have*) Yes, it looks as though we _____ some rain down here in the valley any minute now, doesn't it?

4. **A:** When I walked into the kids' room last night, it looked like a complete mess. (*hit*) Their room always looks as if it _____ by a bomb.

   B: Well, your room doesn't look much better, does it?

5. **A:** I've got some great news. (*get*) It looks as if I _____ married soon. My girlfriend has finally said yes. (*fly*) I feel as if I _____.

   B: Congratulations! I couldn't be happier for you.

6. **A:** What a vain man he is! What a peacock! What arrogance!

   B: (*be*) Yes, he acts as if he _____ God's gift to women.

7. **A:** Ted, you're as pale as a ghost. (*just / see*) In fact, you look as though you _____ one. (*just / lose*) You look as if you _____ your best friend.

B: Well, as a matter of fact, I've just heard some shocking news. (*just / kill*) I feel as

if I _____ myself.

A: Please, Ted, tell me all about it. You can confide in me.

8. A: Do you think, Mom, we can have this leftover stew for dinner?

B: Oh, no, it stinks. (*go*) It smells as if it _____ bad. Let's

just throw it out.

A: Well, it's been in the fridge for more than a week.

9. A: The chicken is dry, the potatoes haven't been cooked enough and the salad

dressing tastes rancid.

B: (*like*) You sound as if you _____ this restaurant, but

don't blame me that we came here. It was your idea, not mine. (*be*) Don't act as if

it _____ my fault.

10. A: (*want*) When I ran into Mark Davis yesterday afternoon, he acted as though he

_____ to speak to me. In fact, he wouldn't even shake

my hand, nor would he even look at me straight in the face.

B: Well, he certainly must have been angry about something.

11. A: Your neighbor is such a pretentious person.

B: Isn't he? (*be*) He's always acting as though he _____ the

richest person on the block, but he hasn't got a nickel.

12. A: Yum, yum, doesn't that smell good?

B: (*cook*) Yes, it smells as though our neighbor _____

something good again. It smells like lamb stew, doesn't it?

13. A: Oh, boy, do I feel just great today. (*be*) I feel, in fact, as if the

world _____ all mine. I've finally found a good job with

decent pay.

B: (*just / inherit*) Well, you look as if you _____ a million

dollars.

14. A: Man, am I tired this evening. (*just / climb*) I feel as though I _____

_____ Mt. Everest.

B: I feel great. (*climb*) I feel as if I _____ Mt. Everest. I feel

like a million dollars.*

15. A: I just love dancing with my girlfriend. She follows so well.

*I feel wonderful.

B: (*float*) Yes, she dances as if she _____ on air.

A: When have you ever danced with her?

16. **A:** Oh, I feel a little dizzy. (*be*) I feel as though I _____ a

little drunk, in fact. But I haven't touched a drop of alcohol.

B: Now, don't be silly. You just haven't eaten anything all day.

17. **A:** This chicken tastes dreadful, doesn't it? Ech!

B: (*fry*) Yes, it tastes as if it _____ in rancid oil, doesn't it?

It smells it, too.

18. **A:** Gosh, I'm tired. (*put through*) I feel as if I _____ a

wringer.

B: So do I. Let's take a break.

☐ 6.26 Clauses of Opinion with *As If* and *As Though*

1.   Adverb **clauses of opinion** (or **clauses of manner**) are introduced by the subordinate conjunctions *as if* and *as though*. If we feel our opinion is true or will probably come true, we use the customary tenses; for example, we use the present tense for present time, the future tense for future time and the past tense or *would* for past time:

> She acts *as if* she's tired, and she should be; she's worked hard today.
>
> My, what dark clouds those are! It looks *as though* we'll have rain soon, doesn't it?
>
> When I got home last night, it looked *as if* we *would* have rain, and we did. It rained all night, in fact.
>
> When I last spoke to him, he sounded *as though* he *was* angry with me, and it turned out that he was.

The modals *may* and *might* also occur in such clauses:

> She acts *as if* she *may* (*might*) go out with me, but I'm not sure.
> Last night it looked *as though* it *might* snow, but it just rained.

2.   Clauses of opinion almost always follow nonaction verbs such as *act, sound, feel, taste* and *smell:*

> **A:** What a beautiful day! Oh, isn't everything just great?
> **B:** My, you certainly *sound as if* you're happy.
> **A:** The baby *smells as if* he's just had his bath.
> **B:** He has, and he had a lot of fun playing in the water. Didn't you, you sweet little thing?

3.   We frequently use nonaction verbs with the preposition *like* with nouns or possessive nouns and pronouns:

> **A:** The baby *looks like* her *mother.*
> **B:** Yes, but her eyes *look like* her *father's,* don't they?
> **A:** His girlfriend *acts like* a princess.
> **B:** Well, he *acts like* a big shot all the time, too.

However, in informal usage we often replace *as if* and *as though* with *like* to introduce clauses of opinion:

> A: Oh, I can barely lift up my feet.
> B: My, you look *like* you're tired.
>
> A: It's gotten so dark so quickly. It looks *like* we'll be having rain any minute now.
> B: Yes, it looks *like* we won't be playing baseball today.

Though it is quite common in everyday speech and writing, strict grammarians consider this use of the preposition *like* as a subordinate conjunction inappropriate in educated speech and formal writing.

4.   Most often we use *as if* and *as though* to introduce clauses that express something that is contrary to fact or reality. The verbs in these clauses take the same form as verbs following *if* in unreal conditions:

> He acts *as if* he *were* a big success, but he's just pretending; actually he's just a big failure.
>
> She looks *as though* she *had* a problem, but she doesn't; she only wants our sympathy.
>
> They act *as though* they *had just won* the lottery, but they don't have a dime in the bank.

7

Complex Sentences: Subordinate Conjunctions and Adjective Clauses

❑ 7.1 *Who* and *That*

Combine each pair of sentences so that the second sentence will become an adjective clause. Use *who* and *that* as subjects. You may do the exercise as shown in the example, or you may use a separate sheet of paper.

Example

A: The person ~~will make millions. He or she~~ invents a new and better mousetrap.* [*who* above "will make millions"; *will make millions* added at end]

B: Well, there are some mice in the kitchen. ~~They~~ need to be caught. ~~And†~~ I have a good trap. ~~It~~ will catch them. [*that* inserted; *that* inserted]

1. A: I've got a darling little dog. He's always hiding my slippers. He's also got a bark. It gets on my nerves.

   B: I've got a cat in my house. She's always scratching the furniture. But she's got a personality. It'll charm you.

2. A: I had a teacher last semester. She had been my father's teacher. Also, she has a daughter. She's my girlfriend now.

   B: Well, I've got a teacher now. She was my grandmother's teacher.

*The symbol ℮ means delete.
†A diagonal slash through a letter means it should be a small (lowercase) letter.

193

3. **A:**   I'm in love with a person. This person doesn't love me.

   B: You must find a relationship. It's more balanced.

4. **A:**   Students don't get good grades. They don't study.

   B: Yes, those students do much better. They do the homework.

5. **A:**   People have little love for themselves. They have little love for others.

   B: Yes, people hate themselves. People hate others.

6. **A:**   What's in the box? It's lying on the kitchen table.

   B: Lobsters. A friend of mine sent them to me. She lives in Maine. She and her husband have a company. It ships lobsters all over the world.

7. **A:**   A person in the army won't do well. He or she can't obey orders. A man or woman must be highly disciplined. He or she is fighting in this army.

   B: Yes, but an army doesn't fight well. It doesn't eat well. This army serves food. It isn't fit for a dog.

8. **A:**   The horses are wild. They live on our ranch in Wyoming.

   B: Well, some of the people are wild, too. They live in my town. A man or woman won't do well in this city. He or she can't get along with many different types of people.

❑ 7.2   *Who* and *That* as Subjects of Adjective Clauses

1.   An **adjective clause** is a dependent clause that modifies a noun in the independent clause of a complex sentence. The relative pronouns *who* and *that*, functioning as subordinate conjunctions, frequently occur as subjects of adjective clauses. We usually use *who* to refer to a person and *that* to refer to an animal or a thing:

> I know *a woman who* can speak seven languages.
> They have *a dog that* is very loyal.
> We're looking for *a machine that* will make our lives easier.

2.   However, in less formal usage *that* may be used to refer to a person:

> Our candidate is a woman *who* (or *that*) will get things done.
> We've got a neighbor *who* (or *that*) plays rock-and-roll on the radio at full volume night and day.

3.   Also, we often use *who* when we are personifying animals or referring to animal pets:

> They have a mule *that* (or *who*) is very stubborn.
> She has a pet monkey *that* (or *who*) is always getting into mischief.

4. When we use *who* or *that* as the subject of an adjective clause, the word replaces the subject that originally appeared in the sentence from which we derived the clause:

> It's hard to find a teenager. *He or she* doesn't like to eat.
> It's hard to find a teenager *who* doesn't like to eat.
>
> I have an alarm clock. *It* is very loud.
> I have an alarm clock *that* is very loud.

5. We call the noun that is modified by an adjective clause the **antecedent** of that clause. Most often an adjective clause follows its antecedent directly:

> There's *the woman* who teaches our grammar class.
> I've got *a report* that needs to be read at once.

6. However, prepositional phrases sometimes follow the antecedent; then an adjective clause follows the prepositional phrase:

> He has *a picture of his wife* that he always carries in his wallet.
> We know *a man in the East* who has connections in the West.
> There are *birds in the tree* that are always singing.

7. Also, an adverb or adverbial expression of time may appear between the antecedent and the adjective clause:

> I saw a movie *yesterday* that scared the pants off me.
> We heard a sermon *a couple of days ago* that inspired us a great deal.

We may use both a prepositional phrase and an adverbial expression of time between the antecedent and the adjective clause:

> I met a woman *at a reception the other night* who reminded me of Greta Garbo.

8. Because of the need to place an adjective clause as close to its antecedent as possible, we quite often need to split the independent clause of a sentence:

> A wild duck cannot fly. It has clipped wings.
> A wild duck *that has clipped wings* cannot fly.
>
> In this city a person has no future. He or she has no friends.
> In this city a person *who has no friends* has no future.

❑ 7.3 Restrictive Versus Nonrestrictive

Combine each pair of sentences with *who, which, whose* or *that*. The second sentence will become either a restrictive or a nonrestrictive clause. Use a comma when it is needed. Use a separate sheet of paper.

Example

A: A child is not normal. He or she is never naughty.

A child who is never naughty is not normal.

B: Our child must be normal. He is often naughty.

Our child, who is often naughty, must be normal.

1. A: Walt Disney is famous all over the world. His movies have enchanted millions and millions of people.
    B: Yes, Disney was a man. He helped people to laugh.

2. A: A writer is a rare person, indeed. He or she can write a book in one draft.
   B: Charles Dickens was supposed to be able to do it. His novels are probably my most favorite of all English novels.

3. A: Christmas depresses many people. It's supposed to be the most popular holiday of the year.
   B: Yes, a lot of people are disappointed. They have great expectations for the holiday season.

4. A: Cats are more independent than dogs. They can take better care of themselves.
   B: Yes, but your apartment is full of hair. It comes from your cat. My dog is much cleaner in the house than your cat. He doesn't shed any hair.

5. A: A friend of mine does nothing but work. His sole interest is in making money. He has an appetite for money. It will never be satisfied. His greed rules his life. It will eventually drive him to an early grave.
   B: I know a person in Chicago. He's just like that.

6. A: Butter is not supposed to be good for your health. It's full of fat.
   B: I know, and eggs are my favorite breakfast food. They are not supposed to be good for your health. However, every Sunday I have eggs. They are fried in butter.

7. A: The poor are asking the government for a better deal. Their standard of living has gone down drastically. Unfortunately, the government can't do anything about the problem. It doesn't have any money. The money isn't coming in anymore. It used to come in from the oil fields. The country is now poor. It used to be one of the richest in the world.
   B: Yes, and the rich are fleeing the country. They have bled the country dry. They are the people. They are responsible for this disaster.

8. A: Alonso Greppo has to work under intense pressure. His boss keeps her eyes on him like a hawk. She's got eyes. They're like radar. And she has a tongue. It never stops wagging.
   B: Yes, but he's got a job. It pays a lot of dough.*

❑ 7.4 Restrictive Versus Nonrestrictive Adjective Clauses; *Which* Versus *That; Whose*

1. There are two types of adjective clauses: **restrictive** and **nonrestrictive**. A restrictive clause restricts or singles out the antecedent in the independent clause of a sentence; it may refer to *some* of a class. A nonrestrictive clause does not restrict or single out; it may refer to *all* of a class. Compare the following:

Restrictive (Some)	Nonrestrictive (All)
The children *who are poor* must be helped.	The children, *who are poor*, must be helped.
The machines *that are broken* must be repaired.	The machines, *which are broken*, must be repaired.

We never use commas with a restrictive clause; with a nonrestrictive clause we always do.

2. Often, when we omit a restrictive clause from a sentence, the true meaning of the statement is lost:

*Money.

Restrictive (Necessary)	**False Statement**
People *who have no tongue* cannot speak.	People . . . cannot speak.
Children *who are honest* don't lie.	Children . . . don't lie.

We may frequently omit a nonrestrictive clause from a sentence because the truth of the statement is not lost:

Nonrestrictive (Unnecessary)	**True Statement**
People, *who can sometimes be difficult,* are usually nice.	People . . . are usually nice.
Children, *who are little people,* must be shown respect.	Children . . . must be shown respect.

 3.   We never use the relative pronoun *that* to introduce nonrestrictive clauses; we use the relative pronoun *which*, which can refer to places, animals or things:

> A giraffe, *which* is the tallest of all existing animals, does not do well in a cold climate.

> My watch, *which* is an antique, keeps perfect time. It was made in Switzerland, *which* is famous for making watches.

Or *which* can refer to groups of people (but never to an individual person):

> The class, *which* started in the middle of January, has made a great deal of progress.
> The crowd, *which* had become violent, suddenly broke down the police barricades.

 4.   We may also use *which* to introduce restrictive clauses; however, its use can be rather formal in tone, and it can look and sound clumsy and unnatural:

> I'm looking for a parrot *that* (sometimes *which*) doesn't speak.
> We like coffee *that* (sometimes *which*) is strong and very hot.

 5.   When we use the relative pronoun *whose* to introduce a restrictive or a nonrestrictive clause, the word is always followed by a noun. *Whose* may refer to animals:

> My dog, *whose tail* is always wagging, is a cheerful fellow.
> Dogs *whose noses* are warm are not well.

Whose may also refer to individual people:

> A person, *whose name* I can't remember, inquired after you.

> A person *whose reputation* is not good will do poorly in this town. Everybody knows everyone here.

And *whose* may refer to groups of people:

> People *whose last names* begin with A always get their gas and electric bills first.
> Some people, *whose addresses* I no longer have, have recently sent me postcards.

 6.   Frequently, nonrestrictive clauses provide extra information that we can leave in or out of a sentence:

> My mother (, *who is an excellent card player,*) plays contract bridge from morning to night. She's a fanatic.

> The Empire State Building (, *which is no longer the tallest building in the world,*) is still probably the most popular building in New York City for tourists to see and visit.

 7.   When the antecedent of an adjective clause is the name of a person, the name of a place or the name of a geographical location, the adjective clause that follows is usually nonrestrictive. The clause is only added information:

Albert Einstein (, *who is recognized as one of the greatest physicists of all time,*) received the Nobel Prize for physics in 1921.

Los Angeles (, *which is jammed with cars all the time,*) is not for people who don't like to drive.

The North Pole (, *which is at the top of the world,*) is a cold and inhospitable place.

8. When an antecedent is preceded by an adjective, which restricts or singles out the antecedent, a nonrestrictive adjective clause usually follows. Again, the clause is only added information:

A beautiful woman (, *who had arrived late,*) walked gracefully into the reception hall.

A lovely-sounding piece of music (, *which I had never heard before,*) was being played by the orchestra.

9. When a noun subject before the verb *be* and a noun after the verb refers to the same person, the second noun is called the **subjective complement**. For example:

Margo Channing [subject] was an *actress* [subjective complement].
Our daughter [subject] is a medical *student* [subjective complement].

In such sentences, we usually put an adjective clause after the noun subject:

Margo Channing, *who was an old friend of mine,* was an actress.
Our daughter *who is living in Chicago* is a medical student.

❑ 7.5 Restrictive Versus Nonrestrictive Adjective Clauses

Using *who, whom, which, whose* or *that*, combine any pair of sentences that you can. Practice omitting relative pronouns when you can. Use a separate sheet of paper.

Example

A: Hi, what's up?
B: I'm reading a letter. I can't believe it.

I'm reading a letter (that) I can't believe.

1. A: Who's the letter from?
    B: It's from a woman. I met her in Miami Beach last winter.

2. A: Grandma, who gave you this beautiful art book?
    B: A man gave that book to me almost sixty years ago. I can't remember his name now. He was a man. I knew him while I was at the university. He was a man. I loved him.

3. A: The gown was not appropriate for the occasion. The First Lady wore the gown to the reception yesterday evening.
    B: I disagree; I thought it was lovely. And the jewelry was lovely. She wore it. And the suit was smashing. She wore it at this morning's press conference.
    C: And the hat was so cute. She had it on. And the purse was just right. She was carrying it.
    D: Oh, yes, the First Lady has impeccable taste. All the clothes are outstanding. She wears them.

4. A: Have you gotten an answer from your friends in Paris?

   B: No, not yet. My letter probably hasn't been received yet. I sent it only a couple of days ago. Letters usually take a week. I send them to Paris.

5. A: His excellent educational background is apparent in his speech and writing. He received it at the best British schools.

   B: He reminds me of a person. I knew him in London years ago.

   A: His wife has also had the same type of education. He married her a couple of years ago.

6. A: The minister of our church is doing a good job. Everyone respects him. His sermons are so inspiring. Everyone in the congregation loves them. And his wife has done so much for the children's program. Everyone adores her.

   B: Well, we have a minister. No one respects him. In fact, he's a man. Everyone in the congregation dislikes him.

7. A: Sir, this car is the finest in the world. You're now driving it. Why don't you buy it? It's a car. You'll love it.

   B: Ha, ha, ha. A Rolls-Royce is a car for the rich. No one in my town owns a Rolls-Royce. I'm going to get a Ford. I can afford to own a Ford.

8. A: The rock star Glory Power has millions of fans. I love his voice. His shows are fabulous. I've seen them many times.

   B: Yes, and all his records are great. I play them all the time.

   A: Me, too. And his band is so great. I just love it.

❑ 7.6 Relative Pronouns as Objects of Verbs; *Whom*

1. In an adjective clause a relative pronoun may be used as the object of a verb:

   > The lecture lasted three hours. No one understood *it*.
   >
   > The lecture, *which no one understood*, lasted three hours.
   >
   > Those students will please come to the front of the room. I am going to call *their names*.
   >
   > Those students *whose names* I am going to call will please come to the front of the room.

2. *Whom*, the object form of *who*, refers only to an individual person:

   > She wants to marry the man. She loves *the man*.
   > She wants to marry the man *whom* she loves.
   >
   > The tenor had the voice of an angel. I'd never heard *the tenor* before.
   > The tenor, *whom* I'd never heard before, had the voice of an angel.

3. In restrictive adjective clauses, *that* can replace *which* or *whom:*

   > These are the things. I bought *these things* yesterday.
   > These are the things *that* (or *which*) I bought yesterday.
   >
   > I learned a lot from the lawyer. I consulted *the lawyer*.
   > I learned a lot from the lawyer *that* (or *whom*) I consulted.

4. In nonrestrictive adjective clauses, *that* cannot replace *which* or *whom:*

   > My company has a fine product. I'm proud to represent *it*.
   > My company, *which* (never *that*) I'm proud to represent, has a fine product.

My psychiatrist charges a great deal. I visit *him* twice a week.
My psychiatrist, *whom* (never *that*) I visit twice a week, charges a great deal.

5. In less formal usage, we may change *whom* to *who:*

She's going to marry a man *who* (or *whom*) she's never met.
His wife, *who* (or *whom*) I don't know, is his second cousin.

6. When a relative pronoun is the object of a restrictive adjective clause, we may omit the word, except for *whose:*

The people were perfectly charming. I met *them* last night.
The people (*who[m]*) I met last night were perfectly charming.

The presents were much appreciated. I gave *them*.
The presents (*which*) I gave were much appreciated.

The fireworks were spectacular. We saw *them* on July 4th.
The fireworks (*that*) we saw on July 4th were spectacular.

7. We cannot omit a relative pronoun from a nonrestrictive clause:

My telegram hasn't been received. I sent *it* a week ago.
My telegram, *which* I sent a week ago, hasn't been received.

The prima ballerina was outstanding. I'd never seen her before.
The prima ballerina, *whom* I'd never seen before, was outstanding.

❑ 7.7 Restrictive Versus Nonrestrictive Adjective Clauses

Using *who, whom, whose, which* or *that,* combine any pair of sentences that you can. Practice using both formal and informal styles. Use a separate sheet of paper.

Example

A: How's your friend Andy Carter doing?
B: The company is making fantastic profits. He's working for it.

The company that he's working for is making fantastic profits.

1. A: Who's been an important person in your life, Madame Toscano?
   B: The great Madame Grimaldi has been responsible for my successful career in opera. I studied with her in Milan. Her teaching methods are superb. I have a great deal of admiration for them. She's a woman. I'm indebted to her.

2. A: Well, General, what do you have to say at this time?
   B: Our country is now free. We've fought for it long and hard. We must applaud our armed forces. We owe a debt to them.

3. A: What's wrong? You're so pale. What was that phone call about?
   B: My dear friend Laura has left me. I'm deeply in love with her.

4. A: Dr. Clark is a remarkable man. I go to him.
   B: Yes, he's a man. I've got a great deal of respect for him.

5. A: Who did Chris Dickens get married to?
   B: He married a woman. He had studied with her at the university.

6. A: Is it true what I hear about your father?

    B: Yes, he's suffering from a disease. There's no known cure for it. We're in a situation. We've got no control of it.

7. A: Who's leading our city? Is it a man? You have trust in him.

    B: The mayor is leading the city. We've got little confidence in his leadership.

8. A: Excuse me, I'd like to speak to E. K. Ewing.

    B: I'm sorry, but the gentleman no longer works for this company. You refer to him.

9. A: Why is your wife quitting her job?

    B: The conditions are making her sick. She's working under them. The man is a monster. She's working for him. The salary is a pittance. She's working for it. The office has no heat or air conditioning. She works in it.

10. A: How was the reception at the White House? You went to it.

    B: Many people had very high positions in the government. I was introduced to them. They were people. I'm very interested in their projects.

11. A: Excuse me, I'd like to get to New Jersey. What's the best way?

    B: There are two tunnels. You can go through them. There's also a bridge. You can go across it. There are also buses and trains. You can go on them. There's also a ferry. You can go on it. If you're brave, there's also the Hudson River. You can swim across it.

12. A: Hush! Don't talk with such a loud voice. The man is a spy. You're standing behind him.

    B: Don't be silly. He's a guy. I work with him.

❑ 7.8 Relative Pronouns as Objects of Prepositions

1. In adjective clauses we often use relative pronouns as the object of a preposition. In formal usage, the preposition precedes the relative pronoun:

> The person did not win the election. I voted *for her.*
> The person *for whom* I voted did not win the election.

> The president has made a mistake. We have a great deal of respect *for him.*
> The president, *for whom* we have a great deal of respect, has made a mistake.

> The office is a very relaxed place. We work in *the office.*
> The office *in which* we work is a very relaxed place.

> My parents are very generous people. I live *in their house.*
> My parents, *in whose* house I live, are very generous people.

2. In informal usage, we place the preposition at the end of the adjective clause, and we may use *who* or *that:*

> The person *whom* (or *who, that*) I voted *for* did not win.
> The president, *whom* (or *who*) we have a great deal of respect *for,* has made a mistake.
> The office *which* (or *that*) we work *in* is a relaxed place.
> My parents, *whose house* I live *in,* are very generous people.

3. When we use a prepositional phrase or an adverbial expression of time in an adjective clause, we place it after the preposition:

> The person whom I voted for *in the last election* did not win.

> John James, whom I traveled with *in Europe a couple of years ago,* is now living in Hong Kong.

4. With restrictive adjective clauses, we may omit the relative pronoun:

> He's the man. I spoke to him at the post office.
> He's the man (*who*[m] or *that*) I spoke to at the post office.
>
> She's the woman. I dream about her at night.
> She's the woman (*who*[m] or *that*) I dream about at night.

5. For many years, traditional grammarians said that we should not put a preposition at the end of a clause or a sentence. Today, however, most speakers and writers consider a preposition in such a position quite acceptable. Compare the following:

Very Formal

> The situation in our European office, *in which* I am very interested, must be discussed at tomorrow's meeting. I have information *about which* no one knows.

Informal

> The situation in our European office, *which* I am very interested *in*, must be discussed at tomorrow's meeting. I have information no one knows *about*.

❑ 7.9 Pronouns as Antecedents; Reviewing Articles and Prepositions

Using *who, whom, which* or *that*, compose a sentence from each set of cue words. You may follow the example and write on this page, or you may use a separate sheet of paper.

Example

A: Who's created this terrible situation?

B: I'm sorry.   it / ~~be~~ *is* / I / ~~be~~ *who am* / to blame.

1. A: You stole my money, not your roommate.

    B: No, no, no.   it / be / she / take / your wallet / not / I

2. A: I should sit in the best seat at the restaurant this evening.

    B: What on earth for?

    A: well / it / be / I / pay / meal / it?

3. A: Most students are studying hard, but some aren't.

    B: it / be / they / be / sorry / later / semester / when / they / take / final examination

4. A: So, you're the number-one man here in the office.

    B: yes / it / be / I / have / power   anyone / get / my way / be sorry / it / later   it /

    be / I / run / show

5. A: class / I / have / your attention / please?   before / final examination / begin / I /

    say / something   anyone / cheat / test / automatically / get / "F"

    B: professor / there / be / no one / this class / cheat / there?

6. A: how / be / party / last night?

    B: everything / they / serve / be / tasteless / everyone / be / there / be / little dull /

    and / nothing / happen / be / interesting

7. A: Why is she changing her phone number?

    B: there / be / someone / always / make / obscene phone calls

8. A: What's wrong?   why / you / always / scratch?

    B: there / be / something / bottom / my foot / itch / lot

9. A: So, your son is a great traveler, I hear.

    B: yes / he / be / only one / family / go / world

10. A: That fellow just won't let anyone help him, will he?

    B: yes / he / just / refuse / to listen / anyone / try / to help him

11. A: Here's the ham, ma'am.   be / there / anything else / you / need?

    B: No, thanks.   that / be / all / I / need / today

12. A: Just who's going to take control of this situation?

    B: worry / thing   it / be / I / handle / it

13. A: I'm afraid I don't have enough money to go to college.

    B: You're a smart young woman.   government scholarships / be / available / those /

    need / financial assistance

14. A: You studied French when you were in high school, didn't you?

    B: yes / but / I / forget / everything / I / learn / unfortunately

15. A: How was the lecture yesterday? What was it about?

    B: Don't ask me.   I / understand / anything / professor / talk

16. A: Who has the combination to the vault in the basement?

    B: I / be / only one / have / it   it / be / only I / have / access / family vault

☐ 7.10 Adjective Clauses Modifying Pronouns

1. In addition to nouns, subject pronouns can occur as the antecedent of an adjective clause. The verb of the adjective clause agrees in person with the antecedent. In such sentences the subject pronouns follow *it* and a form of the verb *be:*

      A: Who's committed this crime? The butler?
      B: Yes, it is *he* who *is* guilty.

      A: Just who is going to win the contest?
      B: It is *I* who *am* going to receive the first prize.

      A: Who broke this vase? Was it the children?
      B: Yes, it was *they* who knocked it over.

2. Besides subject pronouns, we use indefinite pronouns as antecedents of adjective clauses:

      A: What a problem this is!
      B: Yes, *anyone* who can solve it is a genius.

      A: What did you do yesterday?
      B: I went shopping, but *nothing* that I wanted was on sale.

      A: My father is the only *one* in my family who can play chess.
      B: Well, in my family, my father is the only *one* who can't.

3. Demonstrative pronouns also appear as antecedents:

      A: Has the food been salted?
      B: No, but there's salt on the table for *those* who desire it.

      A: What a beautiful watch!
      B: Yes, *this*, which is an heirloom, is my most prized possession.

☐ 7.11 *When* and *Where*

Using *when* or *where*, combine any pair of sentences that you can. You may do this orally or write it on a separate sheet of paper.

> *Example*

      A: July is the month. It really gets hot.

      July is the month when it really gets hot.

      B: And both my wife and I go on a vacation.

1. A: Oh, Mother, you don't ever do anything right.
    B: Oh, I don't, do I? You forget the time. I was changing your diapers. You don't remember the days. I took care of you when you were sick.

2. A: I haven't seen your brother for a long time. Where's he been?
    B: He's now living in Seattle. He's a student at the University of Washington.

3. A: 2062 is the year. Halley's comet returns.
    B: I hope I'm here when it does.

4. A: What are your plans for the time? You retire.
    B: I'm moving to the Southwest. I won't have to shovel snow.

5. **A:** I'm sorry, but I can't lend you any money.
    B: Oh, you can't, can you? Do you forget the times? I've lent you money. Don't you remember the times? You've borrowed my car.

6. **A:** You're moving to Alabama?
    B: Yes, I'm moving to Montgomery. I've already found a job.

7. **A:** Do you remember the time? You were in love the first time.
    B: Yes, it brings back painful memories.

8. **A:** San Francisco is a beautiful city. I once lived.
    B: Yes, it's a city. Beauty surrounds you everywhere.

9. **A:** In Las Vegas you can also lose a lot of money. You can win a lot of money.
    B: Listen, I lost a million when I was there last.

10. **A:** That's a great deal of cash you have there.
    B: Yes, and I'm going to put it in the bank. It'll be safe.

11. **A:** He's finally going to get married, I hear.
    B: I can't believe it. Why, he's a confirmed bachelor. The day will be a miracle. He gets married.

12. **A:** The hospital is now gone. I was born.
    B: The house is now a pet shop. I came into the world.

13. **A:** You're wasting your time and your parents' money.
    B: Oh, Grandpa, I want to have fun. You forget the time. You were a young man. This is the year. I turn 21.
    A: Yes, that is the time. Life is at its best. These are the days. One has no worries.
    B: They're also the times. One has little money. Can I borrow a few bucks?

❑ 7.12 Adjective Clauses Introduced by *When* and *Where*

1. We use *when* in an adjective clause to modify nouns that refer to time:

    I'll never forget *the night when* we danced together the first time.
    I remember well *the time when* we got lost in the forest.
    January 1, 2001 is *the day when* a new century begins.

2. We use *where* to modify nouns that refer to a place:

    They're looking for *a restaurant where* they can get good food at low prices.
    I'm going to rent *a place where* I can store things.
    We live in *Arizona, where* the sun is always shining.
    He works in *a building where* he lives.

3. *When* or *where* can be interchangeable with a preposition plus *which;* the pattern, however, is quite formal:

    This is the year *in which* (or *when*) I turn fifty.
    I'll always remember *the day on which* (or *when*) I first met you.
    The town *in which* (or *where*) I grew up was a farming community.
    The farm *on which* (or *where*) I was raised was a dairy farm.

4. On occasion *that* may replace *when* or *where:*

    We're looking for a place (*that*) we can hang out.
    This is the year (*that*) I'm getting married.

❑ 7.13 Expressions of Quantity

Supply in each blank an appropriate expression of quantity plus *whom, whose* or *which,* or *the* plus a noun plus *of* plus *which.*

(almost) all of	neither of	the bottom of
both of	(almost) none of	the cost of
each of	(only) one (two and so on) of	the purpose of
half of	(only) a few of	the title of
many of	several of	the top of
most of	some of	the value of
much of		

Example

A: Last night at the dinner party, they served three salads, *one of which* upset my stomach.

B: What a coincidence! The same thing happened to me last night.

1. A: The Netherlands, _____ is below sea level, has an elaborate system of dikes and canals.

    B: And there are a lot of windmills, _____ are no longer in use, I believe.

2. A: How's your class?

    B: I've got about sixteen classmates, _____ I like.

3. A: Ha, ha, ha.

    B: What's so funny?

    A: I've just read an article, _____ makes me laugh.

    B: What is it?

    A: "How Much Wood Would a Woodchuck Chuck If a Woodchuck Could Chuck Wood."*

4. A: Now, just what's bothering you?

    B: My neighbor, _____ problems is his alcoholic son, is always complaining to me about his family.

5. A: What's the country like?

    B: Saudi Arabia, _____ is uninhabitable desert, is a huge country. Its people, _____ are Arabs, are devout Muslims.

*An old tongue twister.

6. **A:** My son, _____ friends are single, is always running

    around to parties and different sorts of affairs.

    B: Well, my son, _____ friends are married, leads a very

    quiet life playing bridge. He and his wife are real homebodies.

7. **A:** The government has enlarged its military forces, _____ is

    to put down rebellion.

    B: This move, I believe, _____ is highly questionable, will

    cause the eventual overthrow of the government. The leaders in the government,

    _____ are crooks, should be put up against a wall and

    shot.

8. **A:** That fellow is so picky. He must have tried on at least twenty suits, _____

    _____ he liked.

    B: Yes, he's a very hard person to please.

9. **A:** My roommate, _____ ideas are very eccentric, is driving

    me up the wall. He's a real crackpot.*

    B: So is mine. You wouldn't believe some of his ideas.

10. **A:** Quick, we need a bucket. We've got a leak in the bathroom.

    B: Well, I've got a bucket, _____ leaks, however.

    A: Well, it's an emergency; we can't be picky.

11. **A:** How was the temple's dance for singles last Saturday night?

    B: Well, I met two people, _____ were attractive, intelligent,

    and looking for a long-term relationship, but I wasn't interested. I'm just a

    confirmed bachelor, I guess.

12. **A:** Why didn't you enjoy your stay in Los Angeles?

    B: I stayed with two friends, _____ has a car. You've just

    got to have wheels in L.A.

    A: How was your stay in San Francisco?

    B: Fabulous! I stayed with two friends, _____ has a boat.

13. **A:** Oh, how the government wastes money!

    B: Doesn't it? Why, they're building a dam, _____ is going

    to put this country into debt for years.

14. **A:** Have you got everything for your living room?

*Eccentric.

B: Yes, but I've got a coffee table, _____ is all scratched.

15. A: I have a drawing by Rembrandt, _____ I don't know.

B: No kidding? Shouldn't you get an appraisal? It might be worth millions.

16. A: Here's a pizza, _____ is yours.

B: Yum, yum, yummie, does that smell good!

❏ 7.14 Expressions of Quantity with Adjective Clauses

1. We may combine expressions of quantity such as *some of, most of* and *all of* with *whom, which* or *whose* to form an adjective clause. In writing, a comma is required:

> I have many friends. *All of them* are honest.
> A: Aren't you worried about keeping so much money around your house?
> B: Oh, no. I have many friends, *all of whom* are honest.
>
> They awarded three prizes. *One of them* I won.
> A: How did you do in the contest last night?
> B: They awarded three prizes, *one of which* I won.
>
> I examined a patient yesterday. *One of his problems* is the inability to sleep.
> A: Yes, Doctor, I'm very interested in sleep therapy.
> B: That's a coincidence, Doctor. I examined a patient yesterday, *one of whose problems* is the inability to sleep.

2. As an alternative to adjective clauses with *whose*, we can use *the* plus a noun plus *of* plus *which:*

> I'm reading a book. *Its title* is very strange.
> I'm reading a book *whose title* is very strange.
> I'm reading a book, **the title of which** is very strange.
>
> My neighbors have a barn. *Its side* is painted red.
> My neighbors have a barn *whose side* is painted red.
> My neighbors have a barn, **the side of which** is painted red.

8 Participial Phrases

□ 8.1 Contrasting Adjective Clauses with Participial and Appositive Phrases

Combine each following group of sentences using adjective clauses (*who, whom, whose, that, which, when* and *where*), participial phrases or appositive phrases. Use a separate sheet of paper.

Example

The Great Gatsby has been made into three movies. It is a novel. It was written by F. Scott Fitzgerald.
A: What does your *History of the Movies* have to say about *The Great Gatsby*?
B: Let's see now, what does it have to say?

The Great Gatsby, a novel written by F. Scott Fitzgerald, has been made into three movies.

1. A: The woman was my father's teacher twenty years ago. She is teaching your class.
   B: Yes, Ms. Brooks is my favorite teacher. She was my father's teacher, too.

2. A: The students get the worst grades. They don't do the homework.
   B: Yes, those aren't making much progress. They don't put any effort into their work.

3. A: Do you know or have you ever heard about John J. Withers?
   B: Oh, yes. Withers eventually became an inventor and made millions. He was rejected by every university. He had applied to them. Withers was a genius. His inventions changed the world of electronics.
   A: Oh, I didn't know he was dead.
   B: Yes, Withers died about a year ago. He was hit by a drunk driver. I went to his funeral. It was attended by thousands.

4. A: Oh, most people have some idea of what's going on in the government. They live in the nation.
   B: Yes, but the people have a better understanding of the bureaucracy. They work for the government in Washington, D.C. It is the capital.

5. A: The people will have trouble in the future. They're living in this town. They're not saving any money.

B: Well, my wife and I are two of those people. We spend all of the money. We make it. She and I can't save a dime. We have five kids to feed and clothe.

6. A: English has an alphabet. The alphabet consists of 26 letters. Five of these letters are vowels.
   B: What are the others called, Ms. Kline?
   A: Consonants.

7. A: The nicest people are living in my hometown. They are found in the world. It's the best place on the planet.
   B: How do you know? You've never been to my hometown. It is considered to be the most beautiful place in the United States.

8. A: The electric light bulb was one of the most important inventions of the nineteenth century. It was invented by Thomas Alva Edison. Edison's name is famous all over the world. It is found in almost every child's history book.
   B: What a genius!

9. A: This letter is one of my most prized possessions. It was written almost fifty years ago.
   B: Who wrote it, Grandma?
   A: A man sent it to me. I was deeply in love with him.

10. A: A person in this company won't do well. He or she doesn't have a great deal of energy and ambition.
    B: Well, boss, I'm not one of those people, am I?

11. A: William Blake could never do a selfish thing. He's a very kind and generous person. He's a man. He's known for all his charity and good will.
    B: Yes, old Bill is a great guy. He could never hurt a fly.

12. A: The food at the dinner dance was enough to feed an army. It was served in a buffet style.
    B: And the band was fantastic. It was hired for entertainment.

13. A: The furniture looks very nice. It was delivered yesterday. I have a sofa. It seats twelve people. It was made for me by one of the finest furniture shops in Italy.
    B: That must have cost you a fortune. You can't afford it.

14. A: The people in the company are getting big raises in pay. They are being assigned new jobs.
    B: That's only fair, isn't it? The new jobs require a lot more work. They're getting them.

15. A: What's an essay, Mrs. Jones?
    B: An essay is a short composition. In this composition, a writer tries to persuade a reader to accept a point of view.

16. A: What does your guidebook have to say about Pablo Picasso?
    B: Hmm, let's see. Oh, yes, here it is. Well, it says Pablo Picasso was born in Spain in 1881. He was the foremost figure in twentieth-century art. He was only 15 at the time. He was admitted to the Royal Academy of Art in Barcelona. He spent the latter part of his life in the south of France. He died there in 1977 at the age of 91.

17. A: The ostrich thinks no one can see him when he buries his head in the sand. The ostrich is the largest of all existing birds.
    B: Oh, Grandpa, that's not true, is it?

18. A: Oh, here's an interesting obituary in the *Times*.
    B: Why don't you read it to me?
    A: Carlotta Carmel died peacefully in her sleep on Sunday evening. She was known by millions of fans all over the world. The actress would never admit to her exact date

of birth. She was famous for her great beauty as well as for her fine acting ability. Miss Carmel was a top star on the stage and on the screen for more than sixty years. She was born and raised in New York City. The actress leaves no survivors. She never married.

B: Why, I've never heard of her. Are you making that up?

❏ 8.2 Reducing Adjective Clauses to Participial and Appositive Phrases

1. An adjective clause always contains a subject and a verb:

> The children *who are playing in the playground* are kids from the neighborhood.

A **participial phrase,** which is a **reduction** of an adjective clause, has neither a subject nor a verb:

> The children . . . *playing in the playground* are kids from the neighborhood.

2. Only when an adjective clause has a relative pronoun as its subject, can we reduce the clause to a participial phrase:

> Something *that* is cooking on the stove is smelling up the house.
> Something . . . *cooking on the stove* is smelling up the house.

> The people *who* are living in my town couldn't be nicer.
> The people . . . *living in my town* couldn't be nicer.

3. When a relative pronoun is the object of an adjective clause, the clause cannot be reduced:

> The things (*that*) I bought were all on sale.   [no reduction]
> The students (*whom*) I know are lots of fun.   [no reduction]

4. With a verb phrase in an adjective clause containing a form of the verb *be,* we omit the relative pronoun and the *be* form of the verb to make a participial phrase:

> The butterflies *that are* found in the Amazon are magnificent.
> The butterflies . . . *found in the Amazon* are magnificent.

> The people *who are* living in my town are a hard-working lot.
> The people . . . *living in my town* are a hard-working lot.

We can reduce the participial phrase to an adjective phrase:

> The butterflies . . . *in the Amazon* are magnificent.
> The people . . . *in my town* are a hard-working lot.

And we can reduce the adjective phrase to a single adverb:

> The butterflies . . . *there* are magnificent.
> The people . . . *here* are a hard-working lot.

5. We retain *being,* the passive auxiliary, in continuous participial phrases:

> The homework *that is being assigned now* is due tomorrow.
> The homework . . . *being assigned now* is due tomorrow.

> The men *who are being executed* are innocent of any crime.
> The men . . . *being executed* are innocent of any crime.

6. *Not* precedes the participle in negative participial phrases:

> The accused *who are not found guilty* will go free at once.
> The accused . . . *not found* guilty will go free at once.

The players *who are not practicing now* will be sorry later.
The players . . . *not practicing* now will be sorry later.

7. We sometimes derive *-ing* participial phrases from verbs in adjective clauses that do not contain a form of the verb *be:*

These are diagrams that *explain* different parts of speech.
These are diagrams . . . *explaining* different parts of speech.

Anyone who *doesn't want* to do homework doesn't have to do it.
Anyone . . . *not wanting* to do homework doesn't have to do it.

I'm looking for a school that *holds* evening classes.
I'm looking for a school . . . *holding* evening classes.

8. A participial phrase can be restrictive or nonrestrictive depending on the adjective clause from which it is derived:

Your friends *who are playing in the front yard* are disturbing your father, *who is trying to sleep upstairs.*

Your friends *playing in the front yard* are disturbing your father, *sleeping upstairs.*

My roommate, *who is working all the time,* isn't around much.

My roommate, *working all the time,* isn't around much.

Note: When an adjective clause requires a comma, a participial phrase derived from that clause also requires a comma.

9. Many nonrestrictive adjective clauses can be reduced to **appositive phrases:**

Barbara, *who is tall and thin,* is a fashion model.

Barbara, *tall and thin,* is a fashion model.

Thomas Jefferson, *who was one of the writers of the United States Constitution,* was born and bred in Virginia.

Thomas Jefferson, *one of the writers of the United States Constitution,* was born and bred in Virginia.

❑ 8.3 Participial Phrases Derived from Adverb Time Clauses

When you can, change an adverb time clause to a participial clause.

Example

While ~~Tom was~~ shaving, ~~he~~ Tom was thinking about the night before.

1. Before I took this course, I'd never studied so much grammar.

2. Her husband was working in the garden while she was napping.

3. Since I was told the news, I have been terribly upset.

4. His parents were living in Mexico while he was studying at school.

5. After the children had dinner, they sat down and did their homework.

6. She'd studied a lot of English before she started this course.

7. Since I met my girlfriend, my roommate has been very jealous of me.

Now, using *since, until, while, before, after* or *when,* supply in each blank an appropriate participial phrase.

Example

A: (*tell*) At the hospital last night, _after being told_ the news, the family was in a state of shock.

B: (*hear*) Yes, they all started to cry _after hearing_ it.

8. **A:** (*do*) I never listen to the radio _____ my homework. I find it too distracting.

    B: (*work*) I'm the same way; I must have peace and quiet _____ at my desk, or else I can't concentrate.

9. **A:** (*travel*) _____ in India, I'd never been in such an exotic setting. (*be*) _____ there for a year, I found out a whole lot about myself.

    B: (*hear*) You know, _____ your stories about India, I'm just dying to go to find out for myself.

10. **A:** (*come*) _____ to New York, I'd never ridden on a subway before.

    B: (*come*) Nor had I, but _____ here, I have had to spend a lot of time on the train coming home and going to work.

11. **A:** (*become*) _____ a mother, Maxine has been extremely happy.

    B: (*have*) Yes, she's become more contented _____ a child.

12. **A:** (*make*) _____ a long distance call, it's cheaper to dial the call yourself.

    B: (*call*) Yes, it's also cheaper _____ at night.

13. **A:** (*turn*) _____ fifty, Gregory Boyd's attitude toward life has changed, hasn't it?

    B: (*hit*) Yes, _____ fifty, he feels life has passed him by. His attitude has become very negative.

14. **A:** Why do you have a bandage on your finger?

    B: (*look for*) _____ a pair of scissors in a kitchen drawer, I accidentally cut myself.

15. A: (*elect*) _____, the president has made many fundamental

changes in our society.

B: Yes, some of them are good, but most of them are bad.

16. A: (*enter*) _____the university, she'd never been a particularly

good student.

B: (*start*) Nor had I; however, _____ my studies here, my study

habits have improved a great deal.

17. A: (*fall in*) _____ love, Rod had always been a reckless and

carefree young man; he was always running around.

B: He's now a completely different person, isn't he?

❑ 8.4 Reducing Adverb Time Clauses to Participial Phrases

1. Adverb time clauses may also be reduced to participial phrases:

a. When a verb phrase is continuous, we omit the subject and the auxiliary verb *be:*

When *you are* using electrical appliances, you must be careful.
When using electrical appliances, you must be careful.

She noticed a little bit of gray while *she was* combing her hair.
She noticed a little bit of gray *while combing* her hair.

b. In passive continuous verb phrases, we retain the passive auxiliary:

While *I was* being examined, I wasn't nervous at all.
While being examined, I wasn't nervous at all.

She was crying while *she was* being interrogated.
She was crying *while being interrogated.*

c. If a verb phrase is not continuous, we omit the subject and change the verb to a present participle:

Since *I graduated* from the university, I've been working my head off.
Since graduating from the university, I've been working my head off.

He's been unhappy since *he married* his wife.
He's been unhappy *since marrying his wife.*

After *I get up,* I always make my bed.
After getting up, I always make my bed.

2. In order for us to reduce an adverb time clause to a participial phrase, the subject in the time clause must be the same as the subject in the independent clause. The participial phrase modifies the subject in the independent clause:

Before *she* does anything, *she* will talk to her lawyer.
Before doing anything, she will talk to her lawyer.

He felt better after *he* took his medicine.
He felt better *after taking his medicine.*

3. The adverb time clauses in the following sentences cannot be reduced because the two clauses have different subjects:

The women in the audience were booing while *the men* were applauding.
While *he* is taking it easy, *she* is working her darned head off.

4. When we reduce an adverb time clause containing a noun subject, the noun subject becomes the subject of the independent clause:

> While *my parents* were living in Hawaii, *they* were working on a sugar plantation.
> *While living in Hawaii, my parents* were working on a sugar plantation.

> Since *his sister* got married, *she's* been living away from home.
> *Since getting married, his sister* has been living away from home.

❑ 8.5 Contrasting Participial Phrases

Supply in each blank an appropriate participle made out of the base form given in parentheses.

Example

A: Oh, come on, tell me how you did on the test.

B: (*take*) After _____*taking*_____ it, I felt as though I'd done O.K.
(*study*) However, *not having studied* _____ much, I'm not at all sure how well I did.

1. A: Just how do you know so much about insects, Grandpa?

    B: (*work*) Well, honey, _____ in a garden for more than

    sixty years, I have learned a great deal about them.

2. A: (*hang*) What do you think of the painting _____ over

    the sofa? Do you like it?

    B: (*never / study*) Frankly, _____ much about art, I really

    can't make such a judgment.

    A: No, I don't mean that. How does it appeal to you emotionally?

    B: (*speak*) Well, frankly _____, I think it stinks.

3. A: Why didn't you go on a vacation last summer?

    B: (*have*) My mother, _____ an operation, was still quite

    ill, and I wanted to stay home and take care of her.

4. A: Who's that?

    B: Who?

    A: (*dress / wear*) The man _____ in a gray suit

    and _____ dark glasses,

    (*stand*) _____ in the ticket line.

    B: Why, I can't believe it. It's Rob Rovere, the actor.

A: Oh, he's so cute! He's so adorable!

B: Come on, let's get his autograph.

5. A: Why did the two of you go to Asia last winter?

B: (*already / be*) _____ everywhere in Europe, the Middle East, Africa and Latin America, we wanted to go somewhere different.

6. A: How's your friend Betty Blue doing?

B: Not too well. (*have*) She's new in this town and, _____ many friends, she's a little lonely. (*be*) And I, _____ quite shy, (*live*) know few people _____ in this city I can introduce her to.

7. A: What do you think of that author's new book?

B: (*read*) _____ it yet, I can't say. (*read*) However, _____ all his other books, I think this one will also be good.

8. A: Did you enjoy your trip to India?

B: (*never / be*) Yes, _____ there before, I found it different and exciting. (*already / be*) But my husband, _____ there twice with his second wife, was rather bored, I'm afraid.

A: In India?

B: Yes, even in India. (*be / do*) My husband, _____ everywhere and _____ everything, is quite easily bored.

9. A: How did you do at Berkeley in your first year?

B: (*never / expose*) _____ before to such an intellectual environment, I just couldn't take the constant pressure. It was a mind-boggling experience.

10. A: (*play*) While _____ cards, why do you always get so nervous?

B: (*play*) _____ more times than I care to remember, I always get butterflies* in my stomach as soon as I sit down to play a game of cards.

*A sick feeling.

A: What game do you like best?

B: (*play*) _____ them all, I still think poker is the best.

11. A: How do you like the length of my hemline, Roberto?

B: (*now / wear*) Mom, the hemline _____ by fashionable

women is much shorter than that.

A: I know, but I hate to show my ugly knees.

B: (*look at*) Listen, Mother, _____ the legs of many

women in my time, (*be*) _____ the young and healthy

man I am, I can assure you that you have lovely-looking legs.

A: (*talk*) Roberto, _____ like that, you sound just like

your father, a big flatterer.

12. A: How are you doing in school this semester?

B: (*take*) Well, _____ everything into consideration, I'm

doing O.K. (*be*) However, _____ sick quite a bit this

semester, I'm not getting much above a "C+" in any of my courses. (*have*)

Also, _____ much of a head for math, I'm doing very

poorly in algebra.

13. A: How are things going these days?

B: Not so hot. (*still / make*) My wife and I, _____ any

money in our new business, haven't got a cent to our name.

14. A: What did you do last night?

B: (*feel*) _____ very well, I went to bed early. (*probably /

sleep*) _____ more than 12 hours, I feel like a million

dollars this morning.

A: Hey, great!

15. A: Was last night the first time you'd ever tasted snake?

B: (*not ever / eat*) Yes, and _____ it before, I didn't really

know what to expect.

A: How did you like it?

B: (*eat*) It was O.K., but while _____ it, I just couldn't

get the image of snakes, which I hate, out of my mind.

16. A: How did the meeting go yesterday?

B: (*late / arrive*) Unfortunately, _____, I missed most of it.

☐ 8.6 Perfect Participles

1.   We form a **perfect participle** with (*not*) plus *having* plus (*been*) plus a past participle. The time expressed by a perfect participle is before the time that is expressed by the verb in an independent clause:

> The judge, *having made* a decision at last, *was relieved.*
>
> Their children, *having been trained* well, *behave* like little angels.
>
> The students *not having received* an application *will please go* to the registrar's office.

2.   A **continuous perfect participle** is formed with (*not*) plus *having* plus *been* plus an *-ing* participle:

> Tom Jones, *having been running* after women for years, finally wore down and lost all of his energy.
>
> My husband and I, *not having been living* together for years, know very little about each other.

3.   If the verb in an independent clause expresses present or future time, a perfect participle has the meaning of the present perfect tense:

> The soldier, *having served* (who *has served*) his country loyally, *is* proud.
>
> This refrigerator, *having been reconditioned* (which *has been reconditioned*), *will last* years.

4.   If the verb in an independent clause expresses past time, a perfect participle has the meaning of the past perfect tense:

> The woman, *having been bribed* (who *had been bribed*) a million, informed on her friends.
>
> The boy, *having eaten* (who *had eaten*) too many apples, got sick to his stomach.

5.   Participial phrases that are derived from adjective clauses are most often put after the noun being modified:

> *A person* hoping to make a million had better work hard.
> *The player,* hoping to catch the ball, ended up in the bleachers.
> *The woman,* not having made a reservation, couldn't get a room at the inn.

6.   However, a nonrestrictive participial phrase may also occur in the initial position of a sentence. The subject of the independent clause is the noun that is modified by the participial phrase. A comma is required:

> *Having been written in an easy-to-read style,* **the book** was an instant success with the reading public.
>
> *Not having a college degree,* **her friend** can't find a good job.
>
> *Being a liberal,* **I** most often vote for a democrat.

7.   We must always have a subject in the independent clause that can be used as the subject of the participial phrase; otherwise, the sentence will be confusing. When this confusion occurs, we call the participial phrase a **dangling modifier:**

> *Walking along the street,* there was a car accident.   [Was the car walking along the street?]
>
> *Looking out the window,* there were birds.   [Were the birds looking out the window?]

To clarify these sentences, we could make these changes:

Walking along the street, *I* saw a car accident.

Looking out the window, *she* saw birds in the sky.

8. Once in a while, we use a certain type of participial phrase called a **sentence modifier;** that is, the phrase modifies an entire sentence and does not require a subject:

> *Taking everything into consideration,* the situation in our country isn't as bad as the media say it is.
>
> *Frankly speaking,* that type of painting doesn't appeal to me.
>
> *Considering everything,* life isn't so bad.
>
> *Thinking it over,* a nice leg of lamb or pork instead of a ham might be better for Easter dinner this year.

9. A nonrestrictive participial phrase derived from an adjective clause is also sometimes placed at the end of a sentence. A comma is usually required in writing, and we use a pause in speech:

> All of us were extremely relieved, [pause] *having received news from the battlefront at last.*
>
> The children were thrilled, [pause] *having seen Santa Claus get into a taxi.*
>
> The manuscript is much better, [pause] *having been rewritten.*
>
> The patient seems to have more energy, [pause] *taking vitamins.*

However, sometimes a participial phrase is more closely related to the independent clause, and we omit the comma or the pause:

> David is out in the garage *working on his car.*
>
> Daniel came into the house *carrying a bunch of wood.*

10. We may use a nonrestrictive participial phrase to express result:

> Old Moneybags saved every penny he ever earned, [the result] *becoming the wealthiest man in the county.*
>
> It's been raining for several weeks now, [the result] *leaving the countryside lush and green.*

Or we can use it to express cause:

> At the end of the Wagnerian opera, the audience was exhausted, [why] *having been sitting in their seats for five and a half hours.*
>
> The children aren't at all hungry, [why] *having eaten so much ice cream and cake at the birthday party.*

11. With participial phrases derived from adverb time clauses, we can express time. Note that we may omit the subordinate conjunctions:

> *(While) Driving along the highway,* I saw a great many hitchhikers trying to hitch a ride west.
>
> *(When) Speaking to the customers,* try to be as polite as you can.

When we use *after* with a participial phrase, we may use an *-ing* participle or a perfect participle:

> *(After) Losing (or Having lost) twenty pounds,* the woman looked ten years younger.

12. Adverbs of manner may occur at either the beginning or the end of a participial phrase:

> **Hurriedly** *leaving the room* (or *Leaving the room* **hurriedly**), she slipped and sprained her ankle.
>
> **Completely** *filling his glass* (or *Filling his glass* **completely**), he continued drinking.

13. We always place the adverbs of time, *early* and *late*, at the end of a participial phrase:

> We missed the best part of the show, *having arrived* **late.**
> *Having left the house* **early,** I wasn't able to see my wife.

We may use *now* at either the beginning or the end:

> The boy **now** *playing in the garden* (*playing in the garden* **now**) reminds me of my son when he was a boy.

14. With perfect participles, we can put frequency adverbs before or after the auxiliary *having:*

> *Never having* (or *Having* **never**) *eaten caviar,* I was most eager to try it.
>
> *Always having* (or *Having* **always**) *had the best,* she's become quite willful and spoiled.
>
> *Already having* (or *Having* **already**) *eaten a huge meal,* I didn't want to have anything to eat at the reception.
>
> *Recently having* (or *Having* **recently**) *spent a great deal of money,* she's not spending much money now.

With *not ever*, we may put *ever* after or before *having:*

> *Not* **ever** *having* (or *Not having* **ever**) *been in love before,* the young man doesn't understand the sensation.

15. We often use the adverbs *still* and *yet* in participial phrases:

> **Still** *not being able to speak and write English well,* the student wishes to continue her studies at the institute.
>
> The young man doesn't know much about his job, *not having had much experience* **yet.**

❏ 8.7 Participial Phrases Following *Do, Lose, Spend, Waste, Make* and *Have*

Supply in each blank an appropriate *-ing* participle of your choice.

> ***Example***
>
> A: If I'd had some money on me, I could have made a million *betting* on that game.
>
> B: Oh, please stop your wishful thinking.

1. A: Everyone I know has a hard time _____ a job.

    B: Oh, come on now, not everyone. I certainly don't, do I?

2. A: A lot of money in our city has been spent _____ new schools for our children.

    B: And a lot more should be spent.

3. A: Yes, I have an easy job; all of the work is done _____.

    B: Well, then you don't have to wear out any shoe leather.

4. **A:** Listen, kids, don't waste any time _____ the kitchen and the bathroom.

    B: Oh, Mom, you're a real slave driver.

5. **A:** We had a lot of fun in Europe _____ on the trains.

    B: Yes, isn't it a great way to meet people?

6. **A:** I'm certainly having a hard time _____ my income taxes this year.

    B: Isn't everyone? Who designs those darned tax forms?

7. **A:** More than twenty years were spent _____ that pyramid.

    B: Well, having worked like a slave all my life, I sympathize with the poor people who had to build it.

8. **A:** You know, you're wasting a lot of energy _____ all those bright lights.

    B: Yes, but it's worth it. I like lots of bright lights.

    A: But it's such a waste.

Now supply in each blank a verb phrase plus a noun object plus an *-ing* participle.

Example

A: We just had a terrible time in Europe.

B: What! (*have / a wonderful time / travel*) You *should have had a wonderful time traveling* in Europe; it's just fabulous.

A: Well, it was always raining, and my travel mate and I were always fighting.

9. **A:** Thank God we didn't run out of gas while we were driving across the desert.

    B: Well, we almost did. (*have / a hard time / find*) If we had run out,

    we _____ a gas station

    that was open, since it was in the middle of the night.

10. **A:** Are you serious? You and your wife don't have any savings?

    B: No, not at all. (*spend / all our money / educate*) For the past five years,

    we _____ our three kids,

    all of whom are still at the university.

11. **A:** Grandma, tell me more about your childhood. I love hearing about it.

    B: (*have / a lot of fun / work*) Well, I _____

    _____ in the garden with my mother, your great-grandmother.

12. **A:** Why doesn't your boyfriend ever have any money?

    B: (*lose / all his money / gamble*) Well, he _____

    _____ on stupid investments; also, he's just a spendthrift.

13. A: Yes, sir, that's my motto.

     B: What is?

     A: (*never waste / time / run after*) _____

         rainbows in the sky.

14. A: How come your old boss is in jail?

     B: (*make / millions of dollars / cheat*) Well, he _____

         _____ the government for years, but he finally got caught.

❑ 8.8 Participial Phrases Following Certain Verbs

1.   With certain verbs, we can use *-ing* participial phrases for an adverbial function, in addition to an adjectival function, because they may tell *how*. When we do this, the subject of the verb in an independent clause is also the subject of the participial phrase. We do not need a comma and do not pause in speech:

> **One of us** won a lot of money *betting on that soccer game.*
> **Grandma** does her sewing *sitting in the sun room.*

2.   The noun that precedes the participial phrase is the object of the verb:

> All of us *lost **money*** working on the company's project.
> That student *spends **little time*** rewriting her compositions.

3.   We may place a prepositional phrase between the object and the participial phrase:

> Everyone wastes a great deal of time *at the office* goofing off at the water cooler or at the coffee machine.
> Keiko Uno does all her work *at the store* standing up on three-inch spike heels.

4.   Such sentences often contain passive verb phrases; in this case, the participial phrase follows a verb directly, and it refers to the "unmentioned performer" who performed the action, not to the subject of the sentence:

> My folks spend a lot of time *keeping the house and garden up.*
> A lot of time **is spent** *keeping the house and garden up.*
>
> You're wasting time *worrying about things that can't be changed.*
> Time **is being wasted** *worrying about things that can't be changed.*

5.   We often use the verb *have* plus certain nouns in this pattern:

> He's been having *a hard time* getting used to this place.
> All of us had *a great deal of fun* playing Bingo last night.
> Everyone in the class is having *trouble* trying to make up his or her mind about the future.

Note: We do not usually use the verb *have* in the passive voice.

❑ 8.9 *There*

Place in the first blank the expletive *there* plus a form of the verb *be* plus a subject chosen from the following list. In the second blank place an *-ing* participle made out of the base form given in parentheses. Use an adverb when it is provided.

anybody	anything	something	no one
anyone	someone	nobody	nothing

Example

A: Quick, quick, call the police.

B: What on earth is it?

A: (*mug*) _There's someone_ down on the street _mugging_ a woman.

1. A: What's that?

    B: I have no idea. (*bang*) It sounds as if _____ in the apartment above ours _____ on the floor with a sledge hammer or something like that.

2. A: Why didn't you like your acting class last semester?

    B: (*always / act*) _____ in the class _____ as if he or she were the greatest actor in the world. What egos!

3. A: Our office has been a mess this week.

    B: Why's that?

    A: (*take*) Our receptionist has been sick, and for three days now _____ at the front desk _____ phone calls.

    C: (*give*) Nor _____ at the desk _____ information to the customers.

4. A: You know, Jill, I'm really quite annoyed.

    B: But, why, dear?

    A: (*wait for*) _____ at the station _____ me when I arrived this morning.

    B: (*wait for*) But you didn't call, Jack. If you had, _____ there _____ you. Someone could have driven down to get you. It was your fault, not ours.

Now use the *-ing* participle directly after the subject.

5. A: Why don't you like to stay on campus during the weekend?

    B: (*ever / go on*) _____.

6. A: (*always / guard*) Why _____ your house?

Just the other day I saw three guards at the gate, in fact. Are you in some kind of trouble?

B: No, I just want to be extra careful.

7. A: Last night I left my car for just a few minutes, and when I got back to it, it was all covered with graffiti.

B: (*keep*) _____ an eye on it while you were away. You could have paid a kid on the street a few bucks; he would have done it for you.

A: Are you kidding? It must have been a kid on the street who did it.

8.   [On the phone]

A: Do you keep hearing that beeping sound on the line?

B: (*listen in on*) Yes, _____ our call. Your line isn't tapped, is it?

A: (*do*) _____ something like that, _____? I'm not a spy, am I? I haven't been doing anything illegal, have I?

9. A: Just what is it that you like so much about your office?

B: It's a lot of fun. There's never a dull moment. (*always / happen*) _____ _____.

10. A: I'm going to complain to my landlord.

B: Why?

A: (*ever / guard*) _____ the front gate when I get home late at night.

B: That's terrible. (*always / stand*) _____ there. There are a lot of antisocial elements prowling around this city late at night.

❑ 8.10 Participial Constructions with Expletive *There*

1. A pattern that we frequently use is the expletive *there* plus a form of the verb *be* plus the subject plus an *-ing* participial phrase:

There's *someone* on the phone *asking for you.*
There are *a lot of fans* at the stage door *waiting for the stars of the show to appear.*

The prepositional phrase is often omitted:

There's a dog (*in the backyard*) barking his head off.
There's something (*on the stove*) simmering; I'm making soup.

2. Such participial constructions are derived from adjective clauses:

There are some people (*who are*) *living in that haunted house.*
There's a man in the other room (*who's*) *talking on the phone.*

3. Frequency adverbs are usually placed before the subject:

There's *never anybody* in this hospital taking care of me.
There are *always some people* standing at that corner; it's a bus stop.

4. The adverb *ever* is placed after a negative form of the verb *be:*

We had the pool to ourselves; there *weren't ever* any people swimming in it.
They don't care for gardening; there *isn't ever* anything growing in their garden.

With a negative subject, *ever* follows the subject:

There's *nobody ever* making any trouble in our neighborhood.
There is *nothing ever* happening in this place.

5. Frequency adverbs often appear in questions:

Is there *ever anybody* in your office making trouble?
Are there *always some people* sitting on those benches?

6. These constructions with the expletive *there* can frequently be changed to sentences containing verbs in the present (or the past) continuous tense:

There's nothing happening here.
Nothing *is happening* here.

There was someone standing in the shadows.
Someone *was standing* in the shadows.

Similarly, we can use the present perfect continuous tense:

There's been nobody taking care of the problem.
Nobody *has been taking* care of the problem.

Or we may use other verb forms:

There *should be* someone helping you on the project.
Someone *should be helping* you on the project.

There might have been someone listening in on my phone conversations.
Someone *might have been listening* in on my phone conversations.

❑ 8.11 *Sit, Stand* and *Lie*

In the first blank place an appropriate form of *sit, stand* or *lie.* In the second blank supply an *-ing* participle of your choice.

Example

A: What were you doing when I called?

B: I ____*was sitting*____ at my desk ____*writing*____ a

letter to the president. I wanted to give him a piece of my mind.*

*Complain to him.

1. **A:** What were you doing when the rainstorm hit?

    B: I _____ on the corner _____ you.

    Do you have a good excuse for being so late?

2. **A:** It's too bad we couldn't get tickets for the show.

    B: Yes, if we'd been able to get them, we _____ in the

    theater right now, _____ ourselves.

    A: Instead, we _____ on a street corner on a very rainy and

    cold evening, _____ to get a taxi.

3.   [On the phone]

    A: Hi, Becky, what's up?

    B: Oh, hi, Jason, how are you? What a coincidence! (*just*) I _____

    _____ here in my hammock _____ a little letter

    to you. Funny that you should call at this very moment.

4. **A:** I haven't seen Dan Rivers in ages.

    B: I saw him the other evening on Wilshire in Westwood, where all the movies are.

    A: What was he doing?

    B: (*just*) Oh, he _____ there _____

    the world go by.

5. **A:** Well! It's about time! Since five, I _____ here

    _____ you.

    B: It's not my fault for being so late. Blame Los Angeles traffic.

6. **A:** Where's the baby?

    B: She _____ in her crib _____ a

    nap.

7.   [On the phone]

    A: Hi, it took you so long to answer, I thought you might not be home.

    B: I'm sorry. When the phone rang, I _____ on a ladder

    _____ some pictures on the wall.

8. **A:** Isn't this a lovely picture, children? What do you see in it?

    B: A little girl _____ on the grass _____

    _____ with her little dolly.

    C: And a little boy _____ next to her _____

    _____ a book.

D: And a big boy _____ next to a bicycle _____

_____ a beautiful red kite in his hand.

9. [On the phone]

A: Hi, what's up?

B: You won't believe this, but right now I _____ on my

head _____ a new type of yoga exercise.

A: Ha, ha, ha. You're right. I don't believe it.

❏ 8.12 Participial Constructions Following *Sit, Stand* and *Lie*

1. Participial constructions frequently follow the verbs *sit, stand* and *lie* (meaning "to recline"). A prepositional expression of place often comes between the verb and the *-ing* participle:

> She was sitting *at the desk* daydreaming about nothing.
> He's lying *on the sofa* taking a little cat nap.
> The model stood *in front of the mirror* admiring herself.

2. Often, we put *here* or *there* after the verb:

> **A:** What did you do all day with yourself?
> **B:** I just sat *here* working at my desk.

> **A:** What was his reaction when you told him the story I'd told you?
> **B:** He just stood *there* laughing hysterically.

> **A:** Where's the puppy, Mom?
> **B:** Leave him alone, dear. He's just lying *there* sleeping.

3. Sometimes the participial construction is more loosely connected to the independent clause than it is in the preceding examples. When this occurs, we may put a comma before the participial construction, thereby making a nonrestrictive modifier of the subject of the independent clause:

> We stood at the head of a very long line, *waiting patiently for tickets*.
>
> The large, fat Persian cat lay on the carpet in front of the fire, *softly purring*.
>
> I'll probably be sitting at this desk for the rest of the day, *working on this darned project*.

❏ 8.13 Sense Perception Verbs

Fill in each blank with an appropriate form of a sense perception verb plus an object of the verb plus an *-ing* participle or an infinitive without *to*. When an object is not given in parentheses, the sense perception verb will be in the passive voice followed by an *-ing* participle.

Examples

a. **A:** (*feel / the earth / shake*) Oh, oh, I *feel the earth shaking*.

B: Don't let that bother you; it's just a little tremor.

b. **A:** How do you know your secretary stole your wallet?

B: (*see / take*) She _____ *was seen taking* _____ it off my desk.

1. **A:** What were you doing for such a long time in the park, Bobby?

   B: (*observe / some birds / build*) I had my binoculars, and I _____ _____ a nest. (*watch / them / do*) I had a lot of fun _____ it.

2. **A:** Listen, now don't get nervous, Mr. Smith. (*you / actually / see / the murder / commit*) Last night _____?

   B: (*see / the man / shoot*) Yes, Officer, I _____ _____ the woman.

   A: How many times?

   B: Just once, Officer.

3. **A:** Why was that customer stopped at the store exit by the security guards?

   B: (*see / shoplift*) She _____ by a store clerk just a few minutes before.

4. **A:** You seem to have done everything in your life. (*you / ever / see / a baby / bear*) Tell me something, _____?

   B: Yes, I have, in fact, and it was a wonderful thing to see.

5. **A:** Timmy, what are you doing, standing at their door?

   B: (*just / listen to / our neighbors / have*) Shh, Mom, I _____ _____ a fight.

   A: That's not nice, you little snoop.

6. **A:** (*hear / you / make*) Just a few minutes ago, I _____ _____ a yell in the bathroom. What happened?

   B: (*suddenly / feel / something / crawl over*) I was standing barefoot while I was shaving, and I _____ my foot.

   A: What was it?

   B: A big black spider with hairy legs.

   A: Ugh! I hate spiders.

7. **A:** Why was that guy sitting next to you kicked out of the room during the exam?

B: (*observe / cheat*) He _____.

A: Boy, that teacher has eyes in the back of her head, doesn't she?

8. **A:** Did anything exciting happen while you were on your walk in town?

    B: (*see / a car / hit*) Yes, on the Old Post Road near Greenwich Avenue, I

    _____ a telephone

    pole.

9. **A:** (*you / notice / the woman in a red dress / buy*) In the ticket line a few minutes

    ago, _____ a ticket?

    B: How could I *not* have noticed her? Great-looking woman!

    A: Well, that's my former wife. I don't want to run into her, so let's sit in the

    balcony. (*see / her / go into*) I _____

    _____ the orchestra seats.

10. **A:** I used to be a saleswoman at that store, but they let me go.

    B: Why?

    A: (*overhear / complain about*) Some customers _____

    _____ my service, and I was just fired on the spot. The

    customer is always right, you know.

11. **A:** (*see / Tom Brown / sit*) Yesterday, I _____

    _____ under the banyan tree in front of Town Hall.

    B: (*see / him / sit*) Oh, no, you _____

    _____ there; he's been dead for almost two years now.

    A: I must have seen his ghost.

12. **A:** Now please pay attention, boys and girls. I'd like you to quiet down. Now, listen,

    I'm going to drop this safety pin on the floor. (*hear / it / drop*) You must be as

    quiet as you can so that you _____

    _____. Here goes! [pause] (*you / hear / it / drop*) Well, _____

    _____?

    B: I did, Ms. Baker.

    C: So did I, Ms. Baker.

    D: I didn't.

    E: Neither did I, Ms. Baker.

    A: Well, you're not listening hard enough. Let me try again.

13. **A:** Why did the police arrest your neighbor?

B: (*see / break into*) He _____

someone's apartment through a window.

A: (*see / him / do*) Who _____

it?

B: I did, and it was my apartment.

14. **A:** Doctor, I have a complaint. (*always / hear / something / ring*)

I _____ in my ears. It's

driving me crazy.

B: Does it ever stop?

A: Only when I plug my ears up with cotton, which I have to do at night so that I

can sleep.

B: Hmmm. Let me have a look.

❑ 8.14 Participial Constructions Following Sense Perception Verbs

1. Sense perception verbs can take objects that become the subject of a participial phrase. In this case, the participial construction has an adjectival function. These are the sense perception verbs:

feel	listen to	notice	overhear	watch
hear	look at	observe	see	witness

Have you ever seen *my grandmother* doing the cha cha cha?
We heard *the sad call of the loon* coming from the lake.
Have you ever observed *bees* working in a hive?

2. We may replace the *-ing* participle with an infinitive without *to;* in other words, we make a *to*-less infinitive:

I just couldn't listen to that person *complain* (or *complaining*) anymore.
Did you see that man just *pick* (or *picking*) that guy's wallet?

3. An *-ing* participle or a *to*-less infinitive are usually interchangeable, but there can be a difference in meaning. Compare the following:

a. An *-ing* participle after a sense perception verb emphasizes the duration of an event:

Out in the playground I saw the boy *punching* the other boy [for almost five minutes].

The other night we heard a woman *screaming* [for at least ten minutes].

b. An infinitive without *to* suggests that an event has had little duration, that the action was completed quickly:

I saw him *punch* the boy [with a hard single punch in the jaw].
We heard her *scream* [for not more than three seconds].

4. When a single event expresses almost no duration, we need to use an infinitive without *to:*

I saw a taxi *hit* a pedestrian.   [A taxi couldn't continue to hit a pedestrian.]

5. We sometimes use sense perception verbs in the passive voice:

> We *saw* the thief crawling through our window.
> The thief *was seen* crawling through the window.

> At night we *hear* the frogs croaking.
> At night the frogs *are heard* croaking.

> We *overheard* some people plotting a crime.
> Some people *were overheard* plotting a crime.

6. When a sense perception verb appears in the passive voice, an *-ing* participle almost always follows. However, if we do use an infinitive, it must be an infinitive with *to:*

> Never has that patient been heard *to complain.*

❑ 8.15 *Catch, Discover, Find, Keep* and *Leave*

Supply in each blank an appropriate form of a verb plus a noun or pronoun object plus an *-ing* participle. In some cases the verb will be passive and you will use no object.

> *Example*
>
> A: That darned guy is a real slave driver.
>
> B: How's that?
>
> A: (*keep / his employees / work*) He ___*keeps his employees*___ ___*working*___ under conditions that are unfit for a dog.

1. A: Have you heard what happened to that Mafia guy?

  B: What?

  A: (*finally / find / his bullet-ridden body / float*) The police _____ _____ in the Hudson River.

  B: Those boys really mean business, don't they?

2. A: The paper says the spy is to be hanged.

  B: (*discover / pass*) Yes, he _____

  highly secret papers to the other side. He turned out to be a double agent.

3. A: Why did you send Billy Joe to his bedroom?

  B: (*catch / him / take*) I _____

  some money out of my wallet.

  A: No! Really? (*catch / him / do*) Well, if I _____

  _____ that, I would have given him a good spanking.

4. A: I hear you've lost your job.

B: Yes, but I'm not worried. (*keep / me / go*) My savings _____ _____ for at least six months.

5. **A:** Why didn't you wash the dishes last night?

B: (*just / leave / them / soak*) I didn't have time; I had a lot of studying to do, so I _____ in the sink.

A: Well, everything on the counter is just covered with cockroaches this morning because of your laziness.

6. **A:** My boyfriend and I had an argument down in the lobby just a few minutes ago. I'm still so upset.

B: What happened?

A: Oh, the argument came about just because he's so possessive.

B: How did the argument end?

A: (*just / leave / me / stand*) He slapped my face, and he _____ _____ there in the lobby. I've never felt so humiliated.

B: Listen, Veronica, why don't you tell that big creep to go jump in a lake?

7. **A:** Well, I see your watch has finally turned up.

B: (*find / lie*) Yes, it _____ on the floor in the laundry room by the porter.

8. **A:** I'm glad I got home when I did last night.

B: Why's that?

A: (*catch / the burglar / rifle through*) If I hadn't, I _____ _____ my things.

9. **A:** Where's the dog?

B: (*find / her / lie*) If you go into the bedroom, you _____ _____ on your bed.

A: She's *your* dog. Why isn't she on *your* bed?

10. **A:** Why do those two students have to stay in detention after school today, Mrs. Stern?

B: (*catch / pass*) Well, Mr. Strong, they _____ _____ notes to each other.

A: Is that so serious?

B: (*catch / them / do*) No, but I _____

_____ the same thing yesterday, and the day before, and the day before that.

11. **A:** In that movie, where do the police finally find the murder victim's body?

    B: (*find / lie*) He _____ in a large field of very ripe tomatoes. I'll tell you it's one of the bloodiest and goriest movies I've ever seen.

    A: Ugh! It sounds terrible.

❏ 8.16 Participial Constructions Following *Catch, Discover* and Other Verbs

1. As with sense perception verbs, we can use the verbs *catch, discover, find, keep* and *leave* with a noun or a pronoun object that becomes the subject of an *-ing* participial construction:

> The other day I caught *my roommate* using my toothpaste.
>
> Sir, you will find *your mail and the evening paper* lying on the coffee table in the drawing room.
>
> I need a little snack that will keep *me* going until dinner.
>
> He's lazy and is used to having servants around. When he takes off his clothes, he just leaves *them* lying on the floor.

2. These verbs may appear in the passive voice:

> The children *were left* swimming in the pool by themselves.
> The poor little child *was found* wandering the streets.
> I'm furious; I *was kept* waiting for two hours.

3. Past participles sometimes occur after these verbs:

> When I got back to my parking space, I found my car *towed away.*
> We were left *stranded* in the mountains when we ran out of gas.

9
Causative Verbs

❑ 9.1 *Let, Make* and *Help*

Create an appropriate verb phrase using *let, make* or *help* plus a noun or a pronoun object plus an infinitive with or without *to*. When possible, omit the noun or pronoun object after *help*.

Example

A: Our son is very lazy; he just won't do his homework.

B: (*him / do*) Well, if he were my son, I ___*would make him do*___ it.

1. A: Wasn't it a stormy night last night?

   B: (*the kids / go*) Yes, it was so cold and wet out, I _____ _____ to the movies as they'd planned.

2. A: I moved into my new apartment yesterday. What a big job it was!

   B: (*you / do*) Why didn't you tell me you were moving? If you had, I _____ it.

3. A: Listen, Professor Chang, you're not strict enough with your students. (*them / work*) You _____ harder, _____?

   B: (*me / run*) Listen, _____ my class the way I like. My students are learning, aren't they?

4. A: Doctor Wisdom, my self-esteem is at a very low point, and I can't get along with anybody. (*please / me / understand*) _____ my emotional problems?

   B: Well, I certainly shall try. Where would you like to begin?

234

5. **A:** Gloria Grand says she has millions.

   B: (*her / fool*) Oh, _____ you; she hasn't got a dime to her name. She's just full of baloney.*

6. **A:** Tell me why you're so upset with your roommate.

   B: (*me / do*) He _____ any of the chores around the house.

   A: Doesn't he do anything at all?

   B: (*me / do*) Oh, well, he might make the beds once in a while, but he _____ all of the dirty work.

7. **A:** They're fairly strict parents and insist on good manners.

   B: (*never / their kids / be*) Yes, they _____ rude.

   C: (*their kids / have*) Yes, if only more parents _____ _____ good manners.

8. **A:** Did you give your kids permission to go on that mountain-climbing trip?

   B: (*them / go*) No, but even if I _____, they probably wouldn't have gone. They tend to be a rather lazy lot.

9. **A:** We're going to the mall today and just hang out. Why don't you come along?

   B: I can't. (*my parents / clean up*) I _____ the house and yard today.

   C: Why do you have to do that? It's Saturday.

   D: Right! (*you / stay*) They _____ home on Saturday. It's not fair.

   B: (*almost never / me / go*) Oh, they _____ anywhere on Saturdays. (*always / them / do*) I _____ _____ chores around the house and in the yard. It's my duty, they say.

10. **A:** My roommate is always complaining about such silly things. She drives me up the wall.

    B: (*yourself / bother*) Oh, _____ by her complaining. Just tune her out.†

---

*Nonsense.
†Don't listen to her.

11. A: My parents are so old-fashioned, Aunt Prudence.

     B: Why do you say that?

     A: (*him / sleep*) When my boyfriend visits our house for the weekend,

       they _____ in the guest room. (*us / sleep*)

       They _____ together in my room.

     B: Well, I think they're right. You're not married, are you?

     A: Oh, give me a break, Aunt Prudence, will you? We're no longer living in the

       nineteenth century, are we? You're just as much a hypocrite as they are.

12. A: What's that you're humming?

     B: (*it / be*) It's that old Beatles' song, "_____."

❑ 9.2 *Let,* Make and *Help*

1. We always follow the causative verbs *make* (meaning "compel" or "force") and *let* (meaning "allow" or "permit") with a noun or a pronoun object plus an infinitive without *to:*

> Please don't *make me do* something that I don't want to do.
> The boss *let the staff go* home early; a hurricane was coming.

2. Remember that we use *let's,* the contraction of *let us,* plus an infinitive without *to* for asking permission or making a suggestion:

> A: I'd like to make today a day of accomplishment.
> B: *Let's climb* a mountain, shall we?

3. The verb *help* plus a noun or pronoun object may be followed by either an infinitive with *to* or an infinitive without *to:*

> A friend is *helping me put up* (or *to put up*) a bookshelf in my bedroom.
> Why won't you *help your best friend find* (or *to find*) a decent job?

4. When a noun or a pronoun object after *help* is understood, we very often omit it:

> A computer helps (*us*) to make things easier in our lives.
> A microwave oven helps (*a cook*) to speed up things.

❑ 9.3 Having Someone Do Something

Fill in each blank with an appropriate verb phrase using a pattern with the causative verb *have.*

Example

     A: Oh, these shoes are killing me, and I keep tripping.

     B: (*your shoemaker / put on*) You *should have your shoemaker*

       put on ___ some new heels; those are completely worn down.

1. **A:** Your windows are so dirty. (*someone / wash*) If you don't do them yourself,

   you _____ them.

   B: (*someone / do*) Well, Mom, I _____

   _____ them today, in fact. I would do them myself, but my shoulder is

   killing me today.

2. **A:** Your apartment looks splendid. It's so fresh-looking.

   B: (*anybody / paint*) Thank you, and I _____

   _____ it; I did it myself, the whole place. It took two weeks.

3. **A:** I'm in a lot of trouble with the government now.

   B: I know all about it. I read the newspapers, don't I? (*your lawyer / take care of*) If

   years ago you _____

   things, you wouldn't be in so much trouble now. What a big mistake you made!

4. **A:** Doesn't this silver look a little bit tarnished?

   B: Oh, it certainly does. (*the maid / polish*) I _____

   _____ it right away. We're having guests tonight for

   dinner.

5. **A:** Your hair looks so gorgeous. How full it is!

   B: Thank you. It seems to be growing so fast these days. (*my hairdresser / cut*)

   I _____ it at least four

   times since the beginning of the year.

6. **A:** Your great-grandmother is certainly in a state of good health.

   B: Unbelievable. (*never / anyone / do*) She's now 95, she lives alone and, as long as I

   can remember, she _____

   anything for her. She's always done everything for herself.

7. **A:** You're lucky that you didn't get seriously hurt in your car accident.

   B: (*someone / take care of*) Yes, if that had happened, I _____

   _____ the house. I could never have done it myself.

8. **A:** What a nice restaurant this is! Such a nice atmosphere! Shall we order now?

   B: Let's not. I'm still a little thirsty. (*we / the waiter / bring*) Why _____

   _____ another round of drinks?

   A: I really shouldn't; I'm getting a little tipsy.

9. **A:** I'm going to a dinner party tomorrow evening, and I hate the way my hair looks.

   What shall I do about it?

B: (*your hairdresser / dye*) You _____

_____ it a new and exciting color. (*him / dye*) _____

_____ it red.

A: But that's what it was last month.

B: How about blue?

10. **A:** I painted the living room myself, and it looks just terrible, doesn't it?

B: Well, I hate to have to agree with you, but I'm afraid it does. (*a professional*

painter / paint) You _____

_____ it instead of doing it yourself.

11. **A:** Have you ever noticed her nails? They're always perfectly manicured.

B: (*a manicurist / do*) Yes, she _____

_____ them; she's not very good at doing things manually. She can't

even sew a button on. (*a seamstress / do*) She _____

_____ all of her sewing.

❑ 9.4 Causative Forms with the Verb *Have*

1.   Like *make* and *let*, the verb *have* (meaning "compel") may occur as a causative verb. We frequently use a pattern consisting of a form of the verb *have* plus a noun or a pronoun object plus an infinitive without *to*. We are causing an action that is performed by a "performing agent" other than ourselves:

> I [causer] *had **the mechanic** [performing agent] tune up* my car.
> I [causer] also *had **him** [performing agent] put on* a new muffler.

2.   The pattern can occur in all the tenses and their continuous forms:

> I *have **someone** wash* the windows once a month; I'*m having **someone** do* them to-day, in fact.
>
> I *had **a friend** look over* this letter; actually, I *was having **him** rewrite* it.
>
> I'*ll have **someone** take care of* this situation; in fact, I'*ll have had **someone** take care of* it by the end of the week.
>
> We *have had **the police** investigate* this matter.
>
> If you *had had **a professional mechanic** fix* your car, you wouldn't be having so much trouble with it now.

3.   Modal auxiliaries and related idioms frequently occur in the pattern:

> They'***d better** have **somebody** repair* their roof; it's leaking.
>
> Last week I ***had to** have **my lawyer** change* my will.
>
> We *have **had to** have **somebody** fix* our car twice since we bought it.
>
> You ***must** have **someone** fix* this toaster; it burns the toast. You ***should** have had **someone** fix* it before now.

☐ 9.5 Having Something Done

Supply in each blank an appropriate verb phrase using the pattern described in section 9.6.

Example

A: Do you do your shirts yourself?

B: No, I can't iron very well. (*them / do*) I _*have to have them*_ _*done*_ at a laundry in town—two dollars a shirt.

A: Listen, I'll do them for you for a dollar and a half.

1. A: You bought your Cadillac in 1937? Fantastic! How does it run?

   B: Perfectly. (*it / overhaul*) Of course, I _____ twice since I bought it.

   A: Why, that car must now be worth more than you paid for it.

2. A: Wasn't that a shocking case? Exactly what happened?

   B: It was about ten years ago. (*her husband / murder*) A very wealthy New York socialite _____ by a professional killer.

3. A: I have a brand-new roof, but it leaks.

   B: Who put it on?

   A: I did.

   B: You don't know anything about roofs, do you? (*it / put on*) You _____ by a professional roofer.

4. A: Look at this small growth I have on my left elbow.

   B: Yes, I see it. (*it / check*) You _____, _____?

5. A: My, you get good reception on your TV set.

   B: Yes, and it's an old set. (*I / ever / it / fix*) Not once since I bought it, _____.

6. A: That used car you bought certainly runs well, doesn't it?

   B: Yes, but it looks terrible. (*it / paint*) If I could have afforded it last summer, I _____.

7. A: Oh, this tooth is killing me. It hurts so darned much.

   B: (*it / pull out*) You _____ a long time ago.

8. A: If you could have afforded it, what would you have done last summer?

B: (*a swimming pool / put*) I _____ in my

backyard.

9. **A:** Well, what are your rich neighbors having done now?

B: (*a small swimming pool / put*) They _____

_____ in their living room. (*an alarm system / install*) Also, they

_____ throughout their house. They're

terrified of kidnappers and thieves.

10. **A:** Our neighbors' house is full of termites.

B: (*them / exterminate*) They _____, or else

the whole place might fall down some day.

❑ 9.6 Unmentioned Performing Agent

1. In another causative pattern with the verb *have*, we omit the performing agent, the position of the second object changes, and a past participle replaces the infinitive without *to*. Compare the following:

> We *have a painter paint* the bathroom once a year.
> We *have **the bathroom** painted* once a year.
>
> I *had someone varnish* the bedroom floor.
> I *had **the bedroom floor** varnished*.
>
> She *has had **her seamstress** shorten* all of her dresses.
> She *has had **all of her dresses** shortened*.

2. The performing agent is most often understood, but we sometimes mention it in a *by* phrase when we desire to draw attention to it:

> We have had our bathroom painted *by a world-famous artist.*
>
> He drives a hundred-thousand-dollar Rolls-Royce. He always has it repaired *by the best mechanic in Beverly Hills.*

3. Modal auxiliaries and related idioms frequently occur in this pattern:

> We'*d better* have the bathroom painted.
>
> I *had to* have the bedroom floor varnished.
>
> She has *had to* have all of her dresses shortened.
>
> Her mother, who is very particular, *must* have her hair done by the best hairdresser in town.
>
> You *should* have something done about this problem right away.

❑ 9.7 Getting Something Done

Supply in each blank an appropriate verb phrase using *get* or *have,* whichever is more appropriate. The two words will often be interchangeable.

Example

A: Your house looks so beautiful—almost brand-new.

B: Thanks. (*finally / it / paint*) We ___*finally got it painted*___ a
few months ago.

A: Who did it?

B: My wife and I did it ourselves. We couldn't have afforded professional house
painters.

1. **A:** I've got at least three leaks in the bathroom—serious ones.

   B: (*them / fix*) You _____ right away. You've
   got guests coming for dinner, haven't you?

2. **A:** I laid the concrete sidewalk in front of my house myself.

   B: Yes, and look how it's cracking. Also, it's not level. (*the job / do*) If I'd been you,
   I _____ by a professional.

3. **A:** Oh, I'm so tired; I've been cleaning all day.

   B: Why don't you sit down and rest a while?

   A: I can't. (*the kitchen floor / mop*) I _____
   before my parents come. You know how fussy they are about cleanliness. (*the
   windows / wash*) Also, I _____.

4. **A:** My neighbor says he put the new roof on his house himself.

   B: Baloney! He's just pulling your leg. (*it / do*) He _____
   _____.

5. **A:** I painted the living room myself, and now all the paint is peeling.

   B: (*it / do*) You _____.

6. **A:** It's almost three in the morning. Why don't you go to bed?

   B: I can't. This composition is due tomorrow afternoon, and I've got classes
   tomorrow morning. (*never / it / do*) If I don't do it now, I _____
   _____.

   A: You should do what a student I know does.

   B: What's that?

   A: (*her papers / write*) She _____ by a
   professional writer.

   B: Man, is that dishonest! Also, if she gets caught, she'll get kicked out of school.
   What's wrong with her values?

7. **A:** Doesn't the piano sound terrible?

   B: Ghastly! (*it / tune*) You _____.

8. A: What beautiful clothes Dominique always wears!

    B: (*them / make*) Yes, they look as though she _____

    _____.

    A: Oh, she doesn't have that kind of money.

    B: Well then, she must make them herself.

9. A: What's wrong?

    B: My glasses don't fit right. (*just / them / adjust*) I _____

    _____.

10. A: Your car looks very dirty.

    B: (*it / wash*) Yes, is there anywhere around where I _____

    _____?

    A: I'd be glad to do it for you—for ten dollars.

    B: You're joking. (*it / do*) I _____ at a car

    wash for five.

11. A: Jerry, look at your shoes. They look terrible. (*them / polish*) Why _____

    _____? There's polish in the drawer.

    B: (*just / them / polish*) But, Mom, I _____

    yesterday. It cost me two bucks.

12. A: The kitchen sink is full of dirty dishes.

    B: Oh, leave them until tomorrow morning; I'm dead tired. Let's go to bed.

    A: (*them / wash*) We _____,

    _____? Or otherwise we'll have

    cockroaches everywhere in the kitchen when we get up in the morning.

❑ 9.8 *Get* as a Causative Verb

1. The causative verb *get* (meaning "compel") can replace *have* in the pattern discussed in section 9.6:

> We *get* (or *have*) *the bathroom painted* once a year.
> I *got* (or *had*) *the bedroom floor varnished.*
> She *has gotten* (or *has had*) *all of her dresses shortened.*

2. When we use *have*, there is always the understanding that a performing agent other than ourselves is performing the action. When we use *get*, however, there can be the understanding that we ourselves performed the action. Compare the following:

> I have finally *had* the sink fixed.   (The plumber did it.)
> I should *have* the living room floor refinished.   (I'm calling a painter today.)

VERSUS

I have finally *gotten* the sink fixed.   (I did it myself; I couldn't afford a plumber.)

I should *get* the living room floor refinished.   (I'll have to do it myself; painters are too expensive these days.)

❑ 9.9 Getting Someone to Do Something

Supply in each blank an appropriate verb phrase using the pattern with *get* described in section 9.10.

Example

A: I hear you're going to Europe this summer.

B: (*my parents / lend*) Well, if I _can get my parents to lend_
me some money, I'm going to go.

1. A: (*your dog / stop*) How _____ chasing
    the mail carrier?

    B: I didn't have to do anything; he just stopped doing it.

2. A: (*them / sing*) I love canaries, but how _____
    _____?

    B: Oh, that's easy. I just cover their cages, and they think it's nighttime, and they
    go to sleep.

3. A: My bike is broken, Grandma, so I have to walk to school today.

    B: (*your grandfather / fix*) Dear, why _____
    _____ it? He knows a lot about bikes. He used to fix your father's bikes all
    the time.

4. A: I tried the key, but it wouldn't work. (*the door / open*) I _____
    _____.

    B: I did. It wasn't locked. I just pushed it.

    A: No kidding? How stupid I am!

5. A: I've got a long paper that's due in a week.

    B: (*a friend / do*) Why _____ it for you?

    A: Why, that's completely dishonest. I'd never do such a thing.

6. A: (*our children / eat*) Doctor, how _____
    so much candy?

    B: Easy! You just shouldn't allow them to do it.

    A: Easier said than done, Doctor.

7. A: The kitchen sink is full of dirty dishes; I've got to do them.

   B: (*your kids / wash*) You _____ them.

   Why should they sit around the house all the time doing nothing?

8. A: I was away for a couple of weeks, and all my house plants died.

   B: (*your neighbor / water*) You _____

   them.

   A: Oh, no. Why, we don't even speak to each other.

❑ 9.10 Expressing Persuasion with *Get*

1. In section 9.4 we discussed this pattern: *have* plus a performing agent plus an infinitive without *to*.

> She always *has the maid do* the shopping.
> We usually *have the gardener mow* the lawn on Fridays.

2. With the verb *get* we have this pattern: *get* plus a performing agent plus an infinitive with *to*. When we use *get* in this manner, however, there is the added suggestion that we have had or will have to persuade someone to perform a certain action:

> A: How did you *get* (*persuade*) *your husband to cut off* his beard?
> B: My mother-in-law and I had to do a lot of persuading.
>
> A: How are you going to *get* (*persuade*) *your neighbor to turn down* her radio?
> B: I'm going to call the police; she's beyond any other kind of persuasion.

3. The performing agent may be an animal or a thing:

> A: I can *get my dog to jump over* this stick.
> B: How?
> A: Well, it takes a little bit of persuasion, but he'll eventually do it, and I give him a treat when he does.
>
> A: How did you *get your washing machine to work?*
> B: I just kicked it, and it started going.

4. Negative infinitives frequently occur in this pattern:

> A: How did you get your dog *not to bark?*
> B: I just punished him every time he did it, and he finally got the idea.

10

Complex Sentences: Noun Clauses and Indirect Speech

❑ 10.1 Direct Versus Indirect Objects

Fill in each blank with *to, for* or a horizontal line (meaning no preposition is required).

> ### Example
>
> A: I owe a lot of money ___*to*___ my husband, and I don't know how to pay it back.
>
> B: Well, he shouldn't have lent ___——___ you so much money in the first place.

1. A: They're fussy about where they sit in a restaurant and always reserve the best table _____ themselves.

   B: Yes, but they're so stingy, they always give _____ the waiter a lousy tip.

2. A: Well, dear, what shall we have for dessert tonight?

   B: You haven't baked a cake _____ the family since Christmas. How about chocolate?

3. A: He likes to talk about the past and loves to tell stories _____ his grandchildren.

   B: And he loves to show _____ them old photographs.

4. A: Our neighbors' ten-year-old son is so rude; he never says thank you. They should teach some good manners _____ him.

   B: Well, don't you think they should teach _____ themselves some good manners? Aren't they also very rude at times?

5. A: The owners of the house I want to buy are asking $250,000 for it.

   B: That sounds too high. Offer _____ them $225,000.

6. A: Does your husband do much of the shopping?

245

    B: Rarely, but he does cook _____ the family a nice dinner once in a while.

7. **A:** I don't know what to do. I want to get in touch with Larry Lake, but his phone is out of order.

    B: Why don't you send a telegram _____ him?

8. **A:** We enjoyed our trip, but we got tired of trains, buses and planes.

    B: You should have rented a car _____ yourselves.

    A: Well, we did reserve _____ ourselves a car, but the rental agency fouled up.*

9. **A:** What? Isn't my tip big enough?

    B: Listen, you should give at least 15 percent _____ the waiter, shouldn't you?

    A: Are you joking? Give _____ him that much for such poor service?

10. **A:** Oh, you can't do that. You mustn't sell _____ anybody your house. You've got no other place to live.

    B: But I need the money; I owe _____ everybody in town some money.

11. **A:** What did you do during your vacation?

    B: I knit a sweater _____ my husband, and I made _____ my daughter a new dress.

12. **A:** How was your shopping trip?

    B: Wonderful! I found a beautiful new coat _____ myself. I also found _____ you a nice jacket.

    A: Why, thank you, you always give _____ me such nice presents. Did you buy anything _____ the kids?

13. **A:** He's extremely greedy and stingy, so he doesn't pay much money _____ his workers.

    B: He should give _____ them at least a living wage.

❑ 10.2 Direct and Indirect Objects

1. A noun that is a **direct object** of a verb usually tells *what:*

    She gave her son *a tie.*   (*What* did she give her son?)
    I knit my roommate *a scarf.*   (*What* did you knit your roommate?)

A noun that is an **indirect object** of a verb usually tells *to whom* or *for whom*:

    She gave *her son* a tie.   (*To whom* did she give a tie?)
    I knit *my roommate* a scarf.   (*For whom* did you knit a scarf?)

We use the prepositions *to* and *for* only when a direct object follows the verb:

---

*Made a mistake.

She gave *a tie **to*** her son.
I *knit a scarf **for*** my roommate.

2. These are some verbs followed by a direct object plus a prepositional phrase with *to:*

bring	hand	offer	pay	send	take	tell
give	lend	owe	sell	show	teach	write

3. These are some verbs followed by a direct object plus a prepositional phrase with *for:*

bake	buy	draw	get	make	rent
build	cook	find	knit	paint	reserve

4. We can put the indirect object before a direct object. When we do, we omit the *to* or *for* of the prepositional phrase:

He owed a thousand dollars *to his wife.*

	INDIRECT OBJECT	DIRECT OBJECT
He owed	*his wife*	a thousand dollars.

The artist painted many pictures *for his clients.*

	INDIRECT OBJECT	DIRECT OBJECT
The artist painted	*his clients*	many pictures.

5. A pronoun may be the direct object of a verb:

He owed *it* to his wife.
The artist painted *them* many pictures.

Pronoun direct objects do not usually follow indirect objects:

He owed his wife *a thousand dollars.*   [not *it*]
The artist painted his clients *many pictures.*   [not *them*]

6. Reflexive pronouns frequently appear as the indirect object of a verb:

He made a promise *to himself.*   (He made *himself* a promise.)
They found a fortune *for themselves.*   (They found *themselves* a fortune.)

❑ 10.3 Verbs of Indirect Speech

Supply in each blank the correct form of the verb given in parentheses. When it is required, provide an indirect object of your choice with or without *to.* When it is needed, a subject pronoun is provided in parentheses.

Examples

a. A: (*relate*) This article in *The Christian Science Monitor* ___*relates*___

that the crime rate continues to rise.

  B: Well, I'm not surprised, are you?

b. A: (*claim*) The attorney for the accused ___*has claimed to the court*___ that

her client is innocent by reason of insanity.

  B: That's nonsense. He's not nuts; he's just bad.

1. **A:** I had a date with my boyfriend last night, and look at what I'm wearing now.

    B: (*finally / persuade*) An engagement ring! My, well, well, so you _____ _____ that you should be his wife. Congratulations!

    A: Now listen, it was he who had to do all of the persuading.

2. **A:** (*say / predict*) Look, this article in *The National Enquirer* _____ _____ that a prophet in California _____ _____ the world will come to an end tomorrow.

    B: I'd better cancel my appointments.

3. **A:** Well, Jackie has finally gone to bed and is fast asleep.

    B: (*you / remind*) _____ that she has an early appointment at school tomorrow morning?

4. **A:** My, the children are already sleeping soundly. What on earth did you do to get them to go to sleep so fast?

    B: (*just / tell*) I _____ that I love them, and that seemed to be enough.

5. **A:** What do you think your boss is going to do?

    B: (*hint*) Well, since last month, he _____ that he's going to quit, but I don't believe him.

    A: (*say*) Neither do I. He _____ that he's going to walk out of this office for good ever since I started working here almost twenty years ago.

6. **A:** (*it / forecast*) Andrew, what does the almanac have to say? _____ _____ that we're going to have an easy winter?

    B: (*predict*) Yes, but I _____ that we're going to have a hard winter. Aren't we due for one?

7. **A:** Tony, you don't have any matches, do you?

    B: (*I / always / warn*) Oh, come on, Terry, why smoke? _____ _____ that cigarettes are going to kill you if you don't stop?

8. **A:** I'm sorry, excuse me, but I don't speak Russian. Could you tell me what the customs inspector is saying?

    B: (*explain*) He _____ that you can't enter the Soviet Union because your papers aren't in order.

    A: (*you / tell*) _____ that he must be mistaken?

9. **A:** Do you believe that your neighbor did what the police say he did?

    B: (*swear*) No, he _____ that he's innocent of any

    crime.

10. **A:** (*always / boast*) He _____ that everything he's

    got is the best. He's a big showoff.

    B: (*always / brag*) Yes, and he _____ that he's

    smarter than anybody else.

Now use either *say* or *tell.*

11. **A:** I hear your father is in the hospital.

    B: Yes, I've just been on the phone with Dad's doctor, in fact. She

    _____ that he's getting a lot better. She

    _____ he'll be out of the hospital in a few days.

    A: Good, I'm glad to hear that. _____ that we miss

    him at the country club.

12. **A:** I must be the only one in the office the boss hasn't spoken to. (*he*) What

    _____?

    B: He _____ that the company is going to go out of

    business. We'll be out on the street.

13. **A:** What do your parents think about your plans for the future?

    B: They _____ that they think they stink.

14. **A:** (*your crystal ball*) What _____?

    B: It _____ that you will live to a great age.

15. **A:** I didn't break the vase, Mommy, the cat did. I saw her do it.

    B: Listen, young man, _____ lies.

16. **A:** _____ a riddle, Grandpa, please.

    B: What's black and white and red all over?

❏ 10.4 Noun Clauses as Direct Objects

1. Like adjective and adverb clauses, a **noun clause** is a dependent clause that contains a verb and its subject. We may use it in the same way that we use a noun. For example, we can use a noun clause as the direct object of certain verbs:

INDEPENDENT CLAUSE   DEPENDENT CLAUSE (DIRECT OBJECT)
She has *told us*   *that she has a fortune.*

2. Noun clauses are derived from statements, questions, requests and exclamations. The subordinate conjunction *that* introduces a noun clause derived from a statement, but it may be omitted:

The author has said, *"Revising is half of writing."*
The author has said *(that) revising is half of writing.*

3. An indirect object may precede a noun clause:

INDIRECT OBJECT   DIRECT OBJECT
He's confessed   *to his priest*   that he's committed many sins.

Or the noun clause may immediately follow the verb:

DIRECT OBJECT
He's confessed   *that he's committed many sins.*

4. Noun clauses introduced by *that* can occur as direct objects of **verbs of indirect speech,** some of which appear in the following list. These verbs may be followed by *to* plus an indirect object. When the indirect object is understood, however, we most often omit it.

admit	complain	explain	proclaim	state
announce	confess	hint	relate	swear
brag	declare	indicate	report	whisper
boast	deny	mention	say	write

My boss has complained *(to everyone)* that we're lazy.
They say *(to all of us)* that they're getting a divorce.
She whispered *(to me)* that she knew my secret.

5. The following verbs of indirect speech are most often followed by an indirect object without *to*:

assure	convince	notify	promise	teach	warn
bet	inform	persuade	remind	tell

She's persuaded *the police* that she isn't lying.
They've told *her* that she can go free.

Note: The verb *tell* most often requires an indirect object. However, we also use *tell* in certain idioms without an indirect object, which is optional:

Please *tell (us)* **a story.**
Would you please *tell (me)* **a riddle?**
Don't *tell (anyone)* **our secret.**
Please *tell (us)* **our fortune.**
Tell (your parents) **the truth.**
Never *tell (them)* **a lie.**
A little child can't *tell (people)* **the time.**

6. These verbs of indirect speech cannot take an indirect object:

argue	broadcast	forecast	predict
assert	(dis)agree	maintain	

The weather bureau *has forecast* that we'll have a dry summer.
The professor *maintains* that there are no simple answers.

❑ **10.5** **Following the Rule**

Fill in the blanks with appropriate forms of the verbs given in parentheses. When it is required, observe the rule of sequence of tenses.

Example

A: You seem not to trust the two witnesses in this case.

B: I don't. (*question / tell / lie / say / rob*) I ___*question*___ that
they *have been telling* the truth since this trial began. They
___*were lying*___ when they ___*said*___ that they
___*hadn't robbed*___ the store.

1. **A:**   Reverend James, what has been the most exciting moment in your life?

   B: (*find out / bear*) When I _____ that
   I _____ with a mission in life.

   A: Which is?

   B: To spread the word of the Lord and help the poor.

2. **A:**   Ms. Brooks, what did your student say yesterday morning when he came into the
   classroom without his homework?

   B: (*explain / have / leave / believe*) He _____ that he
   _____ it because he _____ it home by
   mistake, and I _____ him, more or less.

3. **A:**   He's really quite worried about money, isn't he?

   B: (*mind / mind*) Oh, no, he _____ that he has little money, but
   he _____ that he has no girlfriend.

4. **A:**   How did you sleep?

   B: (*dream / chase*) Not well, I _____ all night long that I
   _____ by a pack of wolves.

5. **A:**   Why isn't your girlfriend going to go with you to the concert this afternoon?

   B: (*tell / go / go / tell*) She _____ me that she
   _____ because she _____ to
   the dentist, but I don't think she _____ the truth.

6. **A:**   How was your day, dear?

   B: Not so hot. (*walk / suddenly remember / leave*) When I _____ into my office this morning, I _____ that I _____

_____ my wallet at home. It ruined my day.

7. **A:** There's a great deal of noise from neighborhood traffic in your brother's

apartment, isn't there?

B: (*care*) Yes, but he _____ that there's a lot of noise in his

place. (*care*) He _____, however, that there is very little

light.

8. **A:** I'm very disappointed; I flunked Chemistry 1A.

B: Didn't you expect to?

A: (*study / do / just assume / pass*) No, because I _____

very hard and _____ all my homework, I _____

_____ that I _____.

B: You shouldn't make such big assumptions.

❑ 10.6 Verbs of Mental Activity

1. We also use *that* noun clauses as direct objects of **verbs of mental activity**. Here are the
most common:

assume	discover	guess	(don't) mind	regret
believe	doubt	hear	notice	remember
calculate	dream	hope	pretend	reveal
(don't) care	expect	imagine	prove	think
conclude	feel	indicate	question	see
consider	find out	know	realize	understand
decide	forget	learn	recall	wish

We all *know* that a lasting peace must be found.
She's always *pretending* that she's someone else.
We *assume* that our children are honest and trustworthy.

2. A noun clause does not change in form when a statement is changed into a question:

You know *that you have termites in your house.*
Do you know *that you have termites in your house?*

❑ 10.7 The Rule of Sequence of Tenses

1. The **rule of sequence of tenses** states that a verb in a dependent clause must agree with
a verb in the independent clause of a sentence. When a verb in an independent clause is in its
present form, we need not observe the rule:

I *don't like* this.   She *says* that she *doesn't like* this.
We *did* it.   They *tell* us they *did* it.

However, if the verb in the independent clause is in its past form, we observe the rule of sequence of tenses. Note the use of verb tenses and their continuous forms:

I *am* wrong.   I *felt* that I *was* wrong.
She's *leaving.*   Nobody *knew* that she *was leaving.*
They *did* it.   They *confessed* that they *had done* it.
He *wasn't working.*   I *knew* that he *hadn't been working.*
We *will return.*   We *knew* that we *would return.*
I'll *be seeing* him.   I *doubted* that I *would be seeing* him.
I've *seen* it.   I *told* them I'd *seen* it.
She's *been acting.*   I *didn't know* she'd *been acting.*

2. To observe the rule of sequence of tenses, we must also make modal auxiliaries agree with the verb in the independent clause:

I *can* lift it.   He *boasted* that he *could* lift it.
They *may* move in June.   They *wrote* that they *might* move in June.

a. *Must* for necessity is changed to *had to*:

I *must* change my ways.   She *confessed* that she *had to* change her ways.

We do not change *must* for deduction:

He *must* be sick.   He *said* that he *must* be sick.

b. We do not change *could, should* (ought to) or *might*:

I *couldn't* do it.   I *felt* that I *couldn't* do it.
They *should* leave.   They *knew* that they *should* leave.
We *might* be wrong.   We *felt* that we *might* be wrong.

❑ 10.8 Reporting

Using each direct statement given in quotation marks, compose a noun clause with *that*. Follow the rule of sequence of tenses when it is appropriate.

Example

"I won't ever forget you."

A: What did she say at the airport before you parted?

B: She said _that she wouldn't ever forget me._

1.   "I'm going home because I didn't sleep well last night, and I'm just too

exhausted to work."

A: Why is your secretary putting on her coat?

B: She says _____

_____

"I have a stomachache because I ate something bad last night."

A: She's always got some kind of problem, hasn't she?

B: Yes, just last week, she complained _____

_____

2. "I robbed the Browns' house last month, but I didn't rob the Joneses' house."

A: What happened at the investigation this morning, Detective Livingston?

B: The accused has told us _____

_____

3. "If we're attacked, we'll fight with bricks if it's necessary."

A: Right before that battle in 1974, what did the general say?

B: He said _____

_____

Now do each exercise orally or write it on a separate sheet of paper.

4. A: Your country went through a serious economic crisis last year, didn't it?
   B: Terrible. One Sunday morning, the government suddenly announced, "Starting to-morrow, the million peso note will be worth 10,000 pesos." My father called me up from New York and told me, "You must buy dollars so that you can beat the infla-tion." When I found out, "I can't find any dollars on the open market," I knew, "I'm in a bad situation." Fortunately, my father was able to help me out.

5. A: What did Vera Verlaine say in her last letter from Africa?
   B: That was some months ago; I'm rather worried about her. She said in her letter, "I'm not feeling well now because I've contracted some kind of tropical disease. I'm also working too hard at the mission." I saw Vera's mother the other day, and she said, "I haven't heard from Vera for months, and I'm very worried about her." She also said, "I'm going to contact the State Department if I don't hear from Vera soon."

6. A: People are often wrong in their predictions, aren't they?
   B: They certainly are. For example, Hitler said, "Germany will rule the world," and Churchill said, "The sun will never set on the British Empire."
   A: And a prophet predicted, "The world will come to an end in 1990."
   C: They all turned out to be wrong, didn't they?

7. A: I hear your grandparents have moved.
   B: Yes, I called them up one day a couple of months ago, and they told me, "Our land-lord told us that we have to get out of our apartment by tomorrow morning." So they had to move.
   A: Why, that's terrible. Isn't that against the law?
   B: Well, my lawyer told me, "It isn't, but you can still take the landlord to court for something else." But I didn't want to bother, so I told my grandparents, "My wife and I will find you a nice place." And that's exactly what we did.

❑ 10.9 Indirect Speech

1. **Direct speech** is a speaker's exact words. In writing, we use quotation marks (" ") to enclose the statement:

He said, "*I have nothing but respect for you.*"

Indirect speech, often called **reported speech,** is the restatement of the speaker's exact words:

> He said *that he had nothing but respect for me.*

2.   In indirect speech, the restatement is usually a noun clause. We do not use quotation marks, and we frequently change the pronouns and possessive adjectives from one person to another. Quite often, so that the restatement will remain logical, we must follow the rule of sequence of tenses:

> He said, *"I'm getting tired of living by myself."*
> He told me *that he was getting tired of living by himself.*
>
> *"We're going to be at your house soon,"* they said.
> They told us *that they were going to be at our house soon.*
>
> She said, *"I've received a wonderful present from my father."*
> She said *that she'd received a wonderful present from her father.*

3.   We must often make more than one tense change in a single sentence:

> *"I'm tired because I didn't sleep well,"* he said.
> He complained *that he was tired because he hadn't slept well.*

4.   We may have a series of *that* noun clauses:

> My son says (*that*) his teacher told him (*that*) she didn't believe (*that*) Columbus was the first European to land in the Americas.

5.   We often use *and that* and *but that* to connect a series of noun clauses; we do not usually omit *that:*

> He said, "I'm looking forward to graduation, and I'm getting a lot of job offers."
>
> He told me (*that*) he was looking forward to graduation, *and that* he was getting a lot of job offers.
>
> "I'm having a good time in Rome," he wrote. "I'm studying Italian hard, and I'm getting to know the Romans."
>
> He wrote in his last letter (*that*) he was having a good time in Rome, (*that*) he was studying Italian hard, *and that* he was getting to know the Romans.
>
> "I like my job, but I'm not making much," she said.
>
> She complained (*that*) she liked her job, *but that* she wasn't making much.

6.   We may also connect two noun clauses with just *that:*

> He said, "I'm tired; I'm going to bed."
> He told me (*that*) he was tired, *that* he was going to bed.

7.   When observing the rule of sequence of tenses, we usually change the past tense and its continuous form to the past perfect tense or its continuous form. However, when we restate a dependent clause, there is usually no change:

> He said, "When the phone *rang,* I *answered* it right away."
>
> He told me (*that*) when the phone *rang,* he *answered* (or *had answered*) it right away.
>
> She said, "Even though I *was* tired last night, I *didn't sleep* well."
>
> She told me that even though she *was* tired the night before, she *didn't sleep* (or *hadn't slept*) well.

Note: We do not use a second *that* to restate the independent clause; also note that the verb in the independent clause may be in its past tense or past perfect form.

8.   When following the rule of sequence of tenses, we change future-possible conditionals but not present-unreal conditionals. Compare the following:

He said, "If I'*m* tired this evening, I *won't go out.*"
He said that if he *was* tired that evening, he *wouldn't go out.*

He said, "If I *were* a millionaire, I *would live* on a yacht."
He told me that if he *were* a millionaire, he *would live* on a yacht.

9.   When we are reporting on events that took place in the **near past** (yesterday morning, last night or a few minutes ago), it is not necessary for us to observe the rule of sequence of tenses, because the restatement remains logical:

They said, "We *went* to the movies last night."
They just told me that they *went* to the movies last night.

"I'*m getting* married," she said.
She told me just a while ago that she'*s getting* married.

Also, we do not observe the rule when we are expressing the following:

a.   A universal truth:

The little boy said that three and four *are* seven.
The speaker said that love *is* the major force in the world.

b.   A customary event:

My neighbors said that they *water* their lawn once a week.
Somebody told me that mail *is delivered* twice a day in that town.

c.   A famous quotation or a familiar saying:

"We have nothing to fear but fear itself."
Franklin Delano Roosevelt said that we *have* nothing to fear but fear itself.

"That'*s* the way the cookie *crumbles.*"
He told me that that'*s* the way the cookie *crumbles.*

Note: The "pressure" of the rule of sequence of tenses on the speaker is so great that, through force of habit, we still often observe the rule even when we are referring to the near past, a universal truth, a customary event or a famous quotation or familiar saying.

10.   In indirect speech, when we are speaking of events in the **distant past,** we must observe the rule of sequence of tenses in order to keep the restatement logical. Also, we must often make other changes, most of which are these:

a.   We usually change *this, that, these* and *those* to *the:*

She said, "I want to keep *this* moment to myself."
She said that she wanted to keep *the* moment to herself.

"I found *these* toys in the swimming pool," she said.
She sounded angry when she told the children that she had found *the* toys in the swimming pool.

b.   We most often replace the word *here* with *there* or an expression of place:

"I'm very happy *here,*" he said.
He told me that he was very happy *there.*

He said, "Your daughter sits *here.*"
The teacher told me that my daughter sat *in the first desk of the row.*

c.   We also change:

now to *then*
ago to *before/earlier*
today/tonight to *that day/that night*

yesterday to *the day before/the previous day*
tomorrow to *the following day/the next day*
last week/last month to *the week before/the month before*
tomorrow morning/afternoon to *the following morning/afternoon*
next week/month to *the following week/month*

❑ 10.10 Adjectives Expressing Feeling or Emotion

Supply in each blank an appropriate verb phrase.

Example

A: (*lead*) When my grandmother died last year, she was satisfied that she

_____*had led*_____ a long and happy life.

B: And indeed she did.

1. A: (*be*) After finishing, the surgeon was confident that the operation _____

_____ a success. (*live*) She was sure the patient _____

_____.

B: Unfortunately, she was wrong.

A: (*die*) Yes, it's very sad that the patient _____.

B: And at such a young age, too.

2. A: (*finally / agree on*) Everyone in the world is relieved that a nuclear test

ban _____ by the superpowers.

B: (*occur*) Yes, but everyone is concerned that violations _____.

A: (*happen*) I'm not worried that that _____. (*finally / come*)

I'm convinced that the superpowers _____ to their

senses.

3. A: (*wear*) When Adam and Eve left the Garden of Eden, they were ashamed that

they _____ clothes.

B: (*obey*) They were also ashamed that they _____ God's

command. (*be / eat*) I'm sure that they _____ sorry they

_____ the forbidden fruit.

A: (*do*) I'm sure I _____ the same thing if I had been they.

4. A: (*monitor*) Because of my political activities, I'm afraid my phone calls

_____. (*listen in on*) I'm positive someone _____

_____ my phone conversations.

    B: (*do*) Why, I'm surprised that the government _____ such

a thing. Isn't wire tapping illegal?

5. **A:** What's wrong?

    B: (*turn down*) I'm very disappointed that my girlfriend _____

_____ my proposal of marriage.

    A: (*reconsider*) Listen, you're the biggest catch in town. I'm certain she _____

_____. If she doesn't, she's a fool.

    B: Hey, man, you shouldn't talk about my girlfriend that way.

6. **A:** Well, hello, how are you? Hey, I should be congratulated.

    B: Why's that?

    A: (*choose*) I wasn't sure I _____, but I have been asked to

take over the president's job.

    B: That's great. Congratulations! (*choose*) But I'm not surprised that you

_____. The selection committee couldn't have picked a

better woman.

7. **A:** (*get*) Mrs. Bond, I'm afraid your husband's condition _____

_____ worse. There's now little hope.

    B: (*live*) Oh, Doctor, I was so hopeful that he _____.

8. **A:** Why did you lose your temper with that student, Professor?

    B: (*come into*) Well, first off, I was annoyed that he _____

the class half an hour late. (*even / apologize*) Also, I was irritated that

he _____ when he came into the room.

9. **A:** (*blow up*) When the news came out, the world was shocked that the

embassy _____.

    B: (*happen*) Well, you know, I was afraid that that _____.

(*happen*) In fact, I'm surprised that it _____ a long time

ago.

❑ 10.11 *That* Noun Clauses as Adjective Complements

1. A noun clause introduced by the subordinate conjunction *that* may follow an independent clause that contains a form of the verb *be* plus an adjective expressing feeling or emotion:

> I **am afraid** *that a terrible storm is going to hit us.*
> We**'re thrilled** *that we have a new grandchild.*

2. Such clauses also follow independent clauses containing *it* plus *be* plus an adjective:

> **It's sad** *that your neighbors have decided on a divorce.*
> **It's strange** *that there are no street lights on tonight.*

3. In these sentence patterns, we must often observe the rule of sequence of tenses:

> I *was* very worried that I *had made* a dreadful mistake.
> It *was* sad that the poor children *didn't have* enough to eat.
> I *was* afraid during my vacation that my house *would be robbed.*

4. *That* noun clauses placed after adjectives of feeling or emotion have an adverbial function in that they can answer a question with *why:*

> **A:** *Why* are you so angry?
> **B:** I'm angry that (*because*) my neighbors always make so much noise during the night.

5. We use *that* noun clauses after independent clauses that contain the following adjectives (a partial list):

afraid	confident	envious	glad	jealous	sad
angry	conscious	fearful	(un)happy	positive	sorry
(un)certain	content	furious	hopeful	proud	sure

That noun clauses also may contain these *-ed* participial adjectives (a partial list):

amazed	concerned	disgusted	perplexed	startled
amused	contented	distressed	pleased	stunned
annoyed	convinced	excited	relieved	surprised
ashamed	depressed	impressed	satisfied	thrilled
astonished	disappointed	irritated	shocked	worried

6. With *-ed* participial adjectives, we do not usually omit the subordinate conjunction *that:*

> We are *perplexed that* our son doesn't want to achieve much.
> I'm *disgusted that* my neighbor keeps junk in her yard.

But with the other adjectives, we often do:

> I'm *sure* (*that*) all of you will have a great deal of success.
> It was *sad* (*that*) she had lost all of her possessions in the fire.

❑ 10.12 Wishing and Hoping; Reviewing Prepositions and Articles

Supply in each blank an appropriate verb phrase or auxiliary.

Example

A: Her skin is quite wrinkled from overexposure to the sun.

B: (*spend*) I bet she now wishes she ___*hadn't spent*___ so much time at the beach when she was younger.

1. **A:** Can you donate some money to the poor children of our town?

B: Here's a dollar. (*give*) I wish I _____ more, but I

_____ .

2. A: I'm getting a lot of attention in this company, and everyone shows me a great

deal of respect.

B: (*treat*) I wish that I _____ the way you are. I just can't

seem to get along with people. I wish I _____ , but I

_____ .

3. A: I'm going skiing for the first time this weekend.

B: (*break*) I hope you _____ anything.

A: That's a terrible thing to say. (*be*) I wish that you _____

so sarcastic.

4. A: What a silly man my neighbor is!

B: Why do you say that?

A: (*never / bear*) Oh, for example, he's always saying that he wishes he _____

_____ , and I think he means it.

5. A: She's such a dreamer; her mind is always full of fantasies.

B: (*always wish / be*) Yes, she _____ that she _____

_____ a movie star.

A: She sure has got her head in the clouds.

Now use each set of cue words to compose a sentence. In a few cases, you will need an infinitive. Practice using and not using *that*. You may follow the example and write on this page or use a separate sheet of paper.

Example

A: Their son is going to the city to find a job and live.

B: He's such a reckless young man.   I / hope / he / get / trouble / police *doesn't   into   with the*

6. A: What a racket they're making upstairs!

B: What on earth are they doing?   I / wish / they / quiet

7. A: I have to walk or take the bus everywhere. Sometimes I ride my bicycle. I don't

like the subway.

B: you / wish / you / have / car?

8. **A:** What are your plans?

   B: I / hope / find / good job / when / I / go back / my native country

9. **A:** It's such a cloudy and gray day; it's depressing.

   B: yes / I / wish / sun / come

10. **A:** Well, goodbye everybody, we must rush. Our plane takes off at 8:40, and it takes at least 35 minutes to get to the airport. And look! It's almost quarter to eight.

    B: I / hope / you / get / there / time

    C: I / wish / you / give / yourselves / more time

11. **A:** My husband is in Vancouver on a business trip, and here I am in Toronto freezing to death.

    B: you / wish / you / be / there / him / now?

    A: yes / I / certainly / wish / I / go / but / I / have / lot / things to do / here / Toronto   I / hope / go / his next trip / however

12. **A:** Good morning, sir, may I help you?

    B: yes / thank you / I / wish / see / clock / that / be / display / your Park Avenue window

13. **A:** Here's my composition, Professor. I'm afraid I had to do it in a hurry.   I / wish / that / I / have / more time

    B: Thank you.   if / you / mind / I / wish / speak / you / after class today

14. **A:** Were you being serious when you said what you did at the meeting?

    B: Don't you think I was?   I / hope / that / I / make / fool / myself

15. **A:** How was your grade on your final paper?

    B: Not bad, not good.   I / hope / that / I / get / "A" / but / I / end / "B+" / instead   She's a tough grader.

❑ 10.13 *That* Noun Clauses After *Wish* and *Hope*

1. In what can be a rather formal style, the verb *wish* followed by an infinitive has the same meaning as *want* or *would like:*

A: Excuse me, I *wish to speak* to the ambassador.
B: The ambassador is not in the embassy today, ma'am.

2.   When we use a verb in a *that* noun clause following independent clauses that contain the verb *wish*, it takes the same form as a verb in a present- or past-unreal conditional statement. We may omit *that*:

I *have to work* so hard.   [reality]
I wish (*that*) I *didn't have to work* so hard.   [unreal]

She*'s not feeling* well today.
She wishes (*that*) she *were feeling* better.

He *didn't study* for that course.
He now wishes (*that*) he *had studied* for it.

The teacher *can't work* miracles.
The students wish (*that*) the teacher *could work* miracles.

The meeting couldn't have been longer.
Everyone wishes (*that*) the meeting *could have been* shorter.

3.   We frequently abridge such clauses:

I'm running out of money. I wish I *weren't*.
She doesn't have curly hair. She wishes that she *did*.
He bet all his money on the wrong horse. He wishes he *hadn't*.
I can't make myself invisible. I wish I *could*.
I couldn't be with you. I wish I *could* (*have been*).

4.   We use *that* noun clauses containing the simple past tense or the past perfect tense following *wish* to express unreal conditions. However, we use *wish* followed by *would* plus a base form to represent a wish that is possible to realize in the future. Compare the following:

Reality	Possible to Realize
It's raining.	I wish that it *would stop*.
They haven't served dinner yet.	We wish they *would do* it soon.
The kids are being so noisy.	Don't you wish they *would quiet* down?

5.   We sometimes use *that* noun clauses with *would* after *wish* to make a kind of strong request:

A: Ha, ha, ha.
B: I wish you *would stop* laughing at me.

A: I like lots of fresh air; I keep all the windows open.
B: I wish you*'d close* at least one. It's cold in here.

6.   For events that may occur in the future, we do not make a wish; instead, we hope:

A: I'm leaving on my vacation to Europe tomorrow.
B: I *hope* (*that*) you have a wonderful time.
A: Well, I certainly hope so.

A: Oh, Grandmother, what lies ahead in my future?
B: I *hope* (*that*) you have all of the best, my dear.

7.   If a hope is related to ourselves, we may use either an infinitive or a *that* noun clause:

I hope that *I* will meet the president.
I hope *to meet* the president.

We all hope that *we*'ll become successful and happy.
We all hope *to become* successful and happy.

If a hope is not related to ourselves, we must use a *that* noun clause:

I hope that *the president* will do the right thing.

We hope that *their children* will achieve in school.

8. We may express an **unrealized hope** in the past with *would:*

    We all *hoped* that the project *would be* a great success, but it never was, unfortunately.

    She *hoped* her husband *wouldn't leave* her, but he finally did.

9. We often express a hope about the **present** or **past unknown:**

    I haven't heard from my parents for months. I hope *that they are well and happy.*

    My boss didn't say anything after reading my report. I hope *that his silence wasn't an indication of dislike.*

❑ 10.14 Urgent Matters

Supply in each blank an appropriate verb phrase. Use only the verbs in the following list:

be	find	give	leave	save	sue
continue	find out	have	live	serve	think about
cut off	follow out	hold	pay	shoot	treat
discover	get	keep	play	smoke	type
enter	go into	know	reveal	submit	wait on

Example

A: This contract stipulates that the manuscript ___*be submitted*___ to the publisher by February the first.

B: Why, that's just around the corner.

1. A: The king stood up from his throne and in a loud booming voice demanded that the prisoner's head _____.

    B: That's the way things were done in the fifteenth century.

2. A: The doctor has recommended that the patient _____ the hospital for an operation.

    B: And I agree with his recommendation, but the patient thinks it's better he _____ at home. He feels it's best he _____ near his family.

3. A: Listen, I insist that I _____ at once. I don't have all day to hang around this store.

    B: Yes, sir, of course. May I help you?

4. A: It's such a beautiful day, I propose that the class _____ in the park today.

B: That's a good idea. We'll be able to get a suntan.

5. A: This is highly confidential information. It's essential that it _____

_____ to anyone.

B: Yes, it's best that nobody _____ what our plans are.

We've got fantastic inside information.

6. A: The general has demanded that the enemy spy _____ at

dawn.

B: I know, but some intelligence officers are insisting that she _____

_____ alive for further questioning.

7. A: It is vital to the security of our nation that the enemy _____

_____ any of our military secrets.

B: Yes, it's absolutely necessary that we _____ forever on

our guard.

8. A: Your Honor, please let me speak. I only desire that I _____

_____ a chance to tell my side of the story.

B: Not at this time, please. You'll be able to do so during the cross examination. I

suggest you _____ more patient.

9. A: What does your lawyer have to say?

B: Because of the damage done to our property, he's advised that my company

_____ the government for at least a million.

Now supply in each blank an appropriate pronoun object plus an infinitive.

Example

A: I'm going to drop out of school.

B: Please don't. I urge _____*you to continue*_____ with your studies. Education

is the key to your future.

10. A: My grandfather spends a lot of time in the garage. My grandmother forbids

_____ his pipe in the house.

B: Does he forbid _____ the garage?

11. A: Why do you say that teacher is hard?

B: She requires _____ all of our papers. Also, she

asks _____ two copies along with the original. She has

never explained this requirement.

12. **A:**   Darling, please don't end our relationship. I beg _____

me. I don't know what I'd do without you.

B: But I don't love you anymore. Must I beg _____ me my

freedom? Let me go, please.

13. **A:**   But, General, I can't do that. It would be immoral for me to do so.

B: Major, I order _____ my order, or else you will be shot

along with the rest of the traitors.

14. **A:**   Mommy, I want to go over and see Timmy the Terror.

B: Honey, I must forbid _____ with that boy; he's a very

bad influence on you. I urge _____ anything to do with

him.

Now supply in each blank the preposition *for* plus an appropriate pronoun object plus an infinitive.

Example

A: We need more restrictions on trade.

B: I disagree; it's best ___*for us to have*___ free trade.

15. **A:**   I feel like spending all of my money.

B: You'd better watch out. It's important _____ some

money for a rainy day. It's advisable _____ the future,

isn't it?

16. **A:**   My wife and I don't want to travel around the country changing our jobs all the

time. It's essential _____ a permanent home.

B: Yes, dear, you're right. It's better _____ in a place where

we can have roots.

17. **A:**   I got a promotion last year, and it was very important _____

_____ it when I did.

B: You were almost broke at that time, weren't you?

18. **A:**   I sleep six hours every night.

B: That's why you always look and act so tired. It would be better _____

_____ at least eight hours. It's essential _____

_____ our bodies sufficient rest.

19. A: I didn't make any money last year, so it's not necessary _____

_____ taxes this year.

B: Yes, but it's necessary _____ a job.

☐ 10.15   Verbs and Adjectives of Urgency; the Present Subjunctive

1. We also use *that* to introduce noun clauses that are derived from requests:

> "*Please show your pass.*"
> The guard at the library always insists (*that*) *I show my pass.*

2. Such clauses usually occur after verbs called **verbs of urgency:**

advise	demand	insist	recommend	require	suggest
ask	desire	propose	request	stipulate	urge

3. The verb in a *that* noun clause following a verb of urgency is a base form, traditionally called the **present subjunctive.** *Not* precedes the base form in negative verb phrases. The verb *be* as an auxiliary appears in the passive voice, a pattern that we frequently employ:

Active

I (not) see	we (not) see
you (not) see	you (not) see
he, she, it (not) see	they (not) see

Passive

I (not) be seen	we (not) be seen
you (not) be seen	you (not) be seen
he, she, it (not) be seen	they (not) be seen

4. The verb in a *that* noun clause derived from a request remains a base form regardless of the tense of the verb in the independent clause:

> His doctor *recommends* that he *enter* a clinic at once.
> My lawyer *recommended* that I not *sue* the government.
> The students *demand* they *be given* more control of the school.
> The king *demanded* that I not *refuse* his offer.

5. In less formal (and less urgent) usage, the modal *should* often follows the verb *recommend, advise* or *suggest:*

> My academic advisor *recommended* (*advised, suggested*) that I (*should*) *make* an application to Cornell University.

6. Also in less formal usage, we can use an object plus an infinitive, instead of a *that* noun clause, to follow some verbs of urgency:

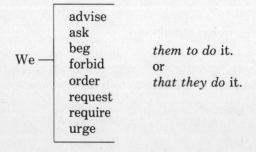

We ⎯ advise / ask / beg / forbid / order / request / require / urge ⎯ *them to do* it.
or
that they do it.

7. We also use *that* noun clauses after independent clauses containing *it* plus *be* plus certain adjectives called **adjectives of urgency.** The verb in such clauses takes the same form as a verb in a *that* clause following a verb of urgency. These are the most common adjectives of urgency:

advisable	better	essential	imperative	mandatory	urgent
best	desirable	good	important	necessary	vital

It is *advisable* that the terms of the contract *be met.*
It is *imperative* that everyone *pay* his or her share of taxes.

8. Less formally, we can follow adjectives of urgency with the preposition *for* plus an object plus an infinitive:

It's advisable *for us to meet* the terms of the contract.
It's imperative *for everyone to pay* his or her share of taxes.

❏ 10.16 More Matters of Urgency

Supply in each blank an appropriate verb phrase. Use the verbs in the following list.

arrive	flee	give	hold	listen	pay	rewrite	sue
be	get	hang	invest	lock up	raise	shoot	wear

Example

A: Well, what's your opinion?

B: I think it's best your mother _____ *listen* _____ to her lawyer's advice that she _____ *sue* _____ her landlord for damages.

1. A: What do you think?

   B: Frankly, there's one thing I don't like about this contract. There's a stipulation that I _____ responsible for any damage to the company's property. That's asking too much.

   A: I agree, and my recommendation is that the contract _____. Their proposal that you _____ responsible is ridiculous. You should propose that they _____ responsible for any damages incurred.

2. A: What a brave thing to write! In an editorial in *The National News,* they more or less make the suggestion that our beloved dictator _____.

   B: Don't you think it's best that that paper's editor _____ the country? Or else he might lose his head.

3. A: How did you become a billionaire?

B: I very wisely listened to my father's advice that I _____

what little money I had in computers.

4. A: What's up?

B: Want to hear the latest news? Our crazy general has issued an order that

everyone in the battalion _____ a uniform on Sunday.

He's nuts.

A: Well, I suggest that he _____ in the stockade.

5. A: Was it difficult to join the Lakewood Country Club?

B: Not at all. There was just the requirement that I _____

two million dollars in dues.

6. A: What does the invitation from the embassy say?

B: There's a request that gentlemen _____ a dinner jacket.

There's an added request that everyone _____ at the

reception before the prime minister's arrival.

7. A: What do you think of that professor?

B: Well, his insistence that everything _____ perfect drives

me crazy, but I'm learning a lot. Also, I like his requirement that everyone

_____ to class on time.

8. A: How did you like my speech, Senator?

B: Beautiful, I particularly liked your recommendation that federal taxes

_____. We need that money for our new social programs.

9. A: Want to hear the latest?

B: Listen, these days it's hard to surprise me.

A: It's our beloved dictator again. He's issued a command that everyone in the

country _____ a day's wages to commemorate his late

wife's birthday.

B: Well, I'd like to issue a command that he _____ in the

nearest public square.

Now supply in each blank an appropriate verb phrase using the verbs *suggest* and *insist* as
verbs of indirect speech. You will often need to follow the rule of sequence of tenses. Use the
following verbs:

| act | be | fire | go | lose | need | quit | shut | submit |
| attend | expect | give | have | make | pass | repeat | steal | turn in |

Example

A: When I spoke to my roommate last, he insisted he _hadn't stolen_ my money, but I didn't believe him.

B: Why, he couldn't have done that; he's way too honest.

10. A: You look upset. What's the problem?

    B: Oh, my history professor insists that I _____ my final paper last week, but I did; I swear I did.

    A: Did he suggest to you, by any chance, that he _____ it?

11. A: Well, last night my roommate suggested that I _____ responsible for her problems with her boyfriend. Of course, I insisted that I _____ anything to do with it.

    B: Oh, are you sure?

12. A: How did you ask your father for a loan?

    B: I didn't ask directly; I just suggested that I _____ a little bit of money.

Now some blanks will require a verb in its present subjunctive form.

13. A: What are you saying?

    B: I'm only suggesting that you _____ a serious mistake when you married your wife.

    A: Listen, I suggest you _____ your mouth before somebody does it for you.

14. A: What was it like to work with Constance Taylor?

    B: Well, I remember she was always insisting she _____ the best actress in the New York theater. Once, when I only suggested that Theresa Todd _____ as well as she did, Constance almost blew her top.*

15. A: Why do you suggest that my husband _____ his job?

    B: I'm only suggesting that he _____ happy where he's now working. I wasn't suggesting that he _____.

16. A: Why are you insisting that I _____ at that meeting?

    B: I'm only making a suggestion that you _____, but when I last

*Got extremely angry.

spoke to your boss, he insisted that the weekly meetings _____

well because of your frequent absences. Certainly, this suggests that he

_____ you to be at tomorrow's meeting.

A: May I make the suggestion that he _____ jump in a lake?

17. A: I don't like this memorandum from the president's special advisory committee.

There's a proposal that everyone on the committee _____ a

raise.

B: Well, I'd like to make the suggestion that everyone on that darned committee

_____ .

18. A: I'm a little depressed. Yesterday, Professor Wise didn't say it directly, but he

suggested that I _____ his course.

B: Why do you think that?

A: Well, I thought that when he suggested that I _____ his

course next fall.

☐ 10.17 Nouns of Urgency

1.   These are some common **nouns of urgency**:

advice	importance	proposal	requirement
command	insistence	recommendation	stipulation
demand	order	request	suggestion

When we use a *that* noun clause after such a noun, the clause requires a verb in its present subjunctive form:

> It is of great *importance* for the world that a vaccine for this disease *be found* as quickly as possible.

2.   Verbs following the nouns *advice, recommendation* and *suggestion* may also occur with the modal auxiliary *should:*

> The author ignored my *suggestion* (*advice, recommendation*) that she (*should*) re-write the entire manuscript for her book.

☐ 10.18 *Suggest* and *Insist* as Verbs of Indirect Speech

The verbs *suggest* and *insist* are sometimes used as reporting verbs in indirect speech. We do not use the present subjunctive form for this, and we must often observe the rule of sequence of tenses:

> "*I'm innocent. I'm not involved in any scandal.*"

> When speaking to the reporters, the former president *insisted* that he *was* innocent, that he *wasn't* involved in any scandal.

"He's guilty. He committed a crime."

At the end of the trial, the judge only *suggested* that the *accused* was guilty. He only *suggested* that he *had committed* a crime.

❑ 10.19 *Whether (or Not)* and *If*

Using each direct yes/no question enclosed in quotation marks as a cue, compose a noun clause introduced by *if* or *whether* (*or not*). You may do this orally or may write on a separate sheet of paper.

Example

"Do I want to go?"

A: It'll be an interesting meeting; some of the best minds at the university are going to be there.

B: I can't decide . . . *whether I want to go or not.*

1. "Is it genuine?"
   A: This painting appears to be a fine work by Rembrandt, yet I've been told it's a copy. Because of the painting's poor condition, it's hard to determine . . . However. I think it is.
   "Is it a genuine Rembrandt?"
   B: You must be right; you're one of the greatest art experts in the world. If you don't know . . . , who does?

2. "Does he have enough food to eat? Does he have enough heat?"
   A: Why are you so worried about the neighbor upstairs?
   B: Oh, it's just that he looks so lonely and poor, and he looks ill. I feel sorry for him. Do you know . . .

3. "Is it going to rain?"
   A: My, those rain clouds on the horizon look threatening.
   B: I've got an umbrella. I don't care . . .

4. "Is he stealing from the company?"
   A: People are saying that your boss is stealing from the company.
   B: Well, knowing him, I really do wonder . . .

5. "Is it good?"
   A: What do you think of this sculpture?
   B: Not having studied much about art, I can't really judge . . . But I know what I like, and I like that.

6. "Was he going to the store?"
   A: Where's your father, dear? Did he go to the store?
   B: I don't know. He went out in a hurry and didn't mention . . .

7. "Are we on the right road?"
   A: Why are you getting out the map again, Dad?
   B: I'm going to try to figure out . . . I don't think we are.

8. "Was she wearing one?"
   A: At the garden party, what kind of hat was the hostess wearing?
   B: Why, to tell you the truth, I didn't even notice . . .

9. "Will he be there?"
   A: Your boss will be here for the meeting tomorrow, won't he?
   B: I don't know. When I last spoke to him, he didn't indicate . . .

10.   "Do you love me?"
    A: Listen, I'm getting tired of your ambivalent attitude. I want to know right now at this very minute . . .
    B: Oh, you silly goose, of course I do.

11.   "Does he want to go with me?"
    A: Of course, your husband wants to go with you to that reception, doesn't he?
    B: Listen, he hasn't even hinted . . .

Now using the example as a guide, compose complete sentences. Use the verbs *ask, say* and *tell* in the independent clauses. You may do this orally or may write on a separate sheet of paper.

Example

"Are you going to be at today's meeting?" "No, I'm not, I have to go to the dentist."

    A: Well, what did she say when you spoke to her on the phone last week?
    B: Well, . . . *I asked her if she was going to be at that day's meeting, and she said that she wasn't, that she had to go to the dentist.*

12.   "Do you want to marry me?" "Yes, I do, I love you very much."
    A: What on earth did John say to my sister a few minutes ago?
    B: Listen, you won't believe this.   . . .

13.   "Did you have a good time at the dance?" "No, I didn't."
    A: Why was your roommate in such a bad mood when he came home the other night? Or is he always like that?
    B: No, but he can be a rather moody guy.   . . .

14.   "Can you drive me to the station?" "No, we can't, our car has broken down, too."
    A: What did you do when your car wouldn't start? Did you go to the neighbors?
    B: Yes, but I didn't have much luck.   . . .

15.   "Will you help me out?" "No, I won't, I don't want to help anyone out, and that includes you."
    A: Your neighbor downstairs is certainly grouchy, isn't he?
    B: You're not kidding. For example, the other day, when I was having some trouble with the garbage cans,   . . .

16.   "Were you born in a happy home?" "Yes, I was, I was born in an extremely happy home."
    A: What was the first thing the psychiatrist asked you?
    B: A very obvious question.   . . .

17.   "Are you carrying any drugs?" "No, I'm not, I'm not a drug user."
    A: What did the police say to you when they suddenly stopped you on the street?
    B: You won't believe this. Do I look like a drug addict?   . . .

❑ 10.20 Noun Clauses Derived from Yes/No Questions

1. In a noun clause derived from a yes/no question, we use the introductory words *whether* or *if. Whether* is more formal:

> *"Do you have a dictionary?"*
> I asked her *whether (if) she had a dictionary.*

2.   When a noun clause is derived from a yes/no question, we place the subject before the verb, drop auxiliaries such as *do* and *did,* and drop the question mark. In order to keep the restatement logical, we must often observe the rule of sequence of tenses:

> *"Did you have a nice time yesterday?"*
> He asked me *whether I'd had a nice time the day before.*
> *"Will you help me?"*
> She wanted to know *if I would help her.*

We retain the question mark if a restatement is a question:

> *Did he ask you* whether you'd had a nice time the day before?
> *Did she want to know* if you'd help her?

Reminder: We also use *if* to introduce conditional adverb clauses.

3.   These are some verbs that take noun clauses with *whether* or *if* as objects:

Verbs of Mental Activity

(don't) care	doubt	learn
choose	find out (discover)	notice
decide	judge	observe
determine	know	wonder

Verbs of Indirect Speech

announce	explain	mention	state
ask	indicate	reveal	suggest
debate	inquire	say	tell

4.   The introductory word *whether* suggests a choice. When we might expect a negative choice with *whether,* we add the words *or not:*

> *"Does the patient have an infectious disease?"*
> The doctors are trying to determine *whether or not* the patient has an infectious disease.
> *"Is the official a criminal?"*
> The report didn't mention *whether or not* the official was a criminal.

5.   For emphasis, and if a noun clause is relatively short, we may put *or not* at the end of the clause:

> *"Does she love me?"*
> I really don't know *whether* she loves me *or not.*
> *"Did he win the first prize?"*
> Didn't he want to know *whether* he'd won the first prize *or not?*

In informal usage, *if* may replace *whether* in this pattern, but only when the clause is very short:

> *"Am I happy?"*
> I don't know *if* I'm happy *or not.*
> *"Do I want it?"*
> She didn't say *if* she wanted it *or not.*

6.   In sentences containing *whether (if)* noun clauses, the verb in the independent clause most often appears in its negative, question or imperative form:

She doesn't care whether she gets a promotion or not.
Do you know if the mail has been delivered yet?
Tell me whether or not you're my best friend.

7.   In indirect speech, we frequently use abridged *that* noun clauses that are derived from short answers made in response to yes/no questions:

> A: "Are you happy?"
> B: "*Yes, I am.*"

She asked me if I was happy, and I told her (*that*) I was.

> A: "Did you go out with anyone while I was away?"
> B: "*No, I didn't.*"

My boyfriend asked me whether I'd gone out with anyone else while he was away, and I told him (*that*) I hadn't.

8.   In direct speech, an independent clause frequently follows a short yes/no answer. For example:

> A: "Arc you happy?"
> B: "Yes, I am, *I couldn't be happier.*"

> A: "Can you go out?"
> B: "No, I can't, *I have homework to do.*"

In indirect speech, these clauses become *that* noun clauses:

He asked her if she was happy, and she said that she was, *that she couldn't be happier.*

He asked me if I could go out, and I told him that I couldn't, *that I had homework to do.*

Note: We cannot omit *that* in this case.

❑ 10.21 More Reporting

Using the direct quotations as cues, compose sentences containing noun clauses introduced by information word(s) or the subordinate conjunction *that.* You may do this orally or may use a separate sheet of paper.

> ### Example
> "What does this word mean?" "I don't know."
> A: Well, what did the teacher say?
> B: I'm really quite surprised.   ...   *I asked him what the word meant, and he said that he didn't know.*

1.   "How old are you?" "I'm fifty."
   A: During the job interview, did your age come up in the discussion?
   B: Just once. ...   My age didn't seem to be of much interest to them.

2.   "How much did you pay for your car?" "It's none of your business."
   A: Boy, how did you get that big black eye? Run into a door?
   B: A complete stranger on the street gave it to me. I guess he didn't like what I said.
   A: Which was?
   B: Well, he just suddenly walked up to me, and . . .

3.   "What's the formula for water?" "It's H_2O."
     A: Well, Kevin, what happened in school today?
     B: In science class I got called on just once, and I was lucky.   . . .

4.   "How much does a BMW cost?" "Much more than we can afford."
     A: Do you think that you and your husband are going to buy a BMW?
     B: Oh, I would love to, but the other day, . . .

5.   "What time do you think that we should start?" "It's up to you. It doesn't make any difference to me."
     A: Why did the meeting last week start so late?
     B: Oh, do you think it started too late? I made out the schedule, you know. When I spoke to my boss about scheduling the meeting, . . .

6.   "What do the symbols in the stained-glass windows mean?" "I don't know, I don't have any idea at all."
     A: During the tour of the cathedral yesterday, did you ask the guide about those interesting-looking symbols in the stained-glass window?
     B: Yes, I did, but she wasn't a very good guide, was she? Not at all knowledgeable. . . .

7.   "What's the shortest distance between two points?" "It's a straight line."
     A: Your neighbors' daughter is quite bright, isn't she?
     B: Brilliant, and she's only three. The other day, for example, . . .

8.   "How much money do you spend on food?"
     A: Your roommate is a very secretive person, isn't he?
     B: Very, he won't even reveal . . .

9.   "Who is he?"
     A: Have you noticed the strange-looking man standing by himself over in the corner of the room?
     B: Yes, odd, isn't he? I don't know . . . , do you?

Now practice the following dialogue and then supply in each blank a noun clause introduced by *whether, if, that* or an *information* word.

10.   A: What are you doing tonight?
      B: I'm just staying home.
      A: Would you like to go to the movies with me?
      B: I can't go out. My parents are at work now, and I must take care of my baby brother, who's sick in bed with the flu.
      A: I can come over to your house while you're babysitting.
      B: That wouldn't be a very good idea because my boyfriend is coming over.

      A: Weren't you thinking about trying to get a date with Marsha?

      B: Yes, so I called her up several weeks ago and asked her _____

_____, and she said _____.

When I heard this, I immediately asked _____

_____,

but she said _____

_____

_____.

I then suggested _____,

but she told me _____

_____.

Now put the noun clauses together with words of your choice. You may do this orally or may use a separate sheet of paper.

11. A: Do you love me?
     B: Yes, I do, but I don't want to marry you. We don't have anything in common.
     A: If we don't get married, both of us will regret it later.
     B: The same thing will happen if we do get married.

12. A: Ms. Crespo, did you get this telegram yesterday?
     B: No, I didn't, Mr. Rogers. I got it last Friday.
     A: Why didn't you give it to me before then?
     B: I'm sorry, but I put it in a drawer, and I just forgot about it.
     A: If something like this should ever happen again, Ms. Crespo, you'll be fired.
     B: You won't have to wait that long, Mr. Rogers. I'm quitting my job right here and now.

❑ 10.22   Noun Clauses Derived from Information Questions

1. An information word (or words) introduces a noun clause derived from an information question:

> "*What* should I do about my future?"
> I don't know *what* I should do about my future.
>
> "*How long* have you known your neighbor?"
> The police asked me *how long* I'd known my neighbor.

2. Remember that the form of a noun clause does not change when it occurs in a question:

> She cares *where she lives.*
> Does she care *where she lives?*
>
> I don't know *what time it is.*
> Do you know *what time it is?*

3. In noun clauses derived from information questions, the verb *be* most often appears at the end of the clause:

> "What time is it?"
> Do you know what time it *is?*
>
> "What is the secret to your great success in life?"
> I asked him what the secret to his great success *was.*

Sometimes, however, such clauses are longer than the preceding examples. When writing, we might put the verb *be* right after the information word:

> "Where *is* the report that you submitted the other day to the committee set up by the prime minister?"
>
> He wants to know where *is* the report that you submitted the other day to the committee set up by the prime minister.

But when speaking, we may keep the verb *be* at the end:

He wants to know where (*is*) the report that I submitted the other day to the committee set up by the prime minister (*is*).

❑ 10.23 More Reporting

Using words of your choice, quote each introductory dialogue indirectly. You may do this orally or may use a separate sheet of paper.

> *Example*
> **a:** Please don't point that gun at me, young lady.
> **b:** Put up your hands, you're being robbed.
>
> **A:** I hear a woman held up Bud Westwood the other night.
> **B:** *Yes, and when she did, Bud told her not to point the gun at him, but then she warned him to put up his hands, that he was being robbed.*

1. **a:** Please don't talk about me behind my back, Roz.
   b: Why, I'd never do anything like that, Josh. Why, I'm one of your best friends.
   a: Ah, Roz, that isn't true.

   A: Well, tell me, how did the argument begin?
   B: . . .

2. **a:** Show me your driver's license, please.
   b: I'm sorry, I don't have it. I left it at home by mistake.
   a: Well, please show me some other kind of identification.
   b: I'm sorry, but I left that home, too.

   A: Well, then what happened?
   B: . . .

3. **a:** Do you live by yourself?
   b: Yes, I do, but I don't like it. It's a little lonely.
   a: Why don't you get a roommate?
   b: Oh, it's difficult to find one. I'm newly arrived on campus, and I know very few people.
   a: Join my social club. You'll meet a lot of new people there.

   A: What were you talking about with the new student?
   B: . . .

4. **a:** What time is it, Gabriel?
   b: Get a watch, Maria.
   a: Why do you have to be so rude?
   b: I enjoy it.
   a: Be more civilized, Gabriel, or I won't ever speak to you again.
   b: I don't care.
   a: If that's the way you feel, I won't.

   A: Now, please tell me, just exactly how did the argument begin? Now try to be as exact as you can.
   B: . . .

❑ 10.24 Commands in Indirect Speech

1. Sentences in the imperative mood (commands) in direct speech are changed in indirect speech to infinitive phrases that are the direct object of the main verb of a sentence. In negatives, we drop the auxiliary verb *do* and place *not* before the infinitive:

> *"Remember my advice."*
> My grandmother told me *to remember her advice.*
>
> *"Don't forget my values."*
> She also told me *not to forget her values.*

We omit *please:*

> *"Please be here on time."*
> She asked me *to be there on time.*
>
> *"Please don't forget our appointment."*
> He almost pleaded with her *not to forget their appointment.*

2. Proper names that appear in direct commands often become indirect objects of the main verb of an indirect statement:

> *"Jason,* please quiet down a bit."
> He *told Jason* to quiet down a bit.
>
> *"Don't rush yourself so much, Barbara."*
> I *told Barbara* not to rush herself so much.

3. A series of infinitives may occur:

> "Sit up straight, look at the interviewer(,) and don't chew gum."
>
> I gave her some advice before the job interview. I told her *to sit up straight, (to) look at the interviewer in the eye(,) and not (to) chew gum.*

Note: The second comma and the second and third *to* are optional.

❑ 10.25 Exclaiming

Using *what* and *how,* make up appropriate exclamatory phrases and sentences. You may do this orally or may use a separate sheet of paper.

Examples

a. A: I'm going to meet the Prime Minister.
B: *How exciting (!)*

b. A: He won't share his toys.
B: *What a selfish kid he is (!)*

1. A: I've been elected president of the High IQ Club.
B: ...

2. A: Thomas True never cheats on his income taxes.
B: ...

3. A: My, you dance very well.
B: ...

4. A: Were you at your son's graduation from Yale?
    B: Oh, yes, . . .

5. A: I'll take three cookies, you can take just one.
    B: Really? . . .

6. A: Here's a photo of Mona Lisa, my new girlfriend.
    B: . . .

7. A: Enrico Caruso was the greatest tenor of all time.
    B: . . .

8. A: Bobby Brains is sixteen and graduating from Harvard.
    B: . . .

9. A: Luda Pavlova is with the Bolshoi Ballet.
    B: I'm her fan. . . .

10. A: She lives in a cave by herself high up in the mountains.
    B: . . .

11. A: Whenever he's asked a question in class, he blushes.
    B: . . .

12. A: Larry Slatkin is almost seven feet tall.
    B: Wow! . . .

13. A: Isn't he a spoiled little boy?
    B: Terribly. . . .

14. A: Vance Vane is always talking to himself about himself.
    B: . . .

15. A: Yes, sir, my brother is the champion of champions.
    B: Yes, . . .

Now, to complete each sentence, make up an appropriate noun clause introduced by *what* or *how.* Use the preposition *about* or *at* when it is required. You may do this orally or may use a separate sheet of paper.

Example

  A: He's such a bragger, isn't he?
  B: You can say that again. He's always boasting . . . *about what wonderful things he's done in his life.*

16. A: Why do you say I was such a brat when I was a child?
    B: Oh, come on, don't you remember . . .

17. A: He's quite a musician, I must say. Don't you think?
    B: Oh, yes, indeed he is. I'm just astounded . . .

18. A: I feel so sorry for Mr. and Mrs. Boyle, my neighbors.
    B: I know, they must be terribly worried . . .

19. A: What a fabulous dancer she is!
    B: You can say that again. I love to be her partner. Why, sometimes I'm just astonished . . .

20. A: Yes, ma'am, may I help you?
    B: I hope so, thank you. I like the merchandise in this store, but I do have a

complaint . . .   Furthermore, I absolutely must complain . . .   And I am indeed astonished . . .

21. A: Children, children, come here, come here. Come see the elephant.
     B: Ooh, ooh. My, just look . . .   And just see . . .
     A: Yes, children, and notice . . .   Also observe . . .

22. A: He's a nice guy, but he's such a bragger, I can't stand him.
     B: Isn't he? He's so boastful . . .

23. A: You know, Mom, my husband has some serious addictions.
     B: I know, dear. I'm just disgusted . . .

24. A: Do you think much about your old school days?
     B: Oh, yes, frequently. I often remember . . .   I'll never forget . . .   Do you remember our English class with Ms. Brooks?
     A: Oh, of course, I will always remember . . .

25. A: Hi, Grandma, how are you?
     B: Well, hi, dear, happy birthday. Just think, you're thirteen, a teenager. My, let me look at you. Why, I'm surprised . . .   And your mother showed me your report card, and I'm very pleased . . .   I'm going to give you five dollars for every "A."

26. A: What! So you say that you don't like the way the house looks?
     B: Yes, that's right, you can say that again. I'm just disgusted . . .   Will you just look . . .   And see . . .

❏ 10.26 Exclamatory Phrases and Sentences

1. An **exclamatory phrase** does not contain a subject or a verb; it ends with an exclamation mark (!). One pattern of exclamatory phrase is *what a (an)* followed by a singular countable noun:

> *What a* sensation!   *What an* artist!

Another pattern is an adjective plus a noun:

> *What a* fantastic sensation!   *What an* accomplished artist!

When the noun is plural or uncountable, the phrase begins with *what:*

> *What* fantastic sensations!   *What* delicious food!

2. An **exclamatory sentence** consists of an exclamatory phrase combined with a subject and a verb:

> What a fantastic sensation *that movie was!*
> What magnificent pictures *that artist paints!*

3. We can use only adjectives (never nouns) in exclamatory phrases with *how:*

> *How* sensational!   *How* magnificent!

However, we may use adverbs as well as adjectives in exclamatory sentences beginning with *how:*

> *How sensationally* everyone acted in the movie!
> *How sensational* they all were!
> *How magnificently* that skyscraper soars into the sky!
> *How magnificent* it is!

❑ 10.27 Noun Clauses Derived from Exclamations

1.   In noun clauses derived from exclamatory sentences, the word order of the exclamation remains the same, but we drop the exclamation mark:

> *"How fast he drives his car!"*
> His parents are worried about *how fast he drives his car.*
> *"What a big scandal it is!"*
> Everyone in town is talking about *what a big scandal it is.*

2.   Noun clauses derived from exclamations occur as objects of verbs and prepositions. As an object of a verb, they most often follow a few verbs of mental activity:

> notice   realize   forget
> observe   see   remember

> *"How merry Santa Claus is!"*
> Just see *how merry Santa Claus is.*
> *"What a delightful time we had then!"*
> Don't you remember *what a delightful time we had then?*

3.   The verb *look* combined with the preposition *at* is frequently followed by a noun clause derived from an exclamation:

> Just *look at* how smoothly your parents are dancing together.
> Would you just *look at* what an amazing trapeze artist he is?

4.   Noun clauses derived from exclamations are often objects of verbs of indirect speech that are combined with the preposition *about:*

> boast about   complain about   think about   worry about
> brag about   talk about   remark about

> He's always *boasting about* what a great fortune he has.
> My boss is always *complaining about* how poorly I do a job.

5.   Noun clauses may also follow the noun form of *complain* and the adjective form of *boast:*

> I've got a *complaint about* how rude the waiter is.
> She's extremely *boastful about* how successful she is.

Note: The noun clause is the object of the preposition.

6.   Such *-ed* adjectives of emotion as *astonished, astounded, disappointed, disgusted, pleased* and *surprised* combined with the preposition *at* often take noun clauses derived from exclamations as objects:

> We're all very *pleased at* what progress we've made.
> Everyone was *astonished at* how fast I had found a new job.

❑ 10.28 Noun Clauses as Subjects

Complete each sentence with a noun clause. Use *the fact* when it is appropriate. You may do this orally or may use a separate sheet of paper.

Example

"She never calls me."

A: *That she never calls me* . . . makes me a little angry, and it also hurts me.

B: I can understand; the woman I love never calls me either.

1. "I can't find a job."
    A: . . . worries me so much; I'm running out of money.
    B: You'll find one soon, believe me. If not, I'll help you out.

2. "How do I sleep?"
    A: . . . bothers my wife a lot, so she often sleeps on the sofa.
    B: What do you mean?
    A: I snore.

3. "Where are our children." "There's so much crime."
    A: . . . concerns both me and my husband. Doesn't it, honey?
    B: Yes, there are a great many dangers in this city. . . . prevents our children from living normal lives.

4. "How old am I?" "How young does one feel?"
    A: What's your age?
    B: I'm sorry, but . . . is a very personal matter. . . . is the important thing in life, not one's age. And I feel great.

5. "Does he have money?" "A man is rich." "What does he think?"
    A: . . . will determine her decision to marry a man.
    B: I disagree, she's not that kind of person. . . . is not important to her. . . . is her major concern.

6. "What are her political views?" "What does she talk about?" "You love her."
    A: Your girlfriend has some strange ideas about politics.
    B: . . . doesn't matter to me; I'm in love with her.
    A: Well, ten years from now, . . . will matter a great deal. . . . doesn't make a good daily topic for conversation at the breakfast table.

7. "Your neighbor has a million dollars." "What kind of character does a person have?" "You have a million dollars." "Do I have money?"
    A: . . . doesn't impress me at all.
    B: Doesn't it?
    A: Of course not. . . . is my major concern.
    B: . . . makes it very easy for you to say that.
    A: That's just not true . . . . doesn't affect my attitude toward other people.

Now make up your own noun clauses.

Example

A: Aren't you worried about the way things are going at the office?

B: _____*What's going on there*_____ . . . doesn't concern me much. I'm married to the boss's daughter.

8. A: Yes, Dad.
    B: Son, I'd like to have a serious conversation with you. . . . disturbs both me and your mother.
    A: Father, I'm almost 35 years old. . . . is a private and personal matter.

9. **A:** Well, what do you think about the story I've just told you about your so-called best friend?

   B: Listen, . . . surprises me much more than you think.

10. **A:** What is something you consider very important?

   B: Well, . . . matters to me a great deal. Also, . . . is of utmost importance to me.

11. **A:** Well, what do you and your close circle of friends think about what's going on in the world?

   B: . . . bothers us tremendously. However, . . . encourages us a great deal.

12. **A:** Your company doesn't pay very well, does it?

   B: Listen, . . . doesn't make any difference to me. I love my job, and I wouldn't give it up for anything. Money isn't everything.

13. **A:** Jane, I can't tell you how thrilled I am. Something good has happened to me at last.

   B: Laura, . . . makes me very happy for you and, I must say, rather envious.

14. **A:** What are some very important things in your life?

   B: Well, . . . means a great deal to me.

❑ 10.29 Noun Clauses in Subject Position

1. A *that* noun clause sometimes occurs in the subject position of a sentence:

   "The accused is guilty of a crime."
   That the accused is guilty of a crime cannot be denied.

   "We are made for each other."
   That we are made for each other is a fact.

When a noun clause appears as a subject, we do not omit *that,* and the clause takes a singular verb.

2. For emphasis, we often add *the fact* to *that:*

   "We are in love."
   ***The fact** that we are in love* is obvious to everyone.

3. We also use *whether or not* and information words to introduce noun clauses that are in subject position:

   "Are you married?"
   In this job application, they ask if I am married.
   ***Whether or not** I am married* is none of their business.

   "Why are you feeling depressed today?"
   ***Why** I am feeling depressed today* is a mystery to me.

4. Noun clauses occur as subjects with only certain verbs:

   a. Linking verbs, especially *be* and *seem:*

   *That she hasn't called me **seems** strange.*
   *That there's hunger in the world **is** a disgrace.*

   b. Causative verbs, such as *make* and *determine:*

   *That he's spying on me **makes** me angry.*
   *What we do in our nation now **will determine** future events.*

   c. Verbs expressing emotion, such as *worry* and *concern:*

That our water supply was low last summer **worried** us all.
That he was losing his hair **concerned** him greatly.

d. The verbs *bother, mean, matter,* and the expression *make a difference:*

What you were doing then **didn't bother** me at all.
How our children do in life **means** everything to us.
Whether or not we went on vacation **didn't matter** to me.
That I'm making more money now **makes a very big difference.**

❑ 10.30 *The Fact That*

Using each set of words enclosed in quotation marks and parentheses, compose a sentence containing a noun clause in either the subject or the predicate position. Use anticipatory *it* when it is needed. Use *that* or *the fact that* when it is required or appropriate. You may do this orally or may use a separate sheet of paper.

Example

"We have terrorism everywhere."   (*frightens us all*)
A: What is a major concern of people in this country?

B: *The fact that we have terrorism everywhere frightens us all. (It frightens us all that we have terrorism everywhere.)*

1.   "She never cleans up after herself."   (*makes me angry*)
    A: Oh, the kitchen is such a big mess. My roommate had a little party last night. ...

    "You're always complaining about your roommate."   (*annoys me*)
    B: Listen, ...   Why don't you find a new one if you don't like her?

2.   "They've lost a good friend."   (*saddens them deeply*)
    A: How does everyone in the office feel about your boss's sudden death?
    B: They've all taken it quite hard. ...

3.   "I hated football."   (*disturbed him*)
    A: I had a big problem with my first husband. ...
    B: I have the same problem with my husband now.

4.   "He has wrinkles."   (*he tries to conceal*)
    A: He's a very vain man, isn't he? ...
    B: Oh, come on, now, be more generous, why don't you? We're all a little bit vain, aren't we?

5.   "My boss worked less and made more than I did."   (*seemed unfair*)
    A: When I worked for that company, ...
    B: Well, then how do you think I feel, working very hard for you and making so little?

6.   "We've won a million dollars."   (*is exciting*)
    A: ...
    B: What's even more exciting is that we don't have to pay taxes on it.

Now add words of your choice in order to complete each sentence.

Example

"They stole my washing machine."   (*overlook*)

A: Why are you going to the police about this matter? Your neighbors are nice people. At least, they appear to be.

B: Listen, are you serious? ... *Don't overlook the fact that they stole my washing machine.*

7. "Poverty causes crime."   (*forget*)
   A: I realize there's poverty in this city, but how does it really affect me?
   B: You must be wearing rose-colored glasses. ...

8. "Our son is a genius."   (*make a difference*)
   A: Oh, you have such a lovely home and such beautiful things.
   B: Yes, we're very lucky. ...

9. "People are starving somewhere."   (*concern*)
   A: Why are you working for that charity organization?
   B: Oh, I'm just a do-gooder, I guess. ...
   A: Yes, there are a lot of hungry mouths in the world.

10. "We've fallen out of love."   (*discuss*)
    A: Our marriage is falling apart, isn't it?
    B: Yes, I'm afraid it is. Perhaps it was inevitable. ...

Now make up your own noun clauses as well.

11. A: Well, tell us, Mr. Sherlock Holmes, what do you have to say about this murder case?
    B: (*suspicious of*) ...

12. A: (*disturb*) ...
    B: Yes, it's a very, very serious problem in this city and in every other city of the country as well.

13. A: Just what is it that you like so much about your husband? Is it his glorious sex appeal? That he is so bright?
    B: (*love*) Oh, no, not at all. ...

14. A: Listen, I wouldn't trust your business partner completely. I've heard a few negative rumors about him. Watch out.
    B: (*aware of*) Oh, I'm not worried about that. ...

15. A: Grandpa, you're still in bed. What's wrong?
    B: Oh, I played tennis all day yesterday, and this morning I'm so stiff and sore that I don't even want to get out of bed.
    A: (*accept*) Grandfather, I've told you time and time again. ...

16. A: No, I don't think my neighbors have such a bright child. Why, he can't even do algebra yet.
    B: (*disregard*) Listen, aren't you expecting too much? ...

17. A: Why do you think you and your roommate get along so well? Are you tolerant of each other's eccentricities?
    B: (*bother*) Yes, that's it in a nutshell. ...

18. A: What is it, Mr. Smith?

B: (*discuss*) You've been a good neighbor over the years, Mr. Jones, taking everything into consideration, but I do have a bone to pick with you.* ...

❑ 10.31 Anticipatory *It; That* Versus *The Fact That*

1. A *that* noun clause in subject position can be somewhat formal in tone. More commonly, in less formal usage, we put such clauses in **predicate position**, following independent clauses introduced by **anticipatory *it***. The use of *that* is optional when there is no loss of meaning (as in the first three examples):

> *That she hasn't called me* seems strange.
> *It* seems strange (*that*) *she hasn't called me.*
>
> *That there's hunger in the world* is a disgrace.
> *It's* a disgrace (*that*) *there's hunger in the world.*
>
> *That he's spying on me* makes me angry.
> *It* makes me angry (*that*) *he's spying on me.*
>
> *That he's losing his hair* concerns him greatly.
> *It* concerns him greatly *that he's losing his hair.*
>
> *That I'm making money* makes a difference.
> *It* makes a difference *that I'm making money.*

2. The modal auxiliary *should* frequently occurs in *that* noun clauses that accompany adjectives and verbs of emotion. This pattern usually appears in the present only:

> That we *should finally reach* the summit *is thrilling.*
> *It is thrilling* that we *should finally reach* the summit.
>
> That our son *should join* the army *shocks us.*
> *It shocks us* that our son *should join* the army.

3. As we have discussed, when a *that* noun clause is in subject position, we may add *the fact:*

> **The fact** *that* the ozone layer is in danger concerns us all.
>
> **The fact** *that* the world's population is getting larger and larger doesn't seem to bother a lot of people.

However, we do not use *the fact* when a *that* noun clause is in predicate position:

> It concerns all of us *that* our environment is threatened.
> It bothers me *that* people don't care enough about their neighbors.

But this is not true in the following cases:

  a. The following verbs must be followed by *the fact:*

accept	discuss	disregard
conceal	overlook	hide

> We must all *accept the fact* that we are only mortals.
> She tries to *conceal the fact* that she's slightly deaf.
> We must *discuss the fact* that our relationship is crumbling.
> Don't *overlook the fact* that I am older and wiser than you.

*A complaint that I wish to discuss with you.

Can we *disregard the fact* that there are homeless here?
I try to *hide the fact* that I have wrinkles.

b. The verbs *like, dislike, hate* and *love* must be followed by *the fact:*

I *like the fact* that my boss is a nice guy, but I *dislike the fact* that he's so stingy.
I *love the fact* that life is so wonderful, but I *hate the fact* that it's so short.

Note: These verbs are also followed by infinitives and gerunds.

c. We can use either *that* or *the fact that* after the following verbs of mental activity:

Don't *forget* (*the fact*) *that* Rome wasn't built in a day.
We all *regretted* (*the fact*) *that* we hadn't invested our time and money more wisely.

d. *The fact* must precede a *that* noun clause when the clause follows a preposition:

We're worried *about* **the fact** *that* our supplies are low.
I am aware *of* **the fact** *that* I am being followed.
He's proud *of* **the fact** *that* he's a self-made man.
They like to boast *about* **the fact** *that* they have ten kids.

❑ 10.32 More *That* Noun Clauses

Make up appropriate *that* noun clauses. You may do this orally or may use a separate sheet of paper.

Example

A: Dr. Frankenstein is a brilliant scientist, but he's mad.
B: Ha, ha, ha. You can say that again. His hypothesis is . . . *that the brain consists of scrambled eggs.*
A: Oh, come now, he's not that crazy, is he?

1. A: Whenever I see her, she always tries to avoid me.
    B: I hate to tell you this, but the reason is . . .
    A: She doesn't like me, does she? Well, the fact is . . .

2. A: Why isn't your roommate married?
    B: Well, I know her pretty well by now, and I think the reason is . . .

3. A: This city is so poorly governed; we live in a state of chaos. Just what's being done with all the taxes we pay?
    B: Don't you think the truth of the matter is . . .

4. A: Granddaddy, how did the world begin?
    B: Well, one belief is . . . ; another is . . .
    A: Which one do you believe, Grandpa?
    B: Well, the fact of the matter is . . .

5. A: How are you going to begin your paper on the plight of the homeless?
    B: Well, Professor, my thesis is . . .

6. A: I've never been to New York City, but I'm dying to go. Tell me what it's like.
    B: Well, one opinion is . . . ; another one is . . .

7. A: General Adams is a brilliant military tactician.
    B: Yes, I'm familiar with his books. One of his theories is . . .

8. A: Well, what's going on in that part of the world?
    B: The situation has become very hot. The latest news is ...

9. A: We're very sorry to hear that you lost your last yacht race in Australia, Captain Waves.
    B: Yes, it was a big disappointment. The major problem was ...

10. A: You've got a lot of faith in your latest campaign, haven't you, Mr. Sales?
    B: I can sell anything, sir. My idea is ...

11. A: Why don't you take a trip around the world?
    B: Well, one thing is ... ; another is ...

12. A: How do you like being married?
    B: One advantage is ...   A big disadvantage is ...

13. A: Well, Mr. Horowitz, how do you do? It's a pleasure to meet you.
    B: Mr. President, sir, I regard it as an honor ...

14. A: What do I have to do when I apply for a visa to that country?
    B: First, you must give proof ... , then you must make it clear ...   Be sure that when you go to the embassy, don't let them get the impression ...

15. A: I can't afford to buy a new car, so I'm going to buy a used one.
    B: Oh, no problem, you can get a good deal, but take care ...

16. A: He says he wants to have a lot of money, but he doesn't seem to be making any efforts to make some.
    B: Oh, listen, don't pay any attention to him. He's got his head in the clouds. He has the idea ...

17. A: Amanda Witherspoon was born with a silver spoon in her mouth. She acts like a princess.
    B: Are you certain? I've always had the impression ...

18. A: Our children are just not doing as well in high school as I'd like them to be.
    B: Now, Samantha, we've got lovely kids, but you must bear in mind ...   Just because you are a genius, doesn't mean that you can take it for granted ...

19. A: Your boss acts as if he were the chairman of the board, yet he's just the manager of a very small department.
    B: Yes, he has an extremely inflated ego. He's of the opinion ... , but he's a terrific boss. If you have a problem, you can count on it ...

20. A: Why do you and your wife live in separate apartments?
    B: When I asked her to marry me, I made it a condition ...

21. A: Sonny wants to borrow the car to take his girlfriend out. Shall we let him?
    B: Why not? He's a responsible young man of eighteen. But make it a condition ... Also, make it clear ...

22. A: Just why are you and your husband working so hard now?
    B: Neither of us has had much formal education, but we want to make it possible ...

❑ 10.33 *That* Noun Clauses Following Certain Nouns and Expressions

1. We can use *that* noun clauses directly after the verb *be* when they follow certain nouns. *That* may be omitted when there is no loss of meaning. These are the nouns:

(dis)advantage	idea	reason	thing
belief	news	theory	truth
fact	opinion	thesis	
hypothesis	problem		

A: How do you like living in the suburbs? Do you miss the city?

B: *One advantage is* that I don't have to breathe the dirty city air; *a big disadvantage is* that I have to commute.

A: Why don't you want to eat in that restaurant?

B: *One reason is* I can't afford it; *another reason is* it's not any good.

2. *That* noun clauses also follow *the fact* (*truth*) *of the matter* plus a form of the verb *be:*

A: Why do you always take a ship to Europe?

B: *The fact of the matter is* that I'm afraid of flying.

A: Why don't you want to live in the country?

B: Well, *the truth of the matter is* I don't like the life-style.

3. *That* noun clauses also follow certain verb plus noun object combinations:

have an idea (meaning "believe")	give (or show) proof
have (or get) the impression	take care (meaning "be careful")
express the view (or opinion)	

A: Her values are all twisted.

B: Yes, she *has an idea* that money can buy everything, and she's wrong.

A: At the meeting everyone was laughing at your jokes.

B: Really? I *got the impression* they were laughing at me.

A: What did the Prime Minister have to say?

B: She *expressed the view* that corruption in the government is only a reflection of corruption in society at large.

4. *That* noun clauses can occur after certain combinations of verbs plus prepositional phrases:

bear in mind (meaning "remember")   be of the opinion

A: What a lazy person he can be!

B: Listen, you've got to *bear in mind* that he's not really well.

A: What a conceited person!

B: Yes, she*'s of the opinion* that she's better than anybody else in town.

5. Certain expressions consisting of verbs combined with the object pronoun *it* are also followed by *that* noun clauses:

depend (or rely, count) on it	regard it (as) an honor
make it a condition	see to it
make (it) clear	take it for granted (meaning "assume")
make it possible	think it probable

A: Remember that my dinner party is tomorrow evening at seven.

B: Yes, ma'am, you *can depend on it* that the food will be delivered.

A: She was very surprised when her husband asked her for a divorce.

B: Yes, she had always *taken it for* granted that he wouldn't walk out on her.

A: What did you tell them at the end of the job interview?

   B: Well, I *made it a condition* that I would stay for a year only if they offered me a million.

6. *Make it a condition* is frequently followed by a verb in its present subjunctive form:

   A: What shall I do before I begin the project?
   B: *Make it a condition* that a contract *be signed.*